INTERACTIONISM:
EXPOSITION AND CRITIQUE
THIRD EDITION

THE REYNOLDS SERIES IN SOCIOLOGY
Larry T. Reynolds, *Editor*
by **GENERAL HALL, INC.**

INTERACTIONISM:
EXPOSITION AND CRITIQUE
THIRD EDITION

Larry T. Reynolds

Central Michigan University

GENERAL HALL, INC.
Publishers
5 Talon Way
Dix Hills, New York 11746

INTERACTIONISM:
EXPOSITION AND CRITIQUE
THIRD EDITION

GENERAL HALL, INC.
5 Talon Way
Dix Hills, New York 11746

Copyright © 1993 by General Hall, Inc.

Publisher: Ravi Mehra
Composition: *Graphics Division,* General Hall, Inc.

LIBRARY OF CONGRESS CATALOG CARD NUMBER: 92–73398

ISBN: 0–930390–65–2[paper]
          0–930390–66–0 [cloth]

Manufactured in the United States of America

Contents

Preface   1

Part One: Symbolic Interactionism   3

I.   **Intellectual Antecedents**   5
        Evolution 6, The Scottish Moralists 9, German Idealism
        10, Pragmatism 13, Charles S. Peirce 17, William James
        as Pragmatist 20, John Dewey as Pragmatist 22,
        Functional Psychology 25, James as Functional
        Psychologist 26, Dewey as Functional Psychologist 29

II.   **The Early Interactionists**   32
        Charles Horton Cooley 32, W. 1. Thomas 39, George
        Herbert Mead 42, Society: Symbols and Role Taking
        49, Self 56, The Elements of Self 60, Mind 63, A
        Brief Summary of Mead's Views 67, Early Inter-
        actionism: Summary Characteristics 70

Part Two: Contemporary Interactionism:
          Major Varieties   73

III.   **The Chicago School**   76

IV.   **The Iowa School**   84

V.   **The Dramaturgical Genre**   95

VI.   **Ethnomethodology**   103

VII.   **Contemporary Interactionism:**
        Summary Characteristics   118

Part Three: A Perspective Critiqued   **128**

VIII.   **Interactionist Self-Criticism**   **129**
Meltzer on Mead's "Sins of Omission" 129, Brittan
on the Metaphysic of Meaning 130, Kuhn on the Evils
of an Oral Tradition 131, Denzin on Methodological
Difficulties 132, Lofland on Analytic Interruptus 133,
Hall on Apolitical Interactionism 134

IX.   **Noninteractionist Critiques**   **135**
Interactionism's Biases: Idealist and Astructural
137, Shaskolsky on Americana and Interactionism
139, Lichtman on the "Quaintness" Question 141,
Huber on the Bias of Emergent Theory 142, Maryl
on Sociology Without Society 145, Collins on Interactionism as Common Sense 146, Gouldner on
Ahistorical, Noninstitutional Interactionism 148,
A Note on the Astructural Bias 154

X.   **The New Studies in Social Organization:**
Overcoming The Astructural Bias by
Christopher Prendergast **and**
John David Knottnerus   **158**
The Astructural Bias 161, Table 1: The Astructural
Bias as a Selection Problem 162, Table 2: The
Astructural Bias as a Displacement Problem 165,
Studies in Social Organization 166, Social Organization
of TV Drama 168, Criminogenic Market Structure 169,
Figure 1: Farberman's Causal Argument 171, Reproduc-
tive Sciences 171, Agricultural Sciences 176, The
Hollywood Film Industry 180, Figure 2: Degrees of
Success in Overcoming the Astructural Bias 181,
Conclusion 182, Notes 184

XI.   **Human Emotions, Social Structure, and Symbolic**
Interactionism by *Bernard N. Meltzer* **and** *Nancy*
J.Herman   **186**
Emotion 187, The Nature of Emotion 190, Types of
Emotions 193, Social Sources of Emotions 195, Social

Consequences of Emotions 199, Unresolved or
Neglected Issues 202, Social Structure 204, Role Theory
210, Negotiated Order 214, Network Analysis and Other
Approaches 221, Unresolved or Neglected Issues 224,
Summary and Appraisal 225, Notes 229

XII. **Some Recent Directions in Symbolic
Interactionism by *Gil Richard Musolf***   **231**
Introduction 231, Postmodernism 231, Major Themes
232, A Postmodern Study 238, Postmodernism
and Interactionism: A Few Similarities 240, Critique
of Postmodern Themes 241, Summary 248,
Structuring Emotions and Reproducing Gender 249,
Emotions 249, The Social Reproduction of Gender
259, Discourse/Conversation-Analysis 261, Dramaturgy
265, Semiotics and SI 272, The Future 278, Conclusion
281, Notes 282

References   **284**
Subject Index   **306**
Name Index   **308**

In memory of
Robert Day,
Nason Hall,
Leslie Lieberman,
and
Andrea Warfield,
scholars and friends

PREFACE

The intent of this edition is the same as that of its predecessors: to offer a quick purview of symbolic interactionism and to briefly discuss both its shortcomings and its considerable strengths. Also in common with the first two editions, the intent is manifestly not to offer a large-scale, comprehensive treatment of the perspective in all its glory. Not all aspects of the framework are subjected to analysis and, of course, not all those that are the object of discussion are treated in sufficient detail, certainly not in the depth which they, in fact, merit. For those seeking a more full-bodied symbolic interactionism, there is simply no substitute for reading the major writings of George Herbert Mead, Charles Horton Cooley, Ellsworth Faris, William I. Thomas, William James, James M. Baldwin, C. S. Peirce, and John Dewey. In some respects, a reading of selected works of Max Weber and Georg Simmel is also called for.

The works of many contemporary symbolic interactionists are well worth the reading. I listed a number, but by no means all, such interactionists in the second edition of this book. I will relist them here and add a few others: Patricia Adler, Peter Adler, Robert Antonio, David Altheide, Lonnie Athens, John Baldwin, Howard Becker, Joel Best, Herbert Blumer, Charles Bolton, Dennis Brissett, Arthur Brittan, Rue Bucher, Lawrence Busch, Spencer Cahill, Aaron Cicourel, Adele Clark, Patricia Clough, Peter Conrad, Carl Couch, Donald Cressey, Arlene Daniels, Fred Davis, Mary Jo Deegan, Norman Denzin, Irwin Deutscher, Mary Lou Dietz, Hugh Duncan, Charles Edgley, Carolyn Ellis, Robert Emerson, Harvey Farberman, Gary Fine, Andrea Fontana, David Franks, Elliot Friedson, Harold Garfinkel, Blanche Geer, Barney Glaser, Daniel Glazer, Erving Goffman, Edward Gross, Jaber Gubrium, Joseph Gusfield, Peter Hall, Nancy Herman, John Hewitt, Arlie Hochschild, Everett Hughes, Hans Joas, John Johnson, David Karp, Lewis Killian, Orrin Klapp, Sherryl Kleinman, David Maines, Peter Manning, George McCall, E. Doyle McCarthy, Peter McHugh, Clark McPhail, Bernard Meltzer, Issei Misumi, Thomas Morrione,

1

Jeffrey Nash, Mary Jo Neitz, Robert Perinbanayagan, John Petras, Ken Plummer, Robert Prus, Laurel Richardson, Julian Roebuck, Arnold Rose, Morris Rosenberg, Earl Rubington, Stan Saxton, Thomas Scheff, Joseph Schneider, William Shaffir, Dmitri Shalin, Tamotsu Shibutani, Gideon Sjoberg, David Snow, Robert Stebbins, Gregory Stone, Anselm Strauss, Sheldon Stryker, Guy Swanson, Ralph Turner, Ted Vaughan, Andrew Weigert, Kirson Weinberg, Eugene Weinstein, Candance West, Norma Williams, Jacqueline Wiseman, William Yoles, and Louis Zurcher.

This is not an exhaustive list of names. There are many more good interactionists around. The perspective is a viable one.

Part One of the present volume details the intellectual antecendents of interactionism (evolution, Scottish moral philosophy, German idealism, pragmatism, and functional psychology) and then details selected writings of the early interactionists (Cooley, Thomas and Mead). Part Two provides a quick sketch of some major varieties of contemporary interactionism (the Chicago and Iowa Schools, dramaturgy, and ethnomethodology).

The third and last part of the book attempts to accomplish a number of things. First, a representative list of interactionists' criticisms of interactionism is presented. Second, a series of noninteractionists' critiques of symbolic interactionism is offered up, including an evaluation by Christopher Prendergast and J. David Knottnerus of selected interactionist ventures into the realms of social structure and organization. Thirdly, Bernard N. Meltzer and Nancy J. Herman provide a symbolic interactionist appraisal of interactionist works on emotions and social structure, as well as a response to critics of the perspective.

Lastly, Gil Richard Musolf attempts to update and keep current the overview of the symbolic interactionist framework. His chapter is titled "Some Recent Directions in Symbolic Interactionism," and it deals with postmodernism, the sociology of emotions, the social reproduction of gender, and very briefly with discourse-analysis and dramaturgy. It also provides a summary of the directions in which interactionism may be heading.

The second edition of this volume was dedicated to the members of the Department of Sociology, Anthropology, and Social Work at Central Michigan University. I inadvertently omitted the names of two good colleagues: Bennie Graves and Lane Mathur.

PART ONE

SYMBOLIC INTERACTIONISM

If one is to depict interactionism accurately in its contemporary manifestations, as well as make some kind of forecast in terms of where it appears to be heading, it is imperative that something also be said about where it came from. Yet, detailing the intellectual antecedents of this orientation is no easy matter. Interactionism is simply not the uniform theoretical framework it is often assumed to be: There are indeed "major variants" of interactionism, variants diverse enough to make the compilation of any list of "common intellectual precursors" or "shared philosophical underpinnings" both a delicate and difficult undertaking. Some idea of the diversity contained within the larger camp of interactionism may be obtained by noting that the following four basic variants of symbolic interactionism have been identified: (1) the Chicago school; (2) the Iowa school; (3) the dramaturgical approach; (4) ethnomethodology.

One author speaks of eight varieties (Warshay, 1971), later reduced to seven, of interactionism (Warshay, 1975), including a field-theory version, a role-theory variant, and an existential and/or phenomenological brand. "Conventional" and "unorthodox" styles of interactionism have been delineated (Vaughan and Reynolds, 1968), and "philosophical anthropology" and "reality construction" have been categorized as deriving from symbolic interactionism (Dreitzel, 1970), as have "labeling theory" and "the sociology of the absurd" (Manis and Meltzer, 1972). Such diversity, and obvious diversity at that, lends support to the remark that "it is difficult to divine what constitutes symbolic interactionism as a theoretical perspective in sociology" (Meltzer, Petras, and Reynolds, 1975).

3

In spite of numerous variations on the basic interactionist theme, it is still possible to speak of interactionism's common intellectual antecedents, for no matter what variant one practices, nearly all of interactionism's practitioners agree that George Herbert Mead is the "true originator" of symbolic interactionism. Mead's views still have a tremendous impact on the work of contemporary interactionists; hence those currents of thought that shaped Mead's ideas continue to influence theirs — no matter which strand of interactionism they adhere to.

One begins, then, with an overview of the intellectual–philosophical precursors of Mead's basic symbolic interactionism. Following this, an outline of Mead's theory is presented. Lastly, the major varieties of contemporary symbolic interactionism are discussed, and an attempt is made to assess the current state of their development.

Chapter 1 INTELLECTUAL ANTECEDENTS

The intellectual precursors of symbolic interactionism are both numerous and diverse. Miller (1973:x), for one, has argued that the primary impetus for interactionism springs both from Darwinism and from that revolt agains introspection that he terms "objective psychology." Others have noted the impact of American pragmatic philosophy on the perspective's initial formulation. The influence of functional psychology during the early stages of symbolic interactionism's development also has been pointed out.

Perhaps the best available listing of the philosophical antecedents of symbolic interactionism in general and of the thought of George Herbert Mead in particular is provided by Jerome G. Manis and Bernard N. Meltzer. These authors specify the following antecedents:
1. Evolutionism
2. German idealism
3. The Scottish Moralists
4. Pragmatism
5. Functional psychology (1978:1–3)

As they directly affected Mead's initial social–psychological interpretation of human behavior, Manis and Meltzer, and David L. Miller would add to the listing above (1) the physiological psychology of Wilhelm Wundt (with its emphasis on the social implications of the gesture) and (2) the writings of those early sociologists who were contemporaries of Mead's and whose ideas also helped lay the foundations for symbolic interactionism (e.g., Cooley, Baldwin, and Thomas). Lastly, both the dramaturgical and ethnomethodological varieties of symbolic interactionism have additional philosophical roots in phenomenology and existentialism (Petras and Meltzer, 1973:1–8).

Only the briefest discussion of the European precursors of symbolic interactionism — evolutionism, the Scottish Moralists,

5

and German idealism – are provided here because symbolic interactionism is, in large measure, a particularly American perspective. And because it is, the American intellectual roots – pragmatism, functional psychology, and the sociologies of Cooley and Thomas – are discussed in somewhat greater detail.

Evolution

The nineteenth-century Darwinian doctrine of evolution was a major source of ideas for the American pragmatists in general and for George Herbert Mead in particular. It was, however, only to selected aspects of Darwin's theory that the founders of interactionism were to direct their attention. Mead, for example, was critical of Darwin's argument concerning emotions and their expression by animals; and Mead, along with most of the key figures in pragmatic philosophy, rejected the one notion deriving from Darwin that Spencer and Sumner had seized on and incorporated in their sociologies – the doctrine of the survival of the fittest. Mead and the pragmatists turned their backs on social Darwinism. In fact, as C. Wright Mills (1966:447) has noted, it was in the process of rejecting both instinctivist psychology and social Darwinism that American pragmatism began to move forward as an "influential variant of sociological reasoning." That strain of social Darwinism that had worked its way into sociology was rejected just as readily by Mead as it was by his pragmatic predecessors and colleagues. Leon Shaskolsky puts it this way: "not for Mead a Summerian jungle society favoring the fittest, but a society undergoing gradual change and held together by the emphatic understanding of interacting individuals" (1970:17).

If Mead and the pragmatists flatly rejected social Darwinism, wherein lay the attraction of Darwin's thought for their respective social theories? Stone and Farberman (1970:17) provide the clue: "For Mead, the attraction was Darwin's emphasis upon process. Indeed, he ignored the *laissez-faire* implications of Darwinism and seized the basic theoretical import: *the same process gives rise to different forms.*" More specifically, Mead was attracted to Darwin's view that a particular relationship existed between the behavior of all living organisms and their environments — namely, that behavior, all behavior, is never accidental, mysterious, or random but is a form of adaptation to the environment. Behavior is performed by organisms, human and otherwise, in the attempt to cope with their environments. Furthermore, as John Dewey (in Mills, 1966:450) noted,". . . all conduct (behavior) is *interaction* between elements of human nature and the environment, natural and social." In this process of interaction, organisms and environments are mutually determinative; they are codeterminants. Manis and Meltzer present the case for codeterminism as follows:

> . . . evolutionary theory conveyed the idea that each organism and its environment fit together in a dialectical relationship, each influencing the nature and impact of the other. That is, the way the environment impinges on an organism is shaped, in part, by the nature of past experiences, and current activity of the organism itself. Environments differ for different organisms, and at times even for the same organism depending upon its activity. The converse of this relationship is also true: Organisms can affect their environment, thereby altering its influence upon them. (1978:2)

Applying the insights of evolutionism discussed above to human beings, one notes that interactionism was to argue that human social life is a *process* of interaction between the person and his or her natural and social environments. As this interaction unfolds, the person's behavior is performed in adaptation to the environment, and person and environment come mutually to influence each other.

The final key formulation drawn from the evolutionary perspective that was to exert a lasting influence on interactionist thought was Henri Bergson's conception of "the reality of qualitative change, emergence, and the coming into being of new forms" (Miller, 1973:28–29). Employing a notion of evolution as a creative and emergent process, Bergson argued that evolution is not solely composed of gradual developments unfolding in a fixed, step-by-step manner. If and when new combinations of behavioral or biological components occur, then radical, abrupt departures from earlier life forms emerge.

Bergson's conception of evolution strongly influenced Mead. In fact, as Miller notes below, Mead is logically constrained to adopt Bergson's basic view:

> Being a process philosopher, Mead must by implication accept the theory of evolution and, more specifically, emergent evolution, which makes room for the emergence of novel events and new biological forms. Each new form requires a new environment, which is to say new environmental characteristics and objects emerge with new forms. In this sense there is a continuous restructuring of the world or part of it. (1973:101)

It is not just Mead who embraced the Bergsonian theory of emergence, ". . . many symbolic interactionists employ the concept of emergence in describing the presumed unpredictability of much human conduct" (Manis and Meltzer, 1978:3). The evolutionary doctrines of process and emergence were employed by Mead and other interactionists not only to deal with overt behavior but also to deal with the phenomena of mind and self. Discussing the impact of the doctrine of evolution with respect to the topic of "mind," Charles Morris put the matter as follows:

> . . . the implication seemed to be that not only the human organism but the entire life of the mind as well had to be interpreted within the evolutionary development, sharing in the quality of change, and arising in the interactivity of organism and environment. Mind had to appear within, and presumably to stay within conduct. (Mead, 1934:ix)

Applying the same basic reasoning to the phenomenon of self, Stone and Farberman were to argue that "social psychology must focus its inquiries on *process,* specifically the *process* of comunication. Different selves (forms) *emerge* from differential participation in the general and universal *process* of communication" (1970:17).

So the evolutionary conceptions of the processual, emergent character of life, the adaptative function of behavior, and the mutually determinative relationship between organisms and environments were to be a part of the intellectual heritage of symbolic interactionism.

The Scottish Moralists

If evolutionism first directed symbolic interactionism's founders' attention to the possibility that minds and selfs, rather than "givens," were emergents, the Scottish Moralists directed the early interactionists toward an even more specific search of the social sources of self and mind. Selfs and minds are social products.

The principal spokesmen of the Scottish Moralists' brand of eighteenth-century philosophy were Adam Ferguson, Henry Homes, David Hume, Francis Hutcheson, John Millar, Thomas Reid, and Adam Smith. The principal significance of the Scottish Moralists for the symbolic interactionists is that the former anticipated many of the key or pivotal social–psychological concepts of the latter. As Manis and Meltzer have pointed out, the Scottish Moralists' concepts of "sympathy" and of the "impartial spectator" clearly foreshadow the interactionists' working concepts of "roletaking" and the "generalized other," and in the writings of Adam Smith are to be found views anticipating the interactionist conceptions of a spontaneous, or "I," component of self, as well as the self's "me," or internalized view of others, component (Manis and Meltzer, 1978:2). Of all the Scottish Moralists, perhaps Adam Smith was the most influential as far as symbolic interactionism is concerned. Smith not only foreshadowed the "I" and "me" concepts of Mead, but his ideas also shaped Charles Horton Cooley's views on the nature of self. One author summarized Smith's influence on Cooley, and through Cooley on Mead, in the following fashion:

> Though Cooley is known as a sociologist, he was definitely influenced by Adam Smith's looking-glass theory of the self. Adam Smith stressed that, in the economic world, the seller must look at himself from the point of view of the buyer, and vice versa, each must take the attitude of the other. Or as Cooley put it, in social behavior we can, through "sympathetic imagination," look at things as others in different situations do, and have the feelings

others have in circumstances actually different from our own. (Miller, 1973:xix)

Furthermore, still by way of stressing the importance of Smith's ideas for interactionism, Miller points out that "Cooley's sympathetic imagination" became, with modifications, Mead's "taking the role of the other" (Miller, 1973:xx). The Scottish Moralists, then, helped provide symbolic interactionism with some of its most indispensable concepts.

German Idealism

According to Manis and Meltzer (1978:2), the principal spokesmen of that variety of German idealism who exerted an influence on George Herbert Mead and symbolic interactionism were Johann Gottlief Fichte, Friedrick Von Schelling, and Immanuel Kant. Here one quickly concedes the correctness of Manis and Meltzer's assertion with respect to Fichte and Schelling. While Kant undoubtedly influenced the thinking of Mead and the interactionists, the nature of this influence — and whether it was, on balance, positive or negative — is not so easy to specify. On the positive side, one can, and should, note that Kant always defended the importance of the individual — clearly a characteristic to be found in the writings of most interactionists. From the Kantian perspective, the individual was never a passive recipient of, or a willing yielder to, pressure applied from a larger natural or social order. To the extent that symbolic interactionism rejected the human image contained in the social-deterministic arguments of the positivists and organicists, Kant's influence was both large and positive. One more point is worth mentioning. In speaking of Kant's theories of the social world, Don Martindale notes, ". . . he tried to reconcile the ideas of a free and simultaneously lawful world" (1960:230). This endeavor is indeed close to the very task that Mead, Dewey, and numerous interactionists were to set for themselves.

On the negative side, Kant assumed an unalterable structure of the mind, and because he did, he was forced to argue for the fixed nature of thought and perception. From Kant's vantage point, forms are logically prior to their objects. This conception

Mead rejected. In fact, Mead's appreciation of Fichte and Schelling derived, in large part, from the fact that they too rejected Kant's views with respect to this matter. Fichte and Schelling did not believe, as Kant did, that forms are logically prior to the rational process. Just as evolutionism had argued that biological forms had origins, so too Fichte and Schelling argued that the forms of perception and thought had their origins, that they did not, in fact, exist prior to their objects. Furthermore, another German idealist, Hegel was making this self same argument. As Hegel profoundly influenced Josiah Royce and, to a lesser extent, John Dewey, and as both Royce and Dewey directly influenced Mead, one could make a case for the argument that Hegel's influence on symbolic interaction was at least as great as Kant's. In an earlier work, Meltzer (1964) mentioned Hegel's influence, and Mead's own words here are instructive: "What the Romantic idealists, and Hegel in particular, were saying was that the world evolves, that reality is in a process of evolution" (1936:154).

The specific Romantic idealists Mead was referring to were Fichte and Schelling. Manis and Meltzer (1978:2) have shown that the influence of German idealism on symbolic interactionism lay in the fact that the idealists had argued that ". . . human beings construct their worlds, their realities." Clearly, Fichte and Schelling believed that human beings inhabited a self-created world. It was Fichte's concept of the "ethical self" and Schelling's discussion of artistic creativity that led each to conclude that the world in which we live was, at least in part, created by ourselves. Lastly, Fichte may have anticipated a central concept of Mead's in that "Fichte's not-self is analogous to Mead's *other* and especially the generalized other" (Miller, 1973:xiv–xv).

Before proceeding to a discussion of the American intellectual antecedents of symbolic interactionism, it is perhaps best to take a quick look at Wilhelm Wundt. Wundt was himself an heir to the tradition of German idealism, and his work on language and gestures was an important source of ideas for the social psychology of George Herbert Mead.

In nineteenth-century Germany, Wilhelm Wundt was one of the leading figures in the field of human psychology. Wundt's doctrines of apperception and psychophysical parallelism were gaining influence in the intellectual community, as were his ideas on folk psychology and on the conducting of laboratory experiments concerned with the workings of basic psychological processes. He established the Psychological Institute, and noted American psychologists came to study there. William James found several of Wundt's ideas especially worthwhile. But it was his reasoning and writing on language and the gesture that was to exert a lasting impact on the perspective of symbolic interactionism. George Herbert Mead would turn to Wundt's conception of the nature of language and especially to Wundt's concept of the gesture. Although Mead borrowed from Wundt, he was nevertheless critical of him. Particularly displeasing to Mead was Wundt's doctrine of psychophysical parallelism, especially his concepts of mind and society. Wundt's theory of society "was based upon the presupposition of the existence of individual minds" (Meltzer, Petras, and Reynolds, 1975:31). Wundt had failed to provide an understanding of the origins of minds in the individuals constituting a society. Mead proposed ongoing activity as the prior content out of which minds emerged; it is out of communicative and interactive processes that minds are formed. But here Mead did turn to Wundt and his concept of the gesture, for ". . . involved in the idea of the gesture is the concept of communication as a social process" (Miller, 1973:xvi). It was in the phenomenon of the gesture that Mead sought the mechanism for the initial rise of the self. Martindale puts the matter in the following terms:

> Following Wundt, Mead took the gesture as the transitional link to language from action, and also as the phenomenon establishing the continuities of human and infrahuman social life. The gesture mediates the development of language as the basic mechanism permitting the rise of the self in the course of ongoing social activity. (1960:335)

From the larger camp of German idealism, then, symbolic interactionism was to draw upon the doctrine that dictated that what Mead termed "the World that is there" was, in fact, a self-created world. People were to be seen as responding to their own working conceptions and definitions of that self-created world and not to the world per se. And from Wundt would be taken the conception of the gesture as the initial phase of the social act — a phase that draws out a response made by the other party or parties in the act, a necessary response for the act's completion. A brief discussion of the American precursors of symbolic interactionism follows.

Pragmatism

If forced to single out the one philosophical school of thought that most influenced symbolic interationism, one would be on safe ground in concluding that pragmatism provides its primary intellectual underpinnings. It is not surprising that pragmatism, "the most influential philosophy in America [and] . . . the most distinctive and major contribution of America to the world of philosophy" should profoundly influence symbolic interactionism (Thayer, 1967:430–431). Symbolic interactionism is, after all, the most distinctively American variety of social psychology, and it is the major contribution of America to the world of sociological theory.

Pragmatism is a philosophy intimately tied to its American social context. In fact, so closely is pragmatism linked to the "American way of life" that George Novak (1975:18) has argued that the methods of pragmatism "belong among such unquestionable values as individual enterprise, monogamy, the two-party system, and big-league baseball." Ruggiero put the case still more directly: "Pragmatism was born in America, the country of 'business,' and is, *par excellence,* the philosophy of the business man" (in Martindale, 1960:297). In somewhat more sophisticated form, Ruggiero's basic argument can be seen again in the following statement:

> The quest for personal material gain was the most powerful and persistent stimulus to economic and social progress [in America]. And the urge to cut down overhead expenses in order to facilitate accumulation manifested itself in all branches of bourgeois activity. This extended to the height of Philosophical thought. Just as the bour-

geoisie repudiated unproductive labor in material production, their thinkers turned away from theories which just-
ified pursuits not immediately productive or gainful. They
demanded that a philosophy prove its worth in practice.
(Novak, 1975:21)

Pragmatism, of course, was the philosophy that strove to prove
its worth in practice. The pragmatists were, however, always
keenly aware of and sensitive to critics who alleged that their
philosophy was an anti-intellectual national philosophy of the
American business class. Perhaps no writer has as succinctly and
eloquently summarized such criticisms as has George Herbert
Mead himself:

Pragmatism is regarded as a pseudo-philosophic formulation of that most obnoxious American trait, the worship of
success; as the endowment of the four-flusher with a faked
philosophic passport; the contemptuous swagger of a glib
and restless upstart in the company of the mighty but
reverent spirit worshipping at the shrine of subsistent entities and timeless truth; a blackleg pacemaker introduced
into the leisurely workshop of the spirit to speed up the process of thinking *sub-specie aeternitatis;* a Ford efficiency
engineer bent on the mass production of philosophical tin
lizzies. (1938:97)

As more than one author points out, pragmatism "does not
completely deserve the unfriendly estimate [that it is] . . . the
philosophy of the business man" (Martindale, 1960:297). As
William Skidmore argues:

Some say it [pragmatism] was a peculiarly American
philosophy because it took a disapproving view of pure
abstraction for its own sake and because it put considerable emphasis on action, as opposed to thinking and
logic, and in general, the mind. This is supposed to be an
American philosophy because America was a place where
there was considerable action, movement, building, and
change, and where traditional philosophical concerns
received little attention. But pragmatism, to its phil-

osophical adherents, did not mean simply "If it works, it's good," as is sometimes said . . . pragmatism was a movement which used the traditional concerns of philosophy as a point of departure from which to defend a somewhat novel way of looking at these problems. (1975:201)

Lest one forget why Martindale qualified his defense of pragmatism by stating that it did not *completely* deserve unfriendly estimates, one can see in the two statements below that such "unfriendly estimates" are not totally misdirected:

[truths] have only this quality in common, that they *pay*.
— William James
A businessman proceeds by comparing today's liabilities and assets with yesterday's, and projects plans for tomorrow by a study of the movement thus indicated in conjunction with study of the conditions of the environment now existing. *It is not otherwise with the business of living.* — John Dewey

It is most difficult to offer the reader a concise yet accurate definition of pragmatism, since pragmatism does not represent "a single unified body of philosophic ideas" (Martindale, 1960: 297). Furthermore, under the differing influences of Peirce, James, and Dewey, pragmatism exhibited some rather profound shifts in its basic formulations, as well as in the direction it was taking as a philosophical movement (Thayer, 1967:431). Pragmatism's critics have offered several short descriptions of pragmatism, such as the one presented here:

What is pragmatism? First pragmatism is what pragmatism does. It is the habit of acting in disregard of solidly based scientific rules and tested principles. (Novak, 1975: 17)

As early as 1808, however, A. O. Lovejoy was able to distinguish between over a dozen possible forms of pragmatism, and, as H. S. Thayer points out, while pragmatism made its initial appearance in a paper titled "How to Make Our Ideas Clear," ". . . pragmatists continued to have so much trouble in doing so"

(1967:431). Perhaps we should accept Thayer's (1967:431, 435) conclusions that pragmatism is "a way of investigating problems and clarifying communication rather than a fixed system of ultimate answers and great truths . . . [hence] a single definitive statement of a single thesis is not to be hoped for."

Thayer's advice aside, one can summarize several key characteristics of American pragmatism:

1. Humans are not passive recipients of stimuli; they are creative, active agents.
2. As people inhabit a world that they themselves have helped shape, even as this self-made world limits and places constraints on the activities of its creators, the world is once again subject to planned change.
3. Subjective experience flows from behavior and does not exist prior to it. From behavior, consciousness and meaning emerge, and an object's meaning resides in the behavior directed toward it and not in the object itself (Manis and Meltzer, 1978:3).
4. The same basic assumptions that shore up and guide empirical science should also guide philosophical analysis.
5. The solution of practical problems and the analysis of social issues should be the prime focus of philosophical concern (Lauer and Handel, 1977:10).
6. It is necessary and desirable to reconcile science with idealism.
7. Action is the means for checking the accuracy of a hypothesis and hence the focus of reality (Weinberg, 1962:403).
8. The best theory of value is the interest theory of value; that is good which satisfies an impulse or an interest.

With this summary of pragmatism's characteristics in mind, it may be best to turn to a discussion of their expression in the writings of a specific set of pragmatists in order to ascertain what relevance they have for symbolic interactionism.

The key founders of pragmatic philosophy in America were Josiah Royce, Charles Peirce, William James, and John Dewey. In terms of its impact on American sociology, the most influential variant of pragmatic philosophy was that emanating from the Chicago school of pragmatism, whose leader was John Dewey, and whose other members included J.H. Tufts, Edward Scribner Ames, James Rowland Angell, Addison Weber Moore, and George Herbert Mead. By stretching the point, the sociologists Albion Small and W. I. Thomas and the economist Thorstein Veblen could also be considered members of the school of Chicago pragmatists. Here one is restricted to dealing with C. S. Peirce, William James, and John Dewey. These three original founders of pragmatism held ideas that directly helped shape Mead's thought, and hence, through Mead, helped shape the structure of symbolic interaction theory. In passing one should note that Royce's ideas of the social source of self and of the affinity between the individual and society (one could not be understood save in reference to the other) were also to have a substantial impact on Mead's theories of self and society. Lastly, one feels constrained to point out, as others already have, that dealing with James and Dewey as representatives of pragmatism does not conclude a treatment of them. Their role as spokesmen of functional psychology is also discussed. Furthermore, one could just as readily treat James and Dewey as "early symbolic interactionists." They are not dealt with as early interactionists, but during the course of discussion of pragmatism and functional psychology, an attempt is made to present those of their ideas that have directly affected symbolic interactionism.

Charles S. Peirce

C. S. Peirce (in Thayer, 1967:431) once asked of William James: "who originated the term *pragmatism,* I or you?" James responded to Peirce's inquiry as follows: "You invented 'pragmatism' for which I gave you full credit. . . ." Yet the label Peirce applied to his philosophy differed from the pragmatism of James, just as Dewey's pragmatism differed considerably from James's. In fact, Peirce became so disenchanted with the development of pragmatism at James's hands that he relabeled his own brand of philosophy *pragmaticism.* John Dewey briefly but accurately summarized the difference between Peirce's and James's varieties of pragmatism in the following terms: "Peirce wrote as a logician and James as a humanist" (Thayer, 1967:434).

Peirce was indeed a logician; and much, much more. In his work one can see in rudimentary form a methodology that transcends the limits of the then-current methodologies by developing a self-reflecting philosophy of science (Habermas, 1970:36). Charles Morris said that "the philosophical task of pragmatism [was] to reinterpret the concept of mind and intelligence in the biological, psychological, and sociological terms which post-Darwinian currents of thought have made prominent . . ." (in Mead, 1934:x). In a very real sense, C. S. Peirce took on this task with the argument that ". . . the technically exploitable knowledge that is produced and tested in the research process of the natural sciences belongs to the same category as the pragmatic knowledge of everyday life acquired through trial and error in the realm of feedback – controlled action" (Habermas, 1970:36).

Peirce began the formulation of the pragmatic criterion of truth: One searched for truth in practice. One could achieve a clear idea of any object only by subjecting that object to experimental treatment and then observing its reaction: "To say that an object is hard is to say that it will not be scratched by other substances" (Ezorsky, 1967:427). The meaning of an object adheres not in the object but in the use we would make of that object, in the practices we would engage in with respect to it, and the experimental handling to which we would subject it. From Peirce's perspective, truth was not an individual matter. Peirce was a realist, not a nominalist. Truth was something to be accepted by the community; therefore, individual judgement would not, and could not, be the real test of truth. Truth was sought in practice because, as Peirce noted, ". . . there is no distinction of meaning so fine as to consist in anything but a possible difference of practice" (in Ezorsky, 1967:427). This dictum was to be widely adopted in American philosophical circles, and its associated notion that the meaning of objects lies solely in the practice (behavior) we direct toward them became a core assumption of symbolic interactionism.

In addition to Peirce's conception of truth, certain other of his ideas were important for the soon-to-be-developed perspective of symbolic interactionism. In particular, Peirce's discussions of thought and language were relevant. Of greatest relevance is his assumption that thought is "a form of behavior initiated by the irritation of doubt and proceeding to some resolution in a state of belief" (Thayer, 1967:433). Peirce's "situation of doubt" as the phenomenon giving rise to thought became Dewey's "indeterminate situation" and Mead's "problematic situation" (Eames, 1973:139). These situations of doubt, indeterminate situations, and problematic situations as existential conditions become "the focal point(s) from which pragmatists developed their method of inquiry"(Eames, 1973:139). Just as Peirce said that truth is established with the arrest of doubt, so too Mead was to say that truth is "synonymous with the solution of the problem . . . judgment must be either true or false for the problem is either solved or it is not solved" (Eames, 1973:139). Of equal importance with Peirce's notion of doubt as the trigger for thought are his ideas on language, specifically on the nature of "signs." Just as Wundt's concept of the gesture is important for interactionist reasoning, so too is the concept of the sign. A sign is a standardized way in which something stands for something else. For Peirce, ". . . the main thing was that signs are socially standardized ways in which something (a thought, word, gesture, object) refers us (a community) to something else (the interpretant — the significant effect or translation of the sign, being itself another sign)" (Thayer, 1967:431). As socially standardized items, signs assume the existence of minds in touch (communication) with one another; this in turn presupposes both the existence of a system of communicating and a human collectivity (society). Here the similarity of Peirce's reasoning to Mead's is obvious.

If it is true that Peirce's influence on symbolic interactionism has been recognized only belatedly, it is perhaps equally true that, apart from direct positive influence on Mead, his greatest influence is on that variety of symbolic interactionism known as the "Iowa school." Peirce's style of pragmatism is not half so much a theory of either truth or meaning as it is a schema, a method, a device for clarifying and unearthing the "empirically significant content of concepts by determining the roles they play in classes of empirically verifiable statements" (Thayer, 1967:433). Hence, Peirce's method clearly foreshadowed the coming of operationalism,verifiability theory, and the preferred methodological posture of Manford Kuhn and other representatives of the Iowa school of symbolic interactionism.

William James as Pragmatist

William James's conception of pragmatism is not only different from Peirce's view but it is so different that it seems almost senseless to classify them as proponents of the same philosophical school of thought. If it is true that pragmatism is more "a way of investigating problems and clarifying communication rather than a fixed system of ultimate answers," then the disparity between Peirce's "way" (or, for that matter, Dewey's) and James's "way" would appear to be even greater (Thayer, 1967:435). Dewey referred to Peirce as a logician and to James as a humanist. In contrasting James with Dewey, it could be said that "Dewey's outlook is scientific and his arguments are largely derived from an examination of scientific method [much like Peirce], but James is concerned primarily with religion and morals" (Martindale, 1960:298). James made pragmatism famous, however, and it was he who successfully proselytized for it as a new philosophy. In the world at large, it was the name of William James that first became synonymous with the word pragmatism.

Two of James's works served to popularize pragmatism in the intellectual community: "Philosophical Conceptions," a lecture delivered in 1898, and *Pragmatism: A New Name for Some Old Ways of Thinking,* a series of lectures delivered in 1906 and published as a book in 1907. It is useful to quickly relate Peirce's position and to contrast it with that of James. When C. S. Peirce spoke of the practical consequence of an idea, activity, or object, he meant results or consequences that the human community could openly, publicly, effectively, and experimentally ascertain. Peirce was a realist; his final court of last resort for the truth was not its being embraced by an individual but its being accepted by the collectivity. James is a nominalist: When he spoke of practical consequences, he meant consequences for the individual; and when he spoke of truth, he meant what was true for the individual. Peirce saw the function of thought as being the eradication of doubt through a clearer perception of reality. For James, thought was not primarily directed at grasping reality; rather, thought gave rise to beliefs and ideas that could satisfy the interests and wants of the individual — regardless of whether or not these beliefs and ideas corresponded to any collectively defined "reality." Peirce's notion of "practical for the community" became in James's hands " practical for the individual"; James's term "practical" referred, and referred exclusively, to the specific impact a given brief or idea had on the life of a concrete individual. Peirce and Dewey were concerned with the generality of truth and meaning, James only with its direct importance for the individual. James is most emphatic on this point: "We cannot reject any hypothesis if consequences useful to [the] life [of the individual] flow from it" (in Martindale, 1960:298). James pushes his argument further: "If the hypothesis of God works satisfactory [for the individual] in the widest sense of the word, it is true [for the individual]" (in Martindale, 1960:298). What satisfies the individual's need is not only good but true. Applying James's pragmatic rule of thumb to James himself, it led him to accept as true "anything that made him happy" (Martindale, 1960:301). What manifestly did not make him happy were the systems of deterministic, scientific explanation. In Don Martindale's words: "The materialistic determinism of nineteenth-century science overwhelmed James with a sense of psychic oppression, and he resolved to make the first act of free will the abandonment of all determinism" (1960:299).

Pragmatists made the attempt to reconcile science with idealism. James was a pragmatist, and so, in spite of his aversion to deterministic science, James too made the attempt. Employing his notion that the truth is that which satisfies needs or interests, he conceded that scientific, experimental methods led to truth because they produced verified ideas. Verified ideas are true, he reasoned, because they "serve our need to predict experience and cope with our environment, scientific truth fulfills our practical interests . . . [hence] the true and the verified are one" (Thayer, 1967:430). James's reconciliation of science and idealism severely restricted both the scope and purpose of science. Ultimately he came out much stronger for idealism and indeterminacy than he did for science and determinism, just as in his social psychology the "social" was forced to take the back seat.

In the pragmatism of William James were to be found all the planks necessary to erect a platform from which to launch a full-fledged assault on those theories perpetrating what Dennis Wrong (1961) would come to call the "Over-Socialized Conception of Man." James never lost sight of either the individual or of the role of creativity in shaping social affairs, and neither did George Herbert Mead. Furthermore, James argued that people "figure out" or give meaning to their surroundings in order to formulate successful "plans of action" for coping with them. The "plans of action" conception of James came to play an important role in Mead's social psychology. It was primarily James's image of people as active and not merely reactive agents that appealed to Mead; James clearly "provided the basis for an image of humans that was congruent with the developing interactionist perspective" (Meltzer, Petras, and Reynolds, 1975:8).

John Dewey as Pragmatist

John Dewey was the titular head of the Chicago school of pragmatism: "Central in the philosophy of this Chicago school was a concern for process, for seeing ideas as part of ongoing activity" (Schellenberg, 1978:42). For Dewey, mental activity was a process, and thought was not an entity but an instrument of response and behavior. Life is caught up with activity, activity and life are synonymous terms. Activity is naturally occurring; and its cause is set by *goals,* which emerge, reemerge, and are altered and modified as organisms constantly adjust and readjust to their environments. These goals or ends, Dewey informs us, are "foreseen consequences which arise in the course of activity and which are employed to give activity added meaning and to direct its future course. They are in no sense ends *of* action. In being ends of *deliberation* they are redirecting pivots *in* action" (in Stone and Farberman, 1970:52). Life is active; people are active. James said it, Dewey said it. It was, in fact, James who turned Dewey toward pragmatism and away from his Hegelian vantage point. Yet although Dewey was intellectually beholden to James, he also rejected many of his views. James had argued that truth is that which gives satisfaction to the individual. From his perspective, it was not necessary that others empirically confirm the individual's "truth." That which satisfied the individual was true; it needed no empirical validation. Dewey's brand of pragmatism dictated that one could not unearth meaning in any notion, idea, or "truth" that could never be empirically verified (Ezorsky, 1967:428). Truth to Dewey was what he termed a "warranted assertion."

Dewey maintained, as Peirce had, that the search for truth is triggered off by doubt, or, to use Dewey's own term, by an *indeterminate situation*. In fact, thought itself starts with an indeterminate situation, with an upset of a previously balanced situation. From Dewey's perspective, every thought, every act flows out of an indeterminate situation and is carried through until such time as the situation is no longer in doubt, no longer indeterminate, no longer unbalanced. When the settlement of doubt is brought about and warranted by inquiry, then the truth is known and we have a warranted assertion. The "warranted assertion" differs from James's "truth" in that it is subject to, and produced by, collective verification — warranted assertion as truth is not an individual matter.

The thought–action process that begins with the *indeterminate situation* and terminates with a *warranted assertion* is the same process for the scientific community as it is for the human community, for, as Morris points out, pragmatism "fails to see any sharp separation or any antagonism between the activities of science and philosophy" (in Mead, 1934:ix). As Mead (1934:ix) put it, ". . . the philosopy of a period is always an attempt to interpret its most secure knowledge." If the world of science is popularly conceived of as concerned with facts while the rest of the world (philosophy included) is supposedly concerned with values, it is Dewey who demonstrates that there is a tremendous continuity between values and facts. The continuity is so great, in fact, that it is nearly impossible to distinguish between "what is objectively real, apart from any human purposes (values) . . . the former [objective reality] is not factually perceived unless it relates to human values facilitating its perception, and the latter [values] require a physical reality of some sort in order to carry meaning" (Thayer, 1967:435).

It is the aim of all thought, all inquiry, to create solutions, goods, satisfactions, and so forth in what was initially a troubled, unbalanced, nonharmonious, and discordant situation. Hence, as Thayer (1967:435) notes, "In this respect all intelligence is evaluative, and no separation of moral, scientific, practical, or theoretical experience is to be made." If we are to comprehend a scientist's use of facts and ideas, we must first understand his or her purposes in beginning the process of inquiry. Similarly, if we are to understand any person's thought or activity, we must come to understand why that thought and activity arose in the first place. Human thought arises when the person sees his or her doubt (indeterminate situation) as a problem. An idea, a thought, is nothing more or less than a proposed solution to the problem. Ideas are plans of action; they are "proposals formed in the context of a problem as a possible solution" (Ezorsky, 1967:429). Ideas in either scientific or practical inquiries coincide with facts when they have "through action, worked out the state of things which [they] contemplated or intended" (Ezorsky, 1967:429). What this means is that Dewey does not see truth (or facts) as immutable; it is meaningless to contend that truth exists separate from or prior to the process of inquiry. From Dewey's perspective, "truth 'happens to an idea' when it becomes a verified or warranted assertion" (Ezorsky, 1967:429). Because of the interactional character of all experience in human society, there could be no fact, no thought, no truth which was antecedent to the person as a thinking being (Meltzer, Petras, and Reynolds, 1975:17). Dewey extended and refined James's conception of individuals as active agents; he went beyond James in elucidating the process by which both thought arises and minds develop in the context of human association. While Dewey's position remained nominalistic, he did go beyond James in demonstrating the relationship between thought, mind, and society. Mead, while drawing heavily on Dewey's work, would, as a realist, go beyond him in depicting the social origins of mind and self in society. But *pragmatism, as* it was *shaped* especially *by* John *Dewey,* would become the *primary* philosophical *foundation* for *symbolic interactionism.* John Dewey would launch the successful attack on those varieties of philosophy that the pragmatists thought little aided human beings in their practical dealings with an emerging, evolving social reality. Among the pragmatists, it was Dewey who argued that the questions posed by traditional philosophy were not worth raising in the first place. Dewey saw human beings, their thoughts, and their societies caught in a larger, interrelated whole; it was he who demonstrated the relativity of philosophical systems in showing their connection with particular kinds of social formations (Meltzer, Petras, and Reynolds, 1975:17).

Dewey set a new task for philosophy, and it was Dewey who made of the philosophical underpinnings of symbolic interactionism the "national philosophy of America" (Novak, 1975:15).

Like Marx, the pragmatists sought to avoid, and often successfully did avoid the use of such artificial dualisms as mind and matter, theory and practice, and experience and nature (Mead, 1934:x). Just as Marx had successfully bridged the people–nature dichotomy, and in so doing proved it to be a false dichotomy, the pragmatists were laying the groundwork for the attempt to bridge the individual–society dichotomy. Pragmatism set a new standard for judging the worth of theory; theories were to be judged on the basis of the fruitfulness of the practical consequences that resulted from their adoption. Among the more significant contributions of pragmatism to the developing theory of symbolic interactionism were its arguments that it is senseless to draw hard distinctions between mind and matter or between society and the individual, as well as its theories of the existential basis of mind, intelligence, and self.

Functional Psychology

In addition to pragmatism, functional psychology was the American-style school of thought that provided intellectual pilings for symbolic interactionism. The principal spokesmen for functional psychology in America were James Rowland Angell, John Dewey, William James, and Charles Hubbard Judd. Of the four, John Dewey and William James had, by far, the largest impact on sociology in general and interactionism in particular; hence only Dewey and James will be singled out for treatment here. But before proceeding to Dewey and James, it may prove worthwhile to specify, in outline fashion, the basic assumptions of the American school of functional psychology. These assumptions are as follows:

1. The process that makes human association (society) possible is the process of linguistic communication.
2. Language not only makes human society possible but is the thing that distinguishes humans from other species; it is a species-specific characteristic of Homo sapiens.

3. Humans are active beings who do not simply respond to stimuli, but select out and pay attention to those stimuli that help to further an ongoing activity.
4. A stimulus embodies no fixed quality of its own; hence the nature of sensation is dependent on the ongoing activity taking place at the time.
5. The mind is not an organ or structure; it is a function that helps the person adapt to his or her environment. Thought is adaptive behavior.
6. Social learning both inhibits and modifies instincts and their expression.
7. Action follows the course of habit until encountering a blockage that, in turn, triggers an impulse that conflicts with the habit; intelligence arbitrates between habit and impulse, thereby securing the release of action.
8. In the formation and development of the individual self, other persons play a key role.

A quick glance at this list reveals that some assumptions of functional psychology overlap with certain basic assumptions of pragmatism. This is hardly surprising in view of the fact that both Dewey and James are widely regarded as being both pragmatists and functional psychologists. James Rowland Angell is also considered by some to be both functional psychologist and pragmatist. Neither should it come as a surprise if it turns out that interactionism shares many assumptions with functional psychology and pragmatism, not merely because they are its intellectual precursors, but because pragmatism is an American philosophy, functional psychology is an American psychology, and symbolic interactionism is either an American social psychology or an American sociology — depending on one's point of view (noninteractionists tend to regard interactionism as social psychological, while many interactionists are pleased to see their perspective as being sociological). I turn now to a brief discussion of the functional psychologies of James and Dewey.

James as Functional Psychologist

The functional psychology of William James is laid out in his 1890 publication, *Principles of Psychology*. In this two-volume work, James sets forth and details the interrelationships that exist between his three pivotal, indispensable concepts: instinct, habit, and self. Now James's treatment of the instinct concept stood in marked contrast to the way in which that concept was handled by the so-called instinct theorists. For the instinct theorists, the most important thing about instincts was that "they were there"; they were essentially fixed faculties of acting unmodified by experience and directed toward the production of certain ends. These instincts, if one concedes their existence in the first place, were of little concern to James. For James, the single most important feature of instincts is that they are inhibited and modified. And, most important, they are inhibited and modified by the action of another of James's key concepts: habits. Habits, in turn, are not part of one's initial biological equipment; they are socially acquired — they are learned. Instincts are socially modified in human beings because Homo sapiens possesses capabilities not characteristic of other species; most notable of these is the ability of the human brain to engage in high-level mental activities such as memory. Because of memory, repeating behavior that was at one time instinctual "can call to mind the performance of the act at that previous time" (Meltzer, Petras, and Reynolds, 1975:4). This kind of behavior, then, must "cease to be blind after being repeated, and must be accompanied with foresight of its end just so far as that end may have fallen under the animal's cognizance" (James, 1890:390).

Therefore, the complexity of a species' behavior is not necessarily related to the number of instincts in its repertoire. A species may have a large number of instincts and yet exhibit a fairly simple system of behavior. Conversely, in the case of humans, instincts are few, but behavior is enormously complex. With respect to human beings, then, ". . . attention should be focused upon the number of *repeated* behavioral experiences that are traceable to a particular instinct" (Meltzer, Petras, and Reynolds, 1975:4). In James's view, ". . . as most instincts are implanted for the sake of giving rise to habits, then, when that purpose has been realized the instincts are destined to simply fade away" (1890:402).

Habits that modify and inhibit instincts are themselves products of the individual's previous experiences, and as such they act to further inhibit the original instinct's range of expression because, as James (1890:394) notes, "When objects of a certain class elicit a certain sort of reaction, . . . [the person] . . . becomes partial to the first specimen of the class on which [he or she] has reacted, and will not afterward react on any other specimen." Not only are humans born with fewer instincts and greater plasticity than other species, but many of the instincts humans do possess come to the fore during a certain developmental period in their lives and then disappear. It is worth noting that, from James's perspective, not only are instincts plastic, subject to inhibition, and prone to fade away, but those instincts we do possess frequently work at cross purposes, cancel each other's effect, or block each other out. Again, instincts are a part of the makeup of Homo sapiens — they are factors helping to determine behavior — but their most important characteristic is that, due to the action of habit, they are modifiable and can be inhibited.

The last key concept of James, at least as far as its direct relevance for symbolic interactionism is concerned, is the concept of *self*. It is most interesting to note James's working conception of self because it is held to by a sizable number of present-day interactionists, and it is flatly rejected by an equally large number of the current practitioners of that perspective. James began by noting that humans had four distinct selves: the self of pure ego, a material self, a spiritual self, and a social self. This notion is, of course, rejected by all contemporary interactionists. Nevertheless, one of James's selves, the social self, became — and pretty much the way James defined it — a key concept for numerous interactionists. In speaking of the social self, he argued as follows:

> Properly speaking, a man has as many social selves as there are individuals who recognized him and carry an image of him in their mind . . . but as the individuals who carry the images fall naturally into classes, we may practically say that he has as many different social selfs as there are distinct groups of persons about whose opinion he cares. (1890:294)

James's *social self* became, for many symbolic interactionists, *the self*. They dropped those "separate types of selves" that were not derived from interaction and were not products of participation in the social milieu, namely, the spiritual, material, and pure ego selves. James's conception of the social self is what has been termed "the multiple entity conception" (Reynolds et al., 1970). Numerous symbolic interactionists, but by no means all of them, would find themselves in basic agreement with James's contention that the individual has more than one self. Some would argue that it is more appropriate to state that the individual has as many selves as there are *groups to which he or she belongs,* rather than to say, as James did, that one has *as many selves as there are groups whose opinion one cares about.* Both definitions are "multiple entity conceptions" of self. Because many interactionists accept the "multiple self" notion, and because all of them agree that basic biological endowments are only seen as they have already been profoundly altered by social experience, James's functional psychology may be said to have exerted a significant impact on interactionism.

Dewey as Functional Psychologist

John Dewey's functional psychology employs a host of concepts, but three stand out as more important than the rest: impulse, habit, and intellect. Of these three, habit and intellect are central, with habit perhaps the most important. Dewey was not, of course, the first spokesman of functional psychology to employ the concept of habit as a central one. William James utilized the concept, but he did so solely for the purpose of dealing with repetitious individual behavior. Dewey was more concerned with the role of social variables in behavior, and as this concern developed on Dewey's part, his basic concepts, habit included, were redefined to reflect that concern. When Dewey (1922:42) eventually defined habit as an acquired predisposition to "*ways* or modes of response, not to particular acts," he was further led to argue that conditions that constitute habit lie in the social order, not in the individual, and because they do, one cannot change habits by merely changing individuals — social conditions too must be altered.

Dewey's three concepts of habit, impulse, and intellect relate to one another in the following manner: Activity runs the path of habit until it is blocked by an obstacle. In the face of blocked activity, impulse emerges and seeks an outlet in activity. In seeking the outlet, the old (habit) and the new (impulse) collide, producing a problem. Intellect mediates between habit and impulse, "thus facilitating the release of action, which will be a projection of existent habits newly combined so as to satisfy the stymied impulse" (Mills, 1966:455). Thus Dewey (1922:30) argued that action, at least blocked action, precedes thought, or as he put it, "The act must come before the thought, and a habit before the ability to evoke the thought at will." It was through the concept of habit that Dewey came to his view on the relationship between the individual and the collectivity. He emphasized the role of social elements in shaping habits, indeed in shaping all behavior, and because he did he was led to conclude further that habits cannot be changed by merely changing individuals — social conditions must also be altered. The social conditions he most ardently sought to alter were those affecting the individual during his or her early years. Specifically, Dewey was concerned with educational institutions and educational processes. *Minds* must be shaped in such a way that they become receptive to the changes necessary if a decent society were to be wrought out of the existing social order. Dewey's conception of mind is crucial here: "Dewey proposed that the mind be viewed as function, with "minded activity" extrapolated from adaptive behavior in an ever-changing environment. This . . . view of the human mind is most congenial with attempts at intelligent social planning" (Meltzer, Petras, and Reynolds, 1975:19).

As Dewey (1971:273) saw it, any view of mind as a fixed and frozen phenomenon stood squarely in the path of social reform because ". . . the most powerful apologetics for any arrangement or institution is the conception that it is the inevitable result of fixed conditions of human nature." In conceptualizing the mind as function, Dewey was moved to argue that the mind's social development was facilitated only through the process of communication, specifically through the use of language. Language enabled individuals to incorporate into their own selves the beliefs, sentiments, and thoughts taken from their respective social environments.

Dewey's contribution to functional psychology in terms of reconceptualizing, reworking, and rethinking its basic concepts and their relationship to one another was enormous — especially with respect to such concepts as mind, impulse, habit, and language. Dewey's other major contribution to functional psychology derives from the classic statement on the reflex-arc concept in psychology. In this work he attacked the stimulus–response conception of human behavior. Interested as he was in the role of interaction in understanding human behavior, he objected to any dualistic notions of stimulus and response in the following words:

> Sensation as stimulus . . . means simply a function, and it will have its value shift according to the special work requiring to be done . . . what the sensation will be in particular at a given time, therefore, will depend entirely upon the way in which an activity is being used. It has no fixed quality of its own. The search for the stimulus is the search for the exact conditions of action; that is, for the state of things which decides how a beginning coordination should be completed. (Dewey, 1896:369)

The attack on the dualism of stimulus and response contained in the above statement paved the way for a view of the role of both individual and social elements in explaining distinctly human conduct. In the functional psychology of John Dewey, the discipline of psychology had stuck its foot in sociology's door.

Charles Horton Cooley

The initial entry into American sociology of several key ideas springing from the functional psychologists, the pragmatist philosophers, and perhaps even the Scottish Moralists was gained through the writings of Charles Horton Cooley. Cooley was a student of John Dewey and was well acquainted with the writings of both William James and James Mark Baldwin. One would have to further agree with those who argue that the parallels between Cooley's views and those of Adam Ferguson, David Hume, and especially Adam Smith are both too strong and too striking not to suggest that Cooley was conversant with the social philosophy of the Scottish Moralists (Stryker, 1980:26). It would appear that the influence of the pragmatists on Cooley was great. Much of his work concerns itself with the *practical* problems people grapple with in a technologically complex society, and indeed it has been argued that:

> In fact, all of Cooley's writings impart the impression that his sociological theorizing on the structure and organization of society was guided by moral principles derived from the pragmatic tradition, and these, in turn were tempered by the reality of social life as interpreted in his sociological theories. (Meltzer, Petras, and Reynolds, 1975:9)

Much philosophy and psychology, then, make their way into early American sociology in the person of Charles Horton Cooley.

Cooley is perhaps best known for introducing sociologists to the concepts *primary group* and *looking-glass self;* yet, from Cooley's perspective, his major contribution was his particular theory of human society — a phenomenon he viewed as being essentially mental in nature (Meltzer, Petras, and Reynolds, 1975:8). Unlike many figures in early American sociology, Cooley did not approach the study of society from the vantage point of the concrete individual and then infer or build up general societal properties based on that individual-centered viewpoint (Bodenhafer, 1920–1921:425–474). Instead, he began with the collectivity or group, for it is from the group that the real basis of individual motivation and behavior comes. In fact, for those concerned with depicting social reality, Cooley warned that the "real person" exists only in what Cooley termed the "personal idea":

> So far as the study of immediate social relations is concerned the personal idea is the real person. That is to say, it is in this alone that one man exists for another, and acts directly upon his mind. My association with you evidently consists in the relation between my idea of you and the rest of my mind. If there is something in you that is wholly beyond this and makes no impression on me it has no social reality. . . . (Cooley, 1902:84)

The individual as a real person thus has no existence independent of the views of others, of other members of the collectivity. One sees in this statement by Cooley evidence of one of the two unique characteristics he attributed to human society: its thoroughly "mental nature." From Cooley's perspective, "The imaginations which people have of one another are the solid facts of society" (1902:87). Society lives in the minds of the members constituting the social unit, and this is precisely what makes the unit something very real as far as that unit's members are concerned: "In actuality, there is no 'mind of society,' but many different minds that exist through a sharing of expectations and patterns of behavior, thereby providing the 'glue' which holds the larger organization together" (Meltzer, Petras, and Reynolds, 1975:9). Cooley put the matter as follows:

> Not in agreement but in organization, in the fact of reciprocal influence of causation among its parts, by virtue of which everything that takes place in it is connected with

everything else, and so is an outcome of the whole. This differentiated unity of mental or social life . . . is what I mean . . . by social organization. (1909:4)

While this quotation, by equating mental and social life, again clearly reveals Cooley's mentalistic conception of society, he also tells us that society manifests a further distinctive characteristic: its "organic nature." A society possesses a structure, and that structure, in turn, displays the characteristics or properties of a complex organism:

It is a complex of forms of processes each of which is living or growing by interaction with the others, the whole thing being so unified that what takes place in one part affects all the rest. It is a vast tissue of reciprocal activity, differentiated into innumerable systems, some of them quite distinct, others not readily traceable, and all interwoven to such a degree that you see different systems according to the point of view you take. (Cooley, 1918:28)

One sees in all these quotations from Cooley concerning his view of the nature of human society that he has pulled off a rather novel feat: He has forcefully attacked both the individualistic and classical organic conceptions of society while retaining key elements of both. He focuses not on individuals but on social organization, but only as the organization is maintained in the imaginations or minds of individuals. He has simultaneously avoided the overpowering social determinism of the classic European organicists and the instinct or propensity-driven human model of the hyperindividualists. Given such a conception of the nature of human collectivities, it is not difficult to see how Cooley was led to conclude that the individual and society are but two sides of the same coin. While Cooley has, in his theory of human society, managed to avoid the dangers inherent in both classic organicism and classic liberalism, his image of society is not without its shortcomings. As Stryker points out, it is Cooley's

way of thinking about social relationships that has been criticized as solipsistic. That is, if imaginations are the solid facts of society, it seems to follow that there are as many societies as there are individual imaginations. If our imaginations differ, how can we get beyond these differences and to what do we refer these differences in order to build general knowledge of society? (1980:27)

Such limitations noted, Cooley nevertheless did something many sociologists fail to do: He developed a methodology compatible with his theory. If "the imaginations which people have of one another are the solid facts of society," it follows that in order to understand best both the nature of society and its workings one must somehow gain access to the "imaginations" of society's members. Furthermore, the sociologist must be certain that it is the imaginations of others that he or she is tapping, not just his or her own imagination imposed on the data. As imaginations are not directly accessible through the mere observation of external behavior, and as these imaginations are, in a sense, only accessible to those who experience them, Cooley put forth a methodology he labeled "sympathetic introspection." One sympathetically comes into contact with others of society's members, one strives to imagine as they imagine, one seeks to uncover the interpretations of and meanings attached to events and objects experienced by members of the collectivity. In short, one places oneself in contact with society's members and sympathetically tries to imagine life as these others live it. One then seeks to detail, describe, and understand the imagination of others, because these imaginations are the solid facts of society. It is not that nonmental factors play no role in influencing human conduct. They do; but from Cooley's perspective, these "material facts" are not nearly as important as those human bonds whose existence depends on the *ideas* society's members have of one another. These are what Cooley called "the social facts." If one would understand society, one must first understand the social facts. One comes to understand social facts by employing the methodology of sympathetic introspection. Given Cooley's views on the nature of human society and how best to approach it, he went on to construct two major concepts that better facilitated his task. These concepts have been of lasting value to symbolic interactionists; they are the *primary group* and the *looking-glass self*. Not only do these two concepts tie directly to

Cooley's image of society, but they also fit in closely with his conception of human nature.

In Cooley's writings, the concepts of self and group are dynamically intertwined. The self develops in a group context, and the group that Cooley called the primary group is the real seat of self-development. Primary groups are triply important: They are the true building blocks for larger and more complex social forms and relationships; they are the mechanisms through which the self evolves; and they are the linkage points between individuals and the larger social order.

Cooley provides the following definition of primary groups:

> By primary groups I mean those characterized by intimate face-to-face association and co-operation. They are primary in several senses, but chiefly in that they are fundamental in forming the social nature of the ideals of individuals. (1909:23)

It is within such groups that the feeling of social unity is first experienced by the child. In the primary group, the person for the first time comes to identify himself or herself as a vital and necessary part of a social unit. Here emerges the sense of belonging that Cooley termed the "we" feeling. Among the more important primary groups are the neighborhood and play groups, and especially the family. From such groups, one's basic motivations as well as one's feelings of self-worth are taken.

As John Petras has pointed out, in Cooley's early works he spoke of three different levels at which human nature can be said to exist (Meltzer, Petras and Reynolds, 1975:11). The first level was largely hereditary in character. At the second level, Cooley dealt with the role played in the motivation of behavior by biology. This second level of human nature was essentially stable, being modified only slowly in an evolutionary process. Lastly, there is a level of human nature that is fundamentally social, and this third level was the object of much of Cooley's attention in his later writings. In speaking of human nature's third level, Petras has remarked:

> This is the human nature that develops with primary groups, and it is here that a link is provided between the

three concepts of primary group, human nature, and looking-glass self. This is the human nature that is characterized not only by the acquisition of ethical standards, but, more importantly, by the development of a sense of self that reflects the definitions of the society as interpreted by the primary groups. At this level human nature is most flexible and, consequently, most susceptible to social influences. It is here that human nature can be seen in its principal aspect, that of *plasticity,* or what Cooley calls "teachability." (Meltzer, Petras and Reynolds, 1975: 11–12)

James Mark Baldwin argued that the child goes through three basic stages in the course of self-development: the projective, subjective, and ejective stages. Baldwin's theory concerning how the self develops influenced both Cooley and Mead in the formulation of their respective theories of the "self," and his theory is one of the earliest and most fruitful expositions on the "social self," on the self as a social product. Although few contemporary sociologists give Baldwin's views the attention they merit, a brief synopsis of them may be helpful here, as Cooley's theory of the looking-glass self owes much to Baldwin's insights.

During the first, or projective, stage of self-development, the child becomes aware or develops a consciousness of others. These others are then classified by the child according to the previous experiences he or she has had with them. A set of regular and sustained contacts with a specific person in the past triggers off quite a different group of perceptions and expectations in the person's presence than those that are given rise to when a still different person confronts the child. In this manner the child comes to distinguish between mother, father, sister, brother, and so on. In the projective stage, then, the child not only becomes aware of others but also begins to categorize these others (Baldwin, 1895).

In the subjective, or second, stage, self-consciousness begins to emerge. It emerges by the child's imitating the behavior of other persons and by then learning of the feeling states that go along with this behavior. In the ejective, or third, stage, the child becomes aware of the fact that others too have feelings. The child "ejects" his or her interpretations and feelings on to other persons. Such ejecting "represents an elementary form of empathy, and it provides a foundation on which Cooley's methodology of sympathetic introspection and Mead's theory of role-taking rest" (Meltzer, Petras and Reynolds, 1975:13). Furthermore, "These processes occur within the context of the 'dialectic of personal growth' that Baldwin believed characterized a lifetime give-and-take relationship constituting the individual and society bond" (Meltzer et al., 1975:13). In Baldwin's writings, then, are to be found ideas that impact on the later theories of both Mead and Cooley: ideas such as the ejecting process, which help lay a base for Cooley's methodology of sympathetic introspection, and the notion of the self as a social product, which foreshadows Cooley's concept of the looking-glass self.

How are we to view the self? Not in isolation. In *Human Nature and the Social Order,* Cooley (1902:91–92) put it as follows: ". . . there is no view of the self, that will bear examination, which makes it altogether distinct in our minds from other persons." The self, then, is an outgrowth of social interaction; it is developed and defined in the course of our interaction with others, especially other members of the "primary group."

From Cooley's vantage point, then, the self is a social product, a product "produced" largely in the primary group. It is a product best labeled a "looking-glass self," in that a child obtains an identity only with the realization that his or her picture, idea, or image of himself or herself "reflects" other people's picture of him or her. In Cooley's terms, what is reflected is the imaginations of others concerning the individual. The self resides in the minds of the members of the collectivity, or society; it constitutes an imaginative fact.

> Persons and society must be studied primarily in imagination. It is true, *prima facie,* that the best way of observing things is that which is most direct; and I do not see how we can hold that we know persons directly except as imaginative ideas in the mind. (1902:86)

The specific social reference for the self, notes Cooley,

> takes the form of a somewhat definite imagination of how one's self — that is, any idea he appropriates — appears in a

particular mind, and the kind of self-feeling one has is determined by the attitude toward this attributed to the other mind. A social self of this sort might be called the reflected or looking-glass self. (1902:151-152)

More succinctly, Cooley (1902:152–153) states, "We always imagine, and in imagining, share, the judgments of the other mind." The social self depicted by Cooley has three basic ingredients: (1) our imagination of how we *appear* to others; (2) our imagination of how others *judge* our appearance; and (3) our resultant self-feelings, which are products of such imaginings.

The above conceptualization of the self and the way it is formed has important consequences: ". . . there is and can be no individuality outside of the social order; individual personality is a 'natural' development from existing social life and the state of communication among the persons sharing that life; and, the expectations of others are central to this development" (Stryker, 1980:29). In the writings of Charles Horton Cooley, especially in his theories of self, society, and human nature, was much food for future interactionist thought.

W. I. Thomas

While Charles Horton Cooley was largely concerned with the process of self-acquisition and self-formation during the childhood years, William Isaac Thomas concentrated on the latter years. His interest in social disorganization and social change led him to be "primarily concerned with the processes through which the adult self came to be redefined" (Stryker, 1980:30). Thomas, among other things, was concerned with developing a theory of human motivation, and especially with developing a motivational theory that dealt directly with the dynamic interaction between the social and individual sources of conduct (Meltzer, Petras and Reynolds, 1975:23).

Thomas began by looking at instincts — sex and food instincts specifically — as the most basic motivational elements in humans. He was then led to look at organic differences between the sexes as basic explanatory factors in behavior. Next he used the concept of "wishes" as the prime explanatory basis for human motivation. Lastly, he turned back to his earlier "definition of the situation" concept as the prime theoretical construct in his theory of motivation. The definition-of-the-situation concept is widely regarded as being the one direct link between W. I. Thomas and the large, growing tradition of symbolic interactionism. However, as Martindale (1960:349) has pointed out, "At every critical point Thomas' affinities are with the pragmatists and symbolic interactionists." Furthermore, as John Petras has noted, Thomas, through his work with Znaniecki, provided "the first large-scale test of many of the propositions that had been developed with respect to the social nature of the self and the role of society in determining individual behavior" (Meltzer, Petras and Reynolds, 1975:22). Thomas's writings on self-society interrelationships, his focus on sympathetic introspection as a methodological tool, his emphasis on self-redefinition in adulthood, and his advocacy of the utilization of personal documents and life histories in sociological research all have exerted a lasting impact on contemporary symbolic interactionism. Such contributions aside, the definition of the situation concept is Thomas's best-known addition to the conceptual inventory of the symbolic interactionists, and it is fitting to conclude this very brief discussion of his work by focusing on this concept.

According to W. I. Thomas, in the course of carrying out the practical activities of everyday life, human beings act in what he termed an "as if" fashion. People always act in an "as if" manner, which is to say that ". . . there is an effort to define each of the paths of contemplated behavior on the basis of what will result if a person follows one path and not another" (Meltzer, Petras and Reynolds, 1975:27). The effort to define, and subsequent deliberation about, paths of potential behavior before carrying out self-determined behavior is what Thomas termed "the definition of the situation." A definition of the situation is formed prior to all "self-determined" action: "An adjustive effort of any kind is preceded by a decision to act or not to act along a given line and the decision is itself preceded by a *definition of the situation* (Thomas, 1937:8).

Very much like the pluralistic behaviorists, Thomas argued that it was the job of the sociologist to study adjustive responses of both individuals and collectivities to other persons and groups. Such adjustments transpire in social situations, and coming between these situations and adjustive responses to them are actors' definitions of the situation. As the same objective situation may lead to different behavior on the part of different persons, and even on the part of the same person on different occasions, Thomas concluded that people do not react to situations or facts in and of themselves. In a sense there are no facts in and of themselves: "Facts do not have a uniform existence apart from the persons who observe them. Rather, the 'real' facts are the ways in which different people come to define situations" (Volkhart, 1951:30).

If sociologists are to deal, then, with the real facts of social life, they must come to grips with "definitions of the situation." These definitions are themselves the real facts of social life; they are the real forces shaping behavior because, as Thomas argued, ". . . if men define situations as real, they are real in their consequences" (1928:572).

None of this is to say that the objective situation itself is unimportant. Both the situation and people's definitions of it, both the "objective" and "subjective" facts of human experience, have to be dealt with by any adequate theory of human behavior. Thomas puts it as follows: "The total situation will always contain more and less subjective factors, and the behavior reaction can be studied only in connection with the whole context, i.e., the situation as it exists in verifiable, objective terms, and as it has seemed to exist in terms of the interested persons" (1928: 572).

So, while objective situations cannot be ignored, neither can people's subjective definitions of them. Both the "life-policies" of individuals as well as their personalities spring from constructed definitions of the situation. Many of the definitions taken on by the individual are, in fact, initially provided by others. Stryker argues as follows:

> Children . . . are always born into an ongoing group that has developed definitions of the kinds of situations faced and has formulated rules of conduct premised on these definitions: moral codes are the outcome of "successive definitions of the situation." Children cannot create their own definitions independently of society, or behave in

those terms without societal interference. And individual spontaneous definitions and societal definitions will always conflict to some extent. (1980:32)

Furthermore, ". . . social as well as personal disorganization are resultants of there being rival social definitions of the situation, none of them fully constraining the person" (1980:32).

All social situations, then, require as key explanatory variables definitions of the situation. When actors' definitions are not amenable to direct asssessment, some method for inferring them must be found. Thomas found such a method in those objects he called "personal documents"—letters, case studies, autobiographies, and life histories. These were the sources that could be expected to reveal the "point of view," the "perspective," the "definition of the situation" of their authors and participants. These personal documents would, from Thomas's vantage point, be a major source of fruitful sociological hypotheses.

William Isaac Thomas, then, would endeavor to (1) explain the proper methodological approach to social life; (2) develop a theory of human motivation; (3) spell out a working conception of adult socialization; and (4) provide the correct perspective on deviance and disorganization. And he would do it all in reference to the definition-of-the-situation idea. In this particular concept he thought he had found one of the real keys necessary to unlock the secrets of human behavior. Apparently, many symbolic interactionists agree with his assessment.

George Herbert Mead

George Herbert Mead was born February 27, 1863, in South Hadley, Massachusetts. He died April 26, 1931, in Chicago, Illinois. The last 38 of his 68 years were spent as a faculty member in the Department of Philosophy at the University of Chicago. There Mead established himself as one of the founding fathers of the symbolic interactionist tradition. So influential have his views become that, if forced to pick a single "founder" of that perspective, he would be the near-unanimous choice of both symbolic interactionists and sociologists of other theoretical persuasions. Indeed, in speaking of Mead, another founding father, his colleague and friend John Dewey (1931:311), noted, "I dislike to think what my own ideas might have been were it not for the seminal ideas which I derived from him." It was, then, not Dewey nor James nor Cooley nor Thomas, but George Herbert Mead who transformed the "inner structure of the theory of symbolic interactionism, moving it to a higher level of theoretical sophistication" (Martindale, 1981:329). Among the major early contributors to the symbolic interactionist viewpoint, Mead would have the greatest influence on the developing interactionist tradition within sociology. And given the disorganized style in which his major works were presented, this was a somewhat surprising development. Although Mead authored a large number of articles in the fields of philosophy, education, sociology, and psychology, at the time of his death he had not written a single book. The reasons for his failure to produce a systematic, book-length statement of his views were no doubt both numerous and complex. Grace Chin Lee suggests one possible reason: "Mead had a certain diffidence that kept him from giving his ideas the finality of printed form or the inflexibility of systematic organization. True to his theory that men do their significant thinking in the course of conservation, he found extemporaneous speaking his best medium" (1945:v).

The problem in coming to grips with Mead, however, lies not only in his failure to produce a systematic book-length manuscript but also in the fact that his language at times tends to be obscure. He often attempts to solve a philosophical problem within the confines of a single lengthy sentence, and consequently, "a sentence is rarely introduced for the sole and deliberate purpose of clarifying a preceding one" (Lee, 1945:4). Moreover, Mead was an innovator, and his language and reasoning are often difficult to follow because, as with most innovators, "they cannot accept the traditional modes of thinking, although the language they must use to convey their meaning is an outgrowth of these modes" (Lee, 1945:2). John Dewey put it as follows: "A great deal of the seeming obscurity of Mr. Mead's expression was due to the fact that he saw something as a problem which had not presented itself at all to the other minds. There was no common language because there was no common object of reference" (in Lee, 1945:2).

Hence, Mead's writing was often obscure and difficult to follow, and he offered up no clear and systematic presentation of his theory. Nevertheless, his views may well have been the right views at the right time at the right place. This, coupled with his bright and inquiring mind, may have led to a victory of substance over style and to his views becoming incorporated in the body of interactional theory in sociology. Intellectually Mead was well equipped to play a leading role in the founding of a theoretical tradition.

Mead received his bachelor of arts degree in 1883 from Oberlin College. His father taught at Oberlin; and his mother, former president of Mount Holyoke College, would do so following her husband's death. On the heels of a four-year stint as teacher, tutor, and surveyor, Mead obtained a master's degree from Harvard in 1888. During his one-year stay at Harvard, he studied with both William James and Josiah Royce. At their hands he received his first systematic exposure to the philosophical tradition of pragmatism and to the notions that ideas are plans of action and that minds arise through use of language.

Completing his M.A., Mead left the United States to study in Germany. While studying both psychology and philosophy, he became acquainted with the German idealist tradition. It was here that Mead became conversant with the work of Immanuel Kant and other major figures in the Romantic idealist camp, especially Hegel, Fichte, and Schelling. Mead was particularly interested in the idealist's emphasis on language, and he was perhaps most impressed by Wilhelm Wundt's views on both language and mythology, especially by Wundt's notion of "the gesture" as that portion of the act that functions as a stimulus to other forms implicated in the same act. The German idealists' theory of personality and their interest in language and communication were instrumental in shaping Mead's own thought and interests, even though he was ultimately to reject many of their arguments.

On his return to the United States, Mead accepted, in 1891, an instructorship in the Department of Philosophy and Psychology at the University of Michigan. Here he became familiar with the work of the school of functional psychology. Mead gained additional exposure to the fields of sociology and social psychology through contact with his colleague and friend Charles Horton Cooley. It was also at Michigan that Mead and John Dewey became not only fellow faculty members but close friends.

In 1894 both Mead and Dewey left the University of Michigan to join the philosophy faculty at the University of Chicago. Here they became an integral part of a developing American philosophy, pragmatism. Their colleagues at Chicago included A. W. Moore, J. H. Tufts, and E. S. Ames in philosophy and W. I. Thomas in sociology. Mead familiarized himself with the theories of "suggestion–imitation" being touted by James Mark Baldwin, Franklin E. Giddings, and the French social psychologist Gabriel Tarde. Mead delved deeper into functional psychology and pragmatism. He began the systematic attack on both individualistic and behavioristic (Watsonian) psychologies, and he was to adopt selected features of the evolutionary theories of Charles Darwin, Jean Baptiste Lamarck, and Henri Bergson. It was also at Chicago that Mead began to embrace certain features of the methodological views being espoused by Alfred North Whithead. Of equal, or perhaps greater, importance, at the University of Chicago Mead began to articulate his own theory of the self (Miller, 1973:xi–xxxiv).

Because Mead never produced a book, one would normally have to piece together his views from a close reading of his many articles and simply be content with the limitations of such an undertaking. But because Mead's students obviously felt he had something eminently worthwhile to say, several made stenographic transcripts of his lectures. These transcripts, together with additional class notes taken by his students, first drafts of unpublished articles, and uncompleted manuscripts, were assembled and published after Mead's death as a series of four books. Only one of these volumes is of prime concern here, because it clearly has had a far larger impact on sociological theory than the other volumes either singly or in combination (Spreitzer and Reynolds, 1973). Before discussing *Mind, Self, and Society,* however, a brief description of the other three books would seem to be in order, as they also are major reference materials for persons interested in providing themselves with a complete picture of Mead's social psychological perspective. It should be kept in mind, as both Lee and Meltzer have pointed out, that all four books are fragmentary, contradictory, and disorganized in nature. As Meltzer (1964:10) notes, ". . . the books consist, in considerable part, of alternative formulations, highly repetitive materials, and sketchily developed ideas." Such repetitions, contradictions, and obscurities are to be expected in collections that are "an aggregation rather than organization" and whose "chief aim is completeness rather than arrangement or interpretation" (Lee, 1945:v).

The first of Mead's posthumously published books was *The Philosophy of the Present*. This book contains the Paul Carus Foundation lectures delivered by Mead shortly before his death. The book appeared in 1932; the lectures were given in 1930; Mead died in 1931. Among other things, the book details Mead's views concerning (1) the parallel nature of social experience and scientific hypotheses; (2) the social consequences, or implications, of "the self"; and (3) the social character of "the present." In general terms, the book was an attempt to spell out the pragmatists' philosophy of history. Perhaps the most important feature of *The Philosophy of the Present* is found in Mead's attempt, or as Lee (1945:vi) put it, Mead's "self-conscious effort," to apply to nature proper the selfsame categories he saw as being operative in the basic workings of human nature. In the terminology of Claude Levi-Strauss, *The Philosophy of the Present* is a cultural representation of nature; the social world is being used in order to explain the world of nature. This book would not mark the last time that a volume by Mead would employ social psychological principles of development in an attempt to "explain" a higher-order phonomenon.

The Philosophy of the Act was published in 1938. For Mead, the basic unit of analysis in the study of human behavior is the *act*. Acts, of which he distinguishes four kinds — automatic, blocked, incomplete, and retrospective — begin with an impulse, or disturbance of equilibrium, and terminate with a goal or objective that provides a release for the impulse. In humans the simple existence of an impulse produces nothing but random activity until the definitions of other persons set goals for it and give to the act its social character. Although the concept of the act, or social act, is indispensable to Mead's social psychology, this particular book seems to be little read and infrequently cited by sociologists. Opinion on the book's merit is sharply divided. Some have argued that this work represents a somewhat systematic statement of the philosophy of pragmatism. Others have argued that the manuscript is a disorganized collection "made up of essays and miscellaneous fragments which are technical and repetitious, obscure and difficult" (Lee, 1945:vi). Nevertheless, in this volume Mead (1938:417) argues both that the *act* is the ultimate unit of existence and that it is the behavior of a person whose "reasons for movement lie within itself," rather than in another. As the social act is a pivotal concept in Mead's social psychology, and as *The Philosophy of the Act* constitutes a substantial part of his treatment of this topic, it is a work that bears some examination by those seeking a fuller treatment of Mead than can be provided in a text such as this.

Movements of Thought in the Nineteenth Century appeared in 1936. It is, for the most part, a series of lectures delivered to Mead's classes in the history of philosophy. These lectures illustrate Mead's ties to, and working knowledge of, various philosophical and sociological schools of thought. This is the most cleanly written and easy to follow of Mead's books; its language is far less technical than that of the others. In a sense, the book approaches a sociology-of-knowledge stance, as Mead tries to relate philosophical systems of knowledge to the times and places in which they arose and were received. One could certainly agree with Martindale's (1981:334) argument that *Movements of Thought in the Nineteenth Century* is one of Mead's most daring analyses, in that he offers his views on analogous developments in the stages of the self and in the process of intellectual history. He deals with the shift from Eighteenth-century rationalism to nineteenth-century Romanticism as if such a movement were the direct parallel to the various stages in the development of the self (e.g., the Romantic discovery of the past is equated with a reflexive discovery of the self). This work represents Mead's attempt to apply the social psychological principles of symbolic interactionism to the analysis of large-scale cultural phenomena. *Movements of Thought in the Nineteenth Century* bears the same relation to symbolic interactionism that "Freud's studies of *Totem and Taboo, Civilization and Its Discontents, The Future of an Illusion,* and *Moses and Monotheism,* bear to psychoanalysis" (Martindale, 1981:334). Such reasoning on Mead's part is perfectly compatible with those styles of interactionist argument that conceive of social organization, culture, and society in somewhat mentalistic terms. Mead's treatment of intellectual history in *Movements of Thought in the Nineteenth Century* directly parallels Charles Horton Cooley's treatment of society in his book *Social Organization.* Both books are examples of one way in which social–psychological principles can be employed in the working out of a higher-level sociological analysis. *Movements of Thought in the Nineteenth Century* should be of interest to those concerned with the development of sociological theory.

The Philosophy of the Act, The Philosophy of the Present, and *Movements of Thought in the Nineteenth Century* are, then, germane to an appreciation of Mead's overall philosophical and sociological system. But most sociologists' acquaintance with Mead's basic perspective rests mainly with the 1934 publication, *Mind, Self and Society.* This volume is the single most complete exposition of Mead's social psychology. He offers in the greatest detail his own views on the nature of the self. *Mind, Self and Society* is a good, representative collection to Mead's thoughts in the sense that his theory " of the self [is] the focal point at which he synthesizes his work in the philosophical and psychological traditions" (Meltzer, Petras and Reynolds, 1975:28). Furthermore, as both Strauss (1964:xiii) and Spreitzer and Reynolds (1973) point out, *Mind, Self and Society* is apparently the only work of Mead's read by many sociologists. At least this is the only work that many of them cite, and even here, when specific page numbers are referred to, they usually are to those portions of the manuscript dealing with the self and not with either mind or society. Meltzer (1964:18) however, is correct when he informs us that ". . . the natural, logical order of Mead's thinking seems to have been society, self, and mind — rather than 'Mind, Self, and Society." This society-to-self-to-mind line of progression is a natural enough one for a person who considers himself to be, as Mead did, a social behaviorist. In fact, the second part of the book's title reads *From the Standpoint of a Social Behaviorist.* It seems wise to follow this natural line of progression by dealing first with Mead's treatment of society. One can then take up the topics of self and mind, in that order.

Society: Symbols and Role Taking

The whole of human experience, the full range of truly human conduct, as Mead sees it, unfolds in the course of human association and only in the association of actors with one other. Life properly human is, in essence, social life, group life. And group life, in essence, is really a matter of cooperative behavior. The group, of course, always precedes the individual's arrival on the scene, and society always survives his or her departure. From Mead's vantage point, those who seek to explain the individual's conduct without first giving due consideration to the collectivity(ies) of which the individual is a part are on a fool's errand. We know from accounts of so-called feral children that although they are Homo sapiens, they are not, strictly speaking, human beings. Their conduct is not that of the person we consider to be human. There are, of course, persons who prefer to isolate themslves from society, to live solely in the company of themselves. But even in their case, society is never really absent; the group is always there, as these people carry with them the essential ingredients of social life; namely, the mental images of the groups and society in which they once dwelled. The life of the hermit is not that of the feral child. The conduct of the recluse and the hermit is molded by past social experiences as well as current mental imagery, itself a product of past social experiences. Their behavior, whether overt or covert, can be understood only by reference to the framework of associations they once participated in with others and now carry about as their repertoire of mental images, images that continue to influence their conduct. Even in the physical absence of others, the others are mentally present and lend to the conduct of the isolate the flavor of the past cooperative endeavors.

But not only human group life is a matter of cooperative behavior; in certain insect societies, cooperation also appears to be the order of the day. Mead, however, distinguishes between forms of human cooperation and those forms of cooperation present in the insect world. He distinguishes between human society and infrahuman collectivities. The biological makeup of insects dictates their behavior; they cooperatively act together in selected ways because they are physiologically organized to do so. A division of labor prevails in insect society that fits together the behavior of individual insects in such a manner as enables the group to engage in fairly numerous cooperative tasks of a somewhat complicated nature. The fact that these cooperative activities are physiologically determined is attested to by the stability, the fixity, and the permanence of those forms of infrahuman conduct. Generation after generation after generation, these patterns persist essentially unchanged. As it goes with insects, so too its goes with other forms of nonhuman cooperation. In speaking of the general patterning of insect society, Meltzer (1964:12) notes that "this picture of infrahuman society remains essentially valid as one ascends the scale of animal life, until we arrive at the human level." And then the picture, according to Mead, changes dramatically.

The social, cooperative life of infrahumans will not serve as either model for or explanation of human social organization. Humans simply enter into too many diverse forms of cooperative association. Furthermore, those forms change over time, emergent forms appear, and the change often comes rapidly. Little fixity is found in human collectivities; behavior tends to be highly variable when contrasted with that of infrahumans. Within the same human collectivity, the experience, conduct, and behavior of people varies. If it varies within a group, it should come as no surprise that it also varies between groups. If human behavior patterns do not spring from the fact that people are physiologically organized so that they must act in certain ways, what, then, allows them to act in concert?

According to George Herbert Mead, humans act in concert because they have the ability to take the other('s) point of view — mentally to place, as it were, themselves in the position of the other, and in so doing to take that person's point of view into account. Human cooperation, then, arises by a process wherein

> . . . (a) each acting individual ascertains the *intention* of the acts of others, and then (b) makes his own response on the basis of that intention. What this means is that, in order for human beings to cooperate, there must be present some sort of mechanism whereby each acting individual: (a) can come to understand the lines of action of others, and (b) can guide his own behavior to fit in with those lines of action.

> Human behavior is not a matter of responding directly to the activities of others. Rather, it involves responding to the *intentions* of others, i.e., to the future, intended behavior of others — not merely to their present actions. (Meltzer, 1964:12)

In short, human beings are able to form a conception of the perspective(s) held by other persons. We can and do act in concert because we share common expectations both for our own behavior and that of others. This leads to Mead's definition of social institutions:

> . . . the institutions of society are organized forms of groups or social activity — forms so organized that the individual members of society can act adequately and socially by taking the attitudes of others toward these activities. (1934:261)

Mead is suggesting again that the basis of group life is located in the ability of humans to take the role and attitudes of others. With the understanding of others' behavior that results from putting oneself in their place, one can structure one's own conduct in such a fashion that it fits in with the conduct of others. Group action consists of individuals putting their separate acts together; joint action is a product of the constructive action of individuals putting their constructs together. In carrying on common action, group members influence themselves and others in similar manner. Mead puts it as follows:

> The very stimulus which one gives to another to carry out his part of the common act affects the individual who so affects the other in the same sense. He tends to arouse the activity in himself which he arouses in the other. He also can in some degree so place himself in the place of the other or the places of others that he can share their experience. Thus, the varied means which belong to complicated human society can in varying degrees enter into the experience of many members, and the relationship between the means and the end can enter the experience of the individual. (1938:137)

Individual behavior is rooted in an "appreciation" of how one is "supposed" to act in a given context — not that one necessarily need go along with his or her appreciation in all situations. The point, however, is that human association, instead of being biologically ordained, is based on people's common understanding concerning how they should act. These understandings are changed, developed, and passed on in the course of people's interaction with one another. Individuals come to learn the collective understandings and patterns of conduct prevalent in the groups to which they belong. This in turn helps make social life, or society, possible. The customs, traditions, and expectations of the collectivity play a large role in helping to shape our feelings, thoughts, and actions. Individuals come selectively to incorporate within themselves the thoughts and feelings of other members of the same society: "The group organization affects very profoundly one's whole organic make-up, feelings, memory, and physiological functions. . . . It is in adjusting ourselves as part of a functioning organization that we develop our thoughts and behavior" (Mimeographed, n.d.:2)

Mead insists in deriving both mind and self from society, rather than the other way around. Social experience, behavior in association with others, is a precondition for the emergence of both selves and minds. In Mead's (1934:227) words, some form of interaction "must have been there in advance of the existence of minds and selves in human beings, in order to make possible the development, by human beings, of minds and selves within or in terms of that process." Here Zeitlin's words bear repeating:

> . . . it is important not to confuse the capacity for mind, intelligence, and self-consciousness with their actual development. The potential capacity was the product of biological evolution; its actualization was a product of social development. One process preceded and made the other possible, but once minds and selve emerged, the two processes became interdependent. (1973:230)

With respect to the higher life forms, Mead (1934:28) reasons that basic biological impulses "involve or require social situations and relations for their satisfaction." By Mead's reasoning, this is certainly no less true of Homo sapiens: Human biological impulses require social relations for their fulfillment. Of special significance are the impulses of hunger and sex. In speaking of the latter, Mead notes that of all the basic impulses, "the one which is most important in the case of human social behavior, and which most decisively or determinately expresses itself in the whole general form of human social organization . . . is the sex or reproductive impulse" (1934:28).

Mead, then, is arguing that in order to meet their basic biological needs, people must enter into definite social connections with one another. They must form societies, and these societies in turn help shape and give form to their human members. As Zeitlin has noted, in terms of tying his view of human biology to his view of human society, Mead likewise emphasizes "the peculiarly human mode of *praxis,* in which the *hand* mediates man's interaction with nature and with other men . . . [Mead] underscores the interdependence of practical experience, mediated by the hand, and the emergence of speech, consciousness, and self-consciousness" (1973:231).

Mead (1934:237) was to argue, then, that "speech and the hand go along together in the development of the social being." Developed social beings, of course, possess both minds and selves, and minds and selves arise, in turn, out of the process of human interaction. Interaction, social experience, behavior, and society come first. There are no preexisting selves and minds that make social experience possible; the latter accounts for the former. What Mead argues in terms of the ontological and temporal priority of social experience over the self holds equally true for the mind:

> It is true that some sort of co-operative activity antedates the self. There must be some loose organization in which the different organisms work together, and the sort of co-operation in which the gesture of the individual may become a stimulus to himself of the same type as the stimulus to the other, so that the *conversation of gestures* can pass over into the conduct of the individual. Such conditions are presupposed in the development of the self. (1934:240)

The italicized words in the statement are of crucial import. Note that Mead speaks of the "passing over" of the conversation of gestures. That is because the conversation of gestures is associated with infrahuman activity, and because ultimately the social life of humans is carried on in terms of language and not in terms of gestures. Gestures have import for human activity, but only to the extent that they become transformed into significant symbols. Gestures become so transformed when they serve as "common signs" to both those who make them and those who perceive them. Such common signs, such mutually understood gestures, are what Mead termed significant symbols:

> Gestures become significant symbols when they implicitly arouse in an individual making them the same responses which they explicitly arouse . . . in . . . the individuals to whom they are addressed. . . . Only in terms of gestures as significant symbols is the existence of mind or intelligence possible; for only in terms of gestures which are significant symbols can thinking — which is simply an internalized or implicit conversation of the individual with himself by means of gestures — take place. (1934:47)

It might do well at this point to contrast the infrahuman conversation of gesture with the more distinctively human mode of interaction between individuals. Infrahumans do not employ significant symbols; rather, they utilize natural signs or signals that may trigger behavior in others. The natural signs, however, have no meaning for the infrahuman who emitted the sign. The signs or signals are not given with the particular intention of calling out a specific response in the other. Infrahumans do indeed adjust themselves to each other by responding to one another's gestures, but infrahuman responses to gestures are products of preestablished tendencies to respond in fixed ways. A gesture calls for an automatic, unreflecting, quick, and direct response by its recipient, but the gesture was not made with any intent of eliciting the response that was forthcoming. Such infrahuman interaction has no room for deliberate, conscious meaning on the part of its participants. Meltzer (1964:13) nicely summarizes the key characteristics of the conversation of gestures and briefly contrasts them with the human mode of interaction in the following manner:

Gestures, at the non-human, or non-linguistic level, do not carry the connotation of conscious meaning or intent, but serve merely as cues for the appropriate responses of others. Gestural communication takes place immediately, without any interruption of the act, without the mediation of a definition or meaning. Each organism adjusts "instinctively" to the other; it does not stop and figure out which response it will give. Its behavior is, largely, a series of direct, automatic responses to stimuli. . . . Human beings on the other hand, respond to one another on the basis of the intentions or meanings of gestures. This renders the gestures *symbolic,* i.e., the gesture becomes something which, in the imaginations of the participants, stand for the entire act.

When a human individual, then, makes a gesture (e.g., draws a gun), the person who is the recipient of the gesture completes in his or her imagination the act that the gesture stands for. The recipient projects the gesture into the future: "I am going to be shot." The human recipient understands the act stood for by the gesture; the gesture's meaning is, so to speak, taken. The intentions of the person making the gesture have been inferred by the gesture's recipient; an interpretation of intent has been made. The act has been imaginatively completed and responded to.

The foregoing paragraph, then, argues that "imaginative activity" is the basis on which human beings respond to one another. Unless each human participant is able to attach the same meaning to the same gesture, however, cooperative, concerted behavior becomes an impossibility. Unless shared meaning, expectation, and understanding are either present or soon arise, unless the imagined section of the act is completed in pretty much the same way, unless parties to interaction come to interpret gestures in similar fashion, cooperative behavior cannot be maintained.

Happily, humans have the ability to respond to their own gestures. Therefore, they can attach to their own gestures the same meaning that others attach to them; the individual can imaginatively complete the act just as others complete it. When shared meanings attach to gestures, they become linguistic elements, significant symbols if you like. A system of significant symbols, of linguistic elements, constitutes a language. Through the use of language, through communication, human society and the human individual interpenetrate. Individuals, because they can respond to their own gestures, can share each other's experiences, can forge a common basis for organized social life, and in cooperation can establish a society. Human behavior in human society is thoroughly social in character, not only because we respond to the behavior of others but because the behavior of others is incorporated in our own behavior — and "ours" is incorporated in "theirs." We respond to ourselves as others respond to us. Because we do, we imaginatively share the behavior of our fellow interactionists. Our relationship with others is a product of our ability to respond to our own gestures and imaginatively to place ourselves in the position of others:

> We are more or less seeing ourselves as others see us. We are unconsciously addressing ourselves as others address us. . . . We are calling out in the other person something we are calling out in ourselves, so that unconsciously we take over these attitudes. We are unconsciously putting ourselves in the place of others and acting as others act. . . . (Mead, 1934:68–69)

Thus is a human society possible, and such a society is the source of the social genesis of both self and mind.

Self

George Herbert Mead was simultaneously an heir to and a critic of several different traditions in both philosophy and psychology. Among the early interactionists, he was the one most heavily influenced by evolutionary thinking. As Petras has argued, "A striking aspect of Mead's work on human behavior is the fact that all of it is conceptualized within a phylogenetic frame of reference . . . [and] the underlying basis for Mead's theories regarding the genesis of the self and the role of society and mind in human behavior evolves out of his working within a phylogenetic framework" (Meltzer, Petras and Reynolds, 1975:28–29). Drawing on Darwin, Lamarck, and Bergson,

Mead would apply the notions of continuity, flux, and emergence to that point on the evolutionary continuum where gestures and symbols meet, where language and communication are birthed, where selfs arise and social differentiation takes the place of physiological differentiation, — where, in short, Homo sapiens become "sorted out" from other members of the phylogenetic kingdom. It is Mead's evolutionary perspective, wedded to the doctrine of emergence and his philosophy of the present, which establishes "the path upon which his theories run from the level of general concepts to the particular application of these, and the sociological theory of the self can be seen as a particular example of the processes discussed in his works in philosophy and psychology" (Meltzer, Petras and Reynolds, 1975:29). In Mead's theory of the self, then, one can catch a glimpse of his overall sociology, philosophy, psychology, and social psychology, as well as see his connection with, reaction to, and criticism of the competing explanations of human behavior offered in his time. Mead not only criticized these diverse, and in some cases extreme, theories of self and behavior but he also borrowed selectively from them. With an increased awareness of the social structuring of human action being felt in social science circles, "there was a need for an explanation of behavioral processes that would incorporate findings from extremes" (Meltzer, Petras and Reynolds, 1975:28). Mead's theory of the self did just that, and in so doing he made an enormous contribution to social psychology.

Three rather different views of the nature of human nature had an impact on Mead's construction of his particular theory of the self: (1) the German idealist approach, embodied in the writings of Wilhelm Wundt; (2) the psychological behaviorist approach, represented by the work of John B. Watson; and (3) the American pragmatist approach, illustrated by the views of John Dewey, and perhaps more directly by those of William James. As Don Martindale suggests, Mead had three basic criticisms of previous theories of the self: "(1) Either they presupposed the mind as antecedently existing to account for mental phenomena (Wundt); (2) or they failed to account for specifically mental phenomena (Watson); and (3) they failed to isolate the mechanism by which mind and self appeared (James and Dewey)" (1981:330). Mead's theory attempts to overcome all three of the deficiencies found in previous conceptualizations of the self.

From the perspective of George Herbert Mead, the most distinguishing, and hence most important, thing about human society is that it is made up of persons with selves. As mentioned previously, Mead argued that (1) human society was possible because individuals could take the role of the other; and (2) human behavior was social in the sense that individuals can respond to themselves as others respond to them, that is, they incorporate in their behavior the response of others, because they are able to respond to their own gestures. The ability to respond to one's own gestures necessarily implies that one possesses a self. If you are capable of acting toward yourself as you act toward others, then you have a self. Simply stated, to possess a self means that you can respond to yourself as an object. It means you have the capacity of gaining perspective on yourself by looking back as others would look on you. You may berate yourself, praise yourself, punish yourself, hate yourself, blame yourself, encourage yourself, and so forth. You may, in short, become the object of your own actions. Through the incorporation of the definitions made by others, a self is formed; hence, the self is formed in the same fashion as are other objects. It is a social product.

When one becomes an object to himself or herself, one has a self, but one can become an object to oneself only by means of language — and language, in turn, is available only in society. The existence of human society necessarily implies the existence of role taking; role taking, in turn, is the underlying mechanism producing the self. Role taking is present whenever significant symbols are employed. A system of significant symbols forms a language, and through the use of language one comes by, or acquires, the definitions and meanings of other parties in society. The definitions and meanings of others provide the means for the individual to view himself or herself as an object. One acquires the meanings and definitions of others through the process of role taking; hence, role taking becomes the basic underlying process giving rise to the self.

Through the process of role taking the individual becomes, in fact, capable of treating himself or herself as an object, becomes capable, as it were, of gaining and maintaining "social distance" from oneself. The self develops during childhood, and childhood activity plays an instrumental role in that development because through initial attempts at role taking, the child begins to gain a modicum of social distance from himself or herself. This takes place through a series of stages, stages in the development of the self.

The first stage can be called the *preparatory,* or *imitation,* stage, although Mead himself fixed no specific label on it. Here the child begins, through the process of meaningless imitation, to gain a small amount of social distance from himself or herself. Without any real comprehension of what he or she is doing, the child imitates, or does, things that others around him or her are doing. A two-year old girl pretending to read a weekly newsmagazine with her father is beginning to extricate herself from herself. She is engaged in the initial process of role taking; she is incipiently placing herself in the position of her father and "acting" like him.

In the second, or *play,* stage, the child gains additional distance by exaggerating the imitation process. Here the child pretends to be somebody he or she is not; the child, in sequential fashion, even pretends to be many people he or she is not. Actual role playing is taking place during the play stage, and the child gains the capability of acting back toward himself or herself in terms of the roles he or she is actually playing. As the child is here in a position to direct activity toward himself or herself by taking the role(s) of the other(s); a self is now being formed. Evidence of this self-formation appears in the form of the child referring to himself or herself as others would, for example, "Mary is tired," or "Bob is a good boy." The instrumental aspect of this process is that the child is beginning to maximize social distance from himself or herself. The child is not only seeing himself or herself from the perspective of others, but is beginning to "take on" those perspectives as his or her own.

During the play stage, a limited number of others have relevance for the child's conduct. The child's configuration of roles is still very unstable, and it "passes from one role to another in unorganized, inconsistent fashion" (Meltzer, 1964:16). The child has yet to develop a consistent, or unitary, vantage point in terms of which to view himself or herself. The child has no unified conception of himself or herself, and so "forms a number of separate and discrete objects of itself, depending on the roles in which it acts toward itself" (Meltzer, 1964:16).

During the last, or *game*, stage the child develops the ability to, and is placed in situations where he or she must, simultaneously take a number of roles — which is to say that several others' expectations must be simultaneously responded to. The child comes to respond to what Mead referred to as the "generalized other"; that is, the child becomes able to see the community of interests as over and against the interests of any one other. The child becomes, as it were, able simultaneously to articulate the whole (the group, society, etc.), to see it as more than the sum of its parts. The child then comes to view himself or herself from the perspective of the interest of the community as a whole. The child comes to grasp that set of values, meanings, definitions, and expectations that are common to the group, community, or society. Once a child has taken on this generalized standpoint, it becomes possible to conduct himself or herself in a consistent, organized fashion. The self can be viewed from a consistent standpoint. As the following statement reveals, the acquisition of a "generalized other" has important consequences:

> This means, then, that the individual can transcend the local and present expectations and definitions with which he comes in contact . . . through having a generalized other, the individual becomes emancipated from the pressures of the peculiarities of the immediate situation. He can act with a certain amount of consistency in a variety of situations because he acts in accordance with a generalized set of expectations and definitions that he has internalized. (Meltzer, 1964:17)

The game state is the completing stage of the self, but while the self is a process that develops in stages, it is a process that also has its own definite structures, or elements.

The Elements of Self

While the self is best conceptualized as a social process within the person, it involves two "distinguishable phases," known respectively as the "I" and the "me" (Mead, 1934:178). The impulsive and spontaneous tendencies of the actor are represented by the "I"; it is the uncertain, unpredictable, unorganized, and undirected component in human experience. It is not too inaccurate to say that the "I" is the spontaneous spark of energy within the individual.

In some respects, the "I" is the most complex and potentially confusing of all Mead's concepts. As Zeitlin points out: "Mead's 'I' involves a paradox: on the one hand it represents freedom, spontaneity, novelty, initiative; on the other hand, however, because the 'I' is essentially biologic and impulsive, it is blind and unconscious, a process we become aware of only when it is a fait accompli" (1973:227).

In a sense, then, the actor never catches sight of himself or herself as "I." The "I" appears to the actor only in his or her memory. When an "I" appears in memory, it has already become a "me." As Mead (1934:174) put it, "If you ask . . . where directly in your own experience the 'I' comes in, the answer is that it comes in as a historical figure." Mead's discussion of the "I" deals heavily with its biologic nature, and as Zeitlin correctly points out, most sociological discussions of Mead's views on the "I" have failed to mention that Mead argues that "the 'I' is a manifestation of human natural needs; it, or the energy behind it, is 'deeply imbedded' in man's biological nature" (1973:228). There would appear to be a tendency on the part of many interactionists to ignore Mead's locating of a phase of the self in natural needs and basic biology in favor of playing up what they take to be the self's thoroughly social nature. Suffice it to say that the "I" is a manifestation of both natural needs and impulses (Mead lists 10), that it is a process of thinking as well as acting (Mead, 1912:405, says it "is identical with the analytic or synthetic process of cognition"), and that, because it represents the truly spontaneous and unpredictable, its existence implies that human beings can never be mere reflections of society and will never be those completely passive agents Dennis Wrong (1961) referred to as oversocialized.

The "me" is the phase of the self that represents the group's common meanings, values, definitions, expectations, viewpoints, and understandings. Depending on the situation, the "me" may comprise a specific other or the generalized other. It represents the incorporated other(s) within the individual person (Meltzer, 1964:17).

Although it would not be exactly correct to say that the "I" disposes, human acts start in the form of the "I" and *tend to terminate* in the form of the "me." One emphasizes the words "tend to terminate" because, as Mead (1934:210) himself noted, while the "me" establishes limits within which the "I" must act, if ". . . the stress becomes too great, these limits are not observed, and an individual asserts himself in perhaps a violent fashion." When this happens the "me" is no longer in control and ". . . the 'I' is the dominant element over against the 'me' " (1934:210). The "I" initiates action and stands for the act before it comes under the influence of those expectations of others incorporated in the "me." While the "me" provides direction to an ongoing act, its initial propulsion comes from the "I." The act itself is a product of the dynamic interplay between the "I" and "me" phases of the self. Conformity would seem to append to the "me" and novelty to the "I"; the "me" represents society's influence on the individual and the "I" the individual's influence on society. The "I" does not appear alone as its action summons up the "me," and in the dynamic interplay between these two phases of the self we are "thus provided with a basis for understanding the mutuality of the relationship between the individual and society" (Meltzer, 1964:17). Without these two phases, both social control and creativity are, as Mead suggests, absent:

> . . . the "I" is always something different from what the situation itself calls for. So there is always that distinction, if you like, between the "I" and the "me." The "I" both calls out the "me" and responds to it. Taken together they constitute a personality as it appears in social experience. The self is essentially a social process going on with these two distinguishable phases. If it did not have these phases there could be no conscious responsibility, and there would be nothing novel in experience. (1934:178)

It is, then, in the "give and take" between the "I" and "me" phases of the self that novel experience becomes possible, while social control becomes, at least in part, self control.

Mind

As Mead (1934:50) noted, ". . . the origin of minds and the interaction among minds become mysteries" if one posits, as Wundt did, the existence of individual minds and then attempts to derive social life and processes from them. Mead (1934:55) rejects this approach and, as he did in the case of the *self,* argues instead that *mind* is *a social product,* or derivative: "Mind arises through communication by a conversation of gestures in a social process or context of experience. . . ." More specifically, it is through communication by means of significant symbols that mind arises. In a sense, "The mind is present only at certain points in human behavior, i.e., when significant symbols are being used by the individual" (Meltzer, 1964:19). Mead summed up this argument concerning both the social derivation of mind and its nature as a process as follows:

> [First] . . . there is an actual process of living together on the part of all members of the community which takes place by means of gestures. The gestures are certain stages in the cooperative activities which mediate the whole process. . . . Given such social process, there is a possibility of human intelligence when this social process, in terms of the conversation of gestures, is taken over into the conduct of the individual. . . . The mind is simply the interplay of such gestures in the form of significant symbols. . . . It is such significant symbols, in the sense of a sub-set of social stimuli initiating a cooperative response, that do in a certain sense constitute our mind, provided that not only the symbol but also the responses are in our natures. (1934:188–190)

The gestures and significant symbols noted by Mead are all important; only by means of them does thinking takes place. This is one way of conceptualizing mind, and it is Mead's way. Thinking involves an internalization of the conversation of meaningful (conventional) gestures, and mind is a process "which manifests itself whenever the individual is interacting with himself by using significant symbols" (Meltzer, 1964:19).

Mead's analysis of mind starts with a consideration of the relationship of the person to his or her environment and ends with Mead's interpreting the mind in behavioristic terms. Mead's behavioristic interpretation of mind sees it "(1) as an organization of responses, i.e., as functional rather than substantive, and (2) as an expression of intelligence rather than wisdom, i.e., as an instrument of action rather than of contemplation" (Lee, 1945:37). The relationship of organisms to their environment is essentially one of adaptation. Continuous adjustments are made to one's surrounding habitat. Because living activity involves selective perception, and because organisms pay attention and adjust only to selected aspects of their environments, Mead assumes that the environment is not exactly the same for all organisms. Because only selected aspects of an environment are responded to, in a sense, the organism plays a role in determining the environment — which is to say that the organism determines which part of the environment it will pay attention to. This, in turn, means that Mead "regards all life as ongoing activity, and views stimuli — not as initiators of activity — but as elements selected by the organism in the furtherance of that activity" (Meltzer, 1964:19). However, the determination of the environment by the infrahuman and unsocialized organism does not involve minded behavior. Although selective in nature, reflective intelligence is not present. Things are quite different at the distinctively human level; as Meltzer (1964:19) points out, here ". . . there is hesitancy, an inhibition of overt conduct, which is not involved in the selective attention of animal behavior." During this period of hesitancy, during this moment of inhibition, mind "exists."

When overt behavior is inhibited, *when one is mentally contemplating alternative courses of subsequent action, when one is assessing the future consequences of present behavior in terms of past experience, then mind is indeed present.* Thinking, or minded behavior, arises in the face of problems, in the light of a blockage of the act: "All analytic thought commences with the presence of problems . . . ." (Mead, 1900:2). Minded behavior is nothing more than contemplating in the light of previous experience the possible consequences of different lines of future conduct before selecting the one alternative to be acted on. Past, present, and future all come together in this process called mind; both hindsight and foresight enter the picture. This process of minded behavior dictates that human beings construct their acts in the course of their execution; they select, organize, and control their responses to their environments. What people are, in fact, responding to are phenomena Mead called "objects." Objects are plans of action, which is to say that humans perceive things in terms of experiences one would have if a plan of action was carried out toward that object. One sees objects in terms of the use to be made of them or the action to be directed toward them. Objects exist only when we indicate them to ourselves. To indicate something to oneself is to take others into account. As "others' definitions" are implicated in our indicating objects to ourselves, objects are largely shared, or social, objects. Hence, while we select the objects which constitute our social environments, we do so on a social as well as an individual basis.

The process of working one's way around a blocked act, the process of *imaginatively rehearsing* one's future behavior, is what Mead termed reflective thought, analytic thought, or, simply, mind. Reflective thought is the process of "the turning back of the experience of the individual upon himself" (1934:134). Such reflective thought, once begun, continues until the individual has selected and embarked upon a new course of action. Mead put it in the following terms:

> [Reflective thought] continues always to be an expression of . . . conflict and the solution to the problems involved. . . . All reflective thought arises out of real problems present in immediate experience, and is occupied entirely with the solution of these problems or their attempted solution. . . . This solution finally is found in the possibility of continuing activity, that has been stopped along old or new lines, when such reflective thought ceases in the nature of the case. (1900:2)

Collective social activity forms the matrix out of which communication arises, and communication is, in turn, the very process out of which mind arises. In the course of interacting with others some initial gestures of the human infant are favorably received. In fairly short order, certain gestures come to have common meanings for both the child and those he or she associates with. These consensually agreed on gestures are called by Mead "conventional gestures." Through such conventional gestures and additional linguistic symbols, the child picks up or learns the definitions and meanings of the collectivity of which he or she is a part, learns to take the role of others, and, in short, comes to possess the ability to think. A socially generated mind enables the person to adjust to the collectivity and, in turn, makes possible the collectivity's continued existence.

The individual, then, engages in minded behavior whenever he or she, through the use of significant symbols, calls out in herself or himself the same response that others would make. This is thoroughly social in both origin and function because these symbols are provided by society. Furthermore, as mental activity entails, in a sense, talking to oneself, one must have a standpoint from which to converse, indicate, and respond. That standpoint too is provided by society—not that it need be uncritically incorporated by the individual. The process is more subtle than that. The standpoint that the individual takes in order to converse with himself or herself is acquired by importing into himself or herself the role of others. Only by indicating to oneself in the role of others does mind arise. When we take the role of the other, we see ourselves as others view us, and hence we are capable of arousing in ourselves the same responses that we call out in others. This is how an internal conversation is made possible, and "it is this conversation with ourselves, between the representation of the other (in the form of the 'me') and our impulses (in the form of the 'I') that constitutes the mind" (Meltzer, 1964:21).

In summary, minds are a process that is both product of, and part of, a still larger ongoing social process. Minds arise in the course of communication and interaction. Yet, as Petras notes, "While the mind emerges out of social interaction, its high level of development among humans depends upon a condition that represents a synthesis of their biological, psychological, and social nature" (Meltzer, Petras, and Reynolds, 1975:31). The "condition" is the ability to respond to one's own gestures and actions. When this condition is arrived at, minded behavior has emerged for the species. When the individual acquires the ability to respond to his or her own behavior, when the individual can turn back his or her own experience upon himself or herself, then mind, or reflective thinking, is also present. It is all a matter of individuals employing significant symbols in order to call out in themselves the same replies that they call out in each other. Given an analysis of mind that sees it as a socially generated process that is, in turn, an emergent from symbolic behavior, it should be evident that "Mead avoids both the behavioristic fallacy of reduction and the individualistic fallacy of taking for granted the phenomenon that is to be explained" (Meltzer, 1964:22).

A Brief Summary of Mead's Views

Perhaps the most distinguishing feature of George Herbert Mead's perspective is that it sees human society as composed, among other things, of individuals who have "selves." The self is a social product in that each individual is born into an ongoing society with its own pattern of symbolic interaction. Employing significant symbols, those who interact with the individual enable him or her to move beyond the simple conversation of gestures stage to the point where actual role taking begins. Through role taking one comes to share others' perspectives. This, in turn, provides the individual with the ability to act toward himself or herself, and eventually such action becomes a product of viewing oneself from the perspective of what Mead termed the "generalized other." One comes to define one's own behavior in terms of the expectations of others, even in terms of the expectations of society as a whole. The *self* develops concurrent with such role taking.

Through the self apparatus, the individual becomes the object of his or her own actions — that is, the individual places on himself or herself the same demands and obligations he or she directs toward others. This is the central mechanism through which and by which the human individual faces and deals with the world. In Mead's view, then, one confronts the world by first, and continually, talking to oneself, or making self-indications, and second by responding to one's own self-indications. Self-indication largely involves an internal conversation between the self's "I" and "me" phases, and whenever such internal conversation, such internal symbolic interaction, transpires, mind is also present, as it is in the course of our symbolic interaction with others.

The general significance of this "self-indication" process would appear to be twofold:

1. To indicate something to oneself is to make that something into an object: the character or meaning of anything is conferred on that thing by the person. People construct meanings relevant to the object; hence, meaning does not inhere in the object itself. Individuals respond to the meanings they attach to objects by formulating what Mead called "plans of action," rather than have objects with preexisting meanings force them to respond in certain ways.

2. Human action is constructed or built up, instead of merely being released. Human social life is a communicative process not just between persons but also in terms of an internal dialogue of assessing and conferring meanings on objects. This whole process enables the person to stand over and against the world of social reality so that one accepts, rejects, or transforms things in terms of how one interprets them to oneself. One interprets things largely on the basis of action one is prepared to direct toward them, instead of this being a stimulus–response. The individual "remakes" each stimulus and responds only to a stimulus of his or her own (social) making. Mead sees people as having a fairly large measure of control over their social lives. People respond to their interpretation of things and not to things themselves; hence, the person can respond differently to the same object on different occasions, but can also respond in the same way to objectively different things if they are similarly defined. Self-indication takes place in a social context, in a context of symbolic interaction. Group action is a focal point of concern, and meaningful action is the product of joint behavior. Group action takes the form of fitting together individual lines of conduct, and in so doing each individual tries to determine the ideas, meanings, and expectations of others. This implies that action is not merely the development or fruition of one's subjective intentions carried through, as Weber argued, because the end product may be diametrically opposed to the individual's original intention. The point being that, from Mead's perspec-

tive, action is something that is constantly being built up; the very nature of interaction makes human affairs highly volatile.

From the perspective of George Herbert Mead, then, human behavior, human action, is built up, or constructed, and the very pattern of society is made by people and hence is not the total determinant of the action that occurs. This approach points to the multitudinous avenues of behavior open to men and women. Mead's approach allows one to examine social stability because it involves studying those similar interpretations that are made repetitiously. These interpretations can and do change, however, because they are made by men and women in action. Many times, joint action does not arise in the way we hope it will, and conflict arises to terminate it; but this in and of itself is both a form of joint action and social change. Mead's approach allows for the study of both stability and change. He offers a different view of social life — one in which we can easily visualize men and women going through the very process of self-indication, interpretation, and interaction that he described. If we would understand these processes of self-indication and interaction, we cannot be content with merely enumerating acts; rather, we must be concerned with explaining and detailing the interpretative process transpiring within and between human beings. This process is best grasped through the methodological device known as *participant observation*.

Mead's contributions to symbolic interactionism are both numerous and diverse. A listing of such contributions, as provided by Bernard N. Meltzer (1964:30–31), would seem a fitting way to conclude this brief section on Mead's social psychology:

1. He clearly stated the essence of the symbolic interactionist viewpoint: Human behavior is behavior in terms of what situations symbolize.
2. He forcefully argued that mind and self are twin social emergents and not biological givens.
3. He illustrated the manner in which language acts as the mechanism for the rise of both self and mind.
4. His concept of the self illuminates the process whereby the individual is both caught up in and extricated from society.

5. His specific functional, processual conception of the mind as the importation within the person of the social process of interaction.
6. His conception of the act as behavior constructed in such a way during the course of activity that individuals can structure or select their own environments.
7. His description of how, through the development of common meanings, understandings, expectations, and objects, a common social world is formed.
8. His demonstration that individuals actually share one another's behavior rather than simply respond to it.
9. His argument, and its implicit methodological implications, that the inner, subjective aspect of behavior is vital for a full understanding of truly human conduct.

Early Interactionism: Summary Characteristics

The most extensive summations of the defining characteristics of early interactionism are perhaps to be found in the writings of John W. Petras (1966:186–213). According to Petras, in spite of the apparent diversity among the major figures now considered to have been the forerunners to, or actual exponents of, an "early interactionism," four basic themes are reflected in their writings. First, all manifested a concern with the role of group factors as key elements in both shaping and understanding behavior. Second, all were concerned with the development of personality and self; and all were cognizant of the fact that biological factors must be dealt with in establishing an adequate theory of motivation. Thirdly, all focused on symbolic behavior, were interested in the means by which people communicated, and were convinced that human society was held together by shared meanings. The fourth and last defining characteristic of early interactionism relates to the kind of research that it generated in sociology. Petras puts the matter as follows:

> Its [early interactionism's] primary influence upon early research came from two directions. First of all, the notion of interaction as a crucial link between the individual and the social group became a subject of concern in several areas.

Secondly, a more direct influence could be noted in the adoption of the method of sympathetic introspection. . . . (Meltzer, Petras and Reynolds, 1975:510)

Clearly, a key contribution of the early interactionists to contemporary sociology was their argument that the group is an all-important factor in the shaping and motivation of behavior. While many of their insights are taken for granted today, such was not the case in their time. American sociology was then dominated by people such as Lester Frank Ward, who used an individual-generated perspective. Ward and others "traced the motivation of behavior to innate tendencies which were then manifested in behavior through the 'natural' fear of pain and the desire to seek after pleasure" (Meltzer, Petras and Reynolds, 1975:48). The instinct theories of motivation were in vogue, and societies were popularly seen as phenomena whose role was to hinder or suppress human nature. The early interactionists helped bring about the decline of the instinct theories of motivation, and they discredited theories that saw an individual–society antagonism as basic to understanding human behavior. Instinct theory and individual–society dualisms have typically gone hand in hand; so, with a single forceful argument the early interactionists undercut the intellectual legitimacy of both positions. In place of the concept *instinct,* they substituted the concept *impulse,* a concept that implies that its "satisfaction can take place only within the bounds of what's called human society" (Meltzer, Petras and Reynolds, 1975:48). In place of an individual and society dichotomy, they opined that the individual and society were, in Cooley's words, but "two sides of the same coin." They attacked the earlier notion that human society is nothing but an aggregation of individuals bound together by physical limitations. Society, they strove to demonstrate, was held together by shared meanings, had about it an organic character, and was both a producer and product of symbolic behavior. How successful were the early interactionists in terms of their views eventually being established in American sociology? Apparently quite successful, for their success "can be measured by the paucity of attention directed toward these aspects of the theory today. Thus, today, no one questions either the importance of the group as a factor in the motivation of behavior or that the sources of motivation do not reside in instincts" (Meltzer, Petras and Reynolds, 1975:52).

Today the concepts of self, role, and identity, among others, capture the attention of those who would test selected aspects of symbolic interaction theory. There has been an increased interest in self-psychology, role theory, and reference group theory. Each has stimulated a growing body of research, but even here, "As far as American sociology is concerned, it was the early formulation of interactionism which provided the basis for each of these subsequent developments" (Meltzer, Petras and Reynolds, 1975:52). Those "subsequent developments" that constitute the major varieties of contemporary interactionism are taken up next.

PART TWO

CONTEMPORARY INTERACTIONISM: MAJOR VARIETIES

As noted at the beginning of this work, and depending on which author one happens to read, there are anywhere from 2 to 15 varieties of contemporary symbolic interactionism. One even suspects that an additional variety or two could be added to the list of 15, if one chose to cut the pie thin enough. The delineation of various varieties, or schools, of interactionism depends on one's identifying among interactionists: (1) differing conceptions of key ideas; (2) either heavy reliance on or unemphasizing of selected key concepts; (3) opposing philosophical viewpoints; (4) varying images of both people and society; and (5) alternate methodological stances.

Primarily on the basis of differences in methodological preferences, for example, Meltzer and Petras (1970) have identified and described what they term the Chicago and Iowa schools of thought. Using the same criteria of differences in preferred methodology alone, Reynolds and Meltzer (1973) distinguish between three sets of symbolic interactionists: participant observers, positivists, and those advocating a combination of methods. Reynolds and his associates, (1970) by focusing only on varying definitions of key or pivotal concepts employed in symbolic interaction theory, first identified what they termed "unorthodox" and "conventional" varieties of interactionism. Reynolds and McCart (1972), employing and refining the same technique, later distinguished between what they labeled the "unorthodox," "semi-conventional," and "conventional" schools.

While the schools, or varieties, of symbolic interactionism specified by Meltzer and Petras and by Reynolds are few in number, others have elected to identify a far larger number of the perspective's variations. Perhaps the two most intensive listings of interactionism's multiple varieties and related variations are provided respectively by Leon H. Warshay and Manford H. Kuhn. Warshay (1971) provides us with the following eight varieties of symbolic interactionism proper:

1. The Blumer school
2. The Iowa school
3. A stress on interaction with deemphasis on language view
4. A role-theory view
5. The dramaturgical school
6. A field-theory version
7. An existential brand
8. Ethnomethodology

The largest single listing is offered by Manford Kuhn (1964). Focusing on what he takes to be the major contradictions and principal points of unclarity in the Meadian tradition, especially in the writings of George H. Mead himself, Kuhn goes on to specify what he takes to be either "sub-varieties," "related orientations," "direct extensions," or "amendments" to the symbolic interactionist framework. Kuhn apparently feels that these "sub and related orientations" are themselves, at least in part, products of the deep-seated contradictions and fundamental ambiguities found within Mead's basic outline of the general interactionist perspective. Kuhn offers the following as variants and related orientations:

> (1) role theory, (2) reference group theory, (3) social and person perception theory, (4) self theory as expounded by Kuhn and his students, (5) phenomenological theory, (6) the Sapir–Whorf–Cassier language and culture orientation, (7) the interpersonal theory of Harry Stack Sullivan, (8) self-consistency theory, (9) self-actualizing theory, (10) the dramaturgical school, (11) cognitive theory, (12) field theory, (13) the developmental theory of Piaget, (14) identity theory, and (15) the self theory of Carl Rogers. (1964:63)

There are, then, numerous varieties of symbolic interactionism and its "related orientations." The four major varieties of symbolic interaction theory seem to be the Chicago school, the Iowa school, the dramaturgical genre, and ethnomethodology. Here one follows the lead of Meltzer, as it is easy enough to agree with his argument that the Chicago and Iowa schools together with dramaturgical and ethnomethodological approaches "more distinctly than the other listed varieties [adopt] a perspective that includes basic constituent elements of the larger framework while, simultaneously, adding or subtracting other elements of a less basic character" (Meltzer, Petras, and Reynolds, 1975:54).

One could also elect to focus on the Chicago and Iowa schools and on the dramaturgical and ethnomethodological approaches because

> . . . as varieties of symbolic interactionism, all of these orientations share the substantive view that human beings construct their realities in a process of interaction with other human beings [and because] . . . each orientation accepts, to some degree, the methodological necessity of "getting inside" the reality of the actor in an effort to understand this reality as the actor does. (Meltzer, Petras and Reynolds, 1975:54–55)

In discussing each of these four kinds of symbolic interaction theory, as in the work of Meltzer, my focus is primarily on the works and ideas of one major exemplar, or exponent, of each perspective. I do this because "to do otherwise would entail a loss of coherence, for a wider coverage would require the inclusion of numerous minor qualifications and reservations" (1975:55). I present the Chicago school first because it is perhaps the largest and best-known camp within the interactionist tradition. I discuss the Iowa school next, and then the dramaturgical approach and ethnomethodology; the latter two are clearly the "newer" of interactionism's four major varieties.

Chapter 3   THE CHICAGO SCHOOL

For an entire generation, the leading spokesman for the Chicago style of symbolic interactionism has been Herbert G. Blumer. Blumer's career spans several decades, and operating first out of the University of Chicago and later out of the University of California at Berkeley, where he is now professor emeritus, Blumer through his writings and especially through his teaching may have exposed more future sociologists to the symbolic interactionist tradition than any other single individual. A list of Blumer's former students reads very much like a "who's who" in contemporary symbolic interactionism. While Blumer is far from being the most widely published of the interactionists, his influence as a teacher of interactionist principles has been unsurpassed in American sociology. During the course of pursuing his own doctorate at the University of Chicago, Blumer came into close contact with such early contributors to the interactionist tradition as Robert Ezra Park and Ellsworth Faris. More important, he was closely associated with George Herbert Mead. In accepting a faculty position in the Department of Sociology at the University of Chicago, Blumer "established himself as the inheritor of Mead's mantle in symbolic interactionism" (Meltzer, Petras and Reynolds, 1975:55). As Don Martindale (1981:354) notes, ". . . it was Herbert Blumer who became the major sponsor of the Meadian point of view in the Chicago department." Blumer coined the term *symbolic interactionism;* it was he who founded the branch of symbolic interactionism that has remained closest to Mead's original position.

From Blumer's vantage point, when discussing human beings it is of paramount importance to note that, first and foremost, humans act on the basis of *meaning*. These meanings, in a sense, are products of collective situations, which is to say that they arise out of interaction with others as the interactive process itself is mediated by language. Through this process, one comes both to see and to take the role of the other and to place on oneself the same demands others place on one. It is therefore also through this process that one comes to view or treat himself or herself as an object. In short, through the interactive process as it is mediated by language one acquires a self. The self, in Blumer's view, is simply that which can be an object to itself. But, as Martindale points out, Blumer is well aware that ". . . individuals remain actors as well as objects, selecting, regrouping, and transforming meanings in light of the situation in which they find themselves. Human groups are joint actions. Culture is how people behave in the course of their joint actions" (1981:354).

Hence, from Blumer's perspective, individual behavior, group conduct, and even culture all come down to this: They are all matters involving meaning and interpretation. By Blumer's (1969:16) reasoning, an individual, a group, a corporation, a complex organization, a nation, or for that matter any collectivity, "needs to construct its action through an interpretation of what is happening in its area of operation." This implies something. If you wish to understand an individual's behavior or a collectivity's actions, you must "get at" the meanings being assigned and the interpretations being made. This is the crucial point for Blumer, because he "continually stressed . . . the reducibility of all social processes, however complex, to meaningful interpersonal behavior" (Martindale, 1981:354). As all social processes are a matter of interpersonal behavior, and as people behave on the basis of meanings, it is imperative, if you wish to understand individual behavior in particular and social life in general, that a distinctive methodology be developed for the study of such behavior.

In addition to defending the interactionist perspective in the face of competing theoretical frameworks such as structural functionalism, behaviorism, entity theories of society, organicism, and all theories proposing a static conception of people and society, Blumer has always seen his major contribution to symbolic interactionism as being an elaboration of its methodology.

Blumer has long argued that sociology needs a distinctive methodology in the social sciences. He has been a strident critic of the positivists in the discipline, and his posture with respect to what constitutes a proper method for sociology clearly sets him apart from Manford H. Kuhn, who for years was the leading exponent of another major variety of symbolic interactionism, the Iowa school. Blumer's (1969:24) disenchantment with a growing tendency for sociologists to equate methodology with "the study of advanced quantitative procedures" is clearly seen in his following remarks:

> . . . much of present-day methodology in the social and psychological sciences is inadequate and misguided. The overwhelming bulk of what passes today as methodology is made up of such preoccupation as the following: the devising and use of sophisticated research techniques, usually of an advanced statistical character; the construction of logical and mathematical models, all too frequently guided by a criterion of elegance; the elaboration of formal schemes on how to construct concepts and theories; valiant application of imported schemes, such as input-output analysis, systems analysis, and stochastic analysis; studious conformity to the canons of research design; and the promotion of a particular procedure, such as survey research, as *the* method of scientific study. I marvel at the supreme confidence with which these preoccupations are advanced as the stuff of methodology. (1969:26–27)

In place of such "preoccupations," Blumer offers a glimpse of a full-bodied methodology involving "(1) a prior picture of the world, (2) a problem, (3) exploration of data and instruments for describing the problematic situation, (4) determination of relations between data, (5) an interpretation of findings, and (6) the use of concepts" (Martindale, 1981:355). As Martindale (1981:355) correctly notes, Blumer's "picture of methodology is similar to that of John Dewey. . . ."

As an alternative to orthodox conceptions of "proper scientific methodology," Blumer proposes a nongeneralizing, or idiographic, function for sociology; he simply seeks to "make modern society intelligible." He desires to understand and explain human behavior; unlike the positivists, he does not seek its prediction and control. Blumer advocates a firsthand acquaintance with social life. Only by such direct exposure to the social life of others can one hope to avoid placing an "outside" and hence inaccurate interpretation on the thought and action of society's members. As one knowledgeable student of social theory points out, for Herbert Blumer:

> The guiding maxim of exploration is to use an ethically allowable procedure that provides the best picture of what is going on: direct observation, interviewing, listening to conversations, reading letters and diaries, securing life histories, examining public records, and even arranging for group discussions and counting items of interest. (Martindale, 1981:355)

From a detailed and intensive examination of the raw data gleaned from either direct observation, letters and diaries, life histories, public records, or discussions, the "meanings" actors attach to social events will be revealed, and when one has "established its meanings one has obtained the most important thing there is to know about social life" (Martindale, 1981:355).

In short, Blumer emphasizes the need for carefully and sympathetically "feeling one's way inside the experience of the actor." If you would understand human behavior, you must first work your way into the worlds of your subjects as they see, interpret, and give meaning to them. People's behavior transpires on the basis of their particular meanings. To understand the behavior, one must first understand the meanings. One best gets at these meanings through the method of sympathetic introspection; one must take the viewpoint of the individual or group whose behavior or action is being investigated. Most important, one must "attempt to use each actor's categories in capturing that actor's world of meaning" (Meltzer, Petras and Reynolds, 1975:58). Intimate understanding of the actor's world is the ultimate goal of such an approach. Intersubjective agreement among investigators is not the prime consideration here. In seeking intersubjective agreement among themselves, Blumer maintains that many sociologists impose a "view from the outside" that fails to capture the "real meanings," which in themselves forcefully mediate and actually determine how human beings respond to those subjects and situations that constitute their social worlds. Although Blumer is well aware that the techniques he advocates for sociology are highly subjective, difficult to teach others, hard to generalize from, and require much skill to employ successfully, he stands by them in the face of much opposition from the advocates of "scientific methodology" in the discipline. Those who extol the virtues of quantitative, generalizing, "hard" methodology, by Blumer's reasoning, miss the whole point of a viable sociology. Their techniques fail to capture the actor's meanings, and when your sociological investigations fail to catch the meanings actors attach to objects and situations, you have, as Blumer sees it, truly come up empty-handed.

Because Blumer puts much stock in people's ability to mold and remold their social worlds, and because his view of social reality puts him on the extreme fluidity end of the fluidity-stability societal dichotomy, he can favor and logically posit the use of what he terms "sensitizing concepts" rather than concepts that are operationally defined. As Sjoberg and Nett (1968:59) point out: "That Blumer objects to operational definitions of concepts and advocates the use of 'sensitizing concepts' is consistent with his image of social reality." As Blumer contrasts "sensitizing concepts" with "definitive concepts" (operational concepts), he notes that the latter provide exact prescriptions of what to see, while the former merely offer suggested social alleyways and avenues along and around which one may look. Sensitizing concepts are best for sociology because they enable the sociologist to grasp in observation and preserve in analysis what is distinctive about the phenomenon under investigation. In Blumer's terms, sensitizing concepts are superior because they allow one to work "with and through the distinctive nature of the empirical instance, instead of casting the unique nature aside . . ." (1969:8). As Meltzer notes, ". . . the student of human conduct moves from the abstract concept to the concrete distinctiveness of the instance; for he or she must use the distinctive expression in order to discern the common" (Meltzer, Petras and Reynolds, 1975:60). Blumer puts it as follows:

> Because of the varying nature of the concrete expression from instance to instance we have to rely, apparently, on general guides and not on fixed objective traits or modes of expression. To invert the matter, since what we infer

does not express itself in the same fixed way, we are not able to rely on fixed objective expressions to make the inference. (1969:8)

As Blumer seeks relevant understanding in a world he feels is characterized largely by its processual, change-inducing nature, he rejects the use of "variables" in sociological analysis because of their "mechanistic implications of a static-stimulus–response image of human behavior" (Meltzer, Petras and Reynolds, 1975:61).

Because Blumer consistently views human behavior as creative, and because it always has about it an indeterminate, spontaneous, and unpredictable quality, he favors techniques and concepts that allow one to deal with the dynamic interplay that transpires between the emergent, or spontaneous, aspects of the self, on the one hand, and its socially derived facets on the other. That is largely why he prefers direct observation and sensitizing concepts to quantitative methods, operational definitions, and variables. As Bernard N. Meltzer has argued, Blumer's image of people leads him to a particular methodology, and as that methodology has already been briefly discussed, a more detailed look at Blumer's image of people should prove useful at this point (Meltzer, Petras and Reynolds, 1975:61).

With respect to the nature of human nature, Blumer probably follows Mead's treatment, given conventional interpretations of Mead, closer than most contemporary symbolic interactionists. In fact, Blumer remains so close to Mead's original position that one author has dubbed him the "founder of the orthodox branch of symbolic interactionism" (Martindale, 1981:354). From Blumer's vantage point, and very much in common with Mead, the most distinctive feature of human society is that it is made up of individuals who have selves. And the self, according to Blumer, has two components best conceived of as analytically distinguishable phases, namely, the "I" and the "Me." The "I" represents the individuals's impulsive tendencies. The "I" is the spontaneous, the unregulated, or initial facet of human experience. It represents "the undisciplined, unrestrained, and undirected tendencies of the individual, which take the form of diffuse and undifferentiated activity [represented, for example, by] . . . one's immediate impulse of anger upon having been struck by another" (Meltzer, Petras and Reynolds, 1975:61). The other, as it is incorporated within the person, is represented by the self's "Me" phase. The "Me" component embraces the group of definitions, meanings, and attitudes prevalent within the collectivity (the group or society). On a specific occasion, the "Me" represents the generalized other (the group or society); in another situation, the "Me" may represent not the generalized other but a specific other. In the usual course of things, each act starts in the form of an "I" and ends in the form of a "Me." The "I" constitutes the initiation of the act before the act comes under the influence or control of the expectations of others as incorporated in the "Me." Propulsion is the function of the "I," direction the function of the "Me." According to Blumer, the act is the product of a dialectical relationship between impulses triggering it off and the "Me" phase of the self that provides its guidance. Because of this dialectical exchange, or interplay, the act "cannot be accounted for by factors which precede the act" (Blumer, 1962:183). The act begins with an impulse that comes from within; it does not begin as a response to some outside stimulus.

As one author sees it, "It is not entirely clear from Blumer's work whether the indeterminacy that characterizes human conduct is the product simply of the exploratory, improvising, and impulsive I or is a more complex emergent from the interaction between the I and the Me" (Meltzer, Petras and Reynolds, 1975:62). What is clear is that either the "I" itself or the interplay between the "I" and "Me" could be the source of much spontaneity. Given Blumer's view that the self is not simply a summation of the "I" and "Me" aspects, in seeking an explanation for indeterminacy one could and probably should pay as much attention to the dialectical interplay between the "I" and the "Me" as to the impulsive nature of the "I" itself. As Meltzer has argued, the Chicago school in general, and Blumer in particular, conceives of both society and self in largely processual terms (Meltzer, Petras and Reynolds, 1975:62). Society is an arena of interaction, not a static state of affairs, and by Blumer's reasoning, any theory that fails to acknowledge this basic fact will "face grave difficulties in view of the formative and explorative character of interaction as the participants judge each other and guide their own acts by that judgment" (1953:199).

Just as society is, in essence, a process rather than a mechanical structure, so too is the self, the latter being a ceaseless process of interaction between its "I" and "Me" phases. This interplay between the "I" and the "Me" is a reflexive process during which the individual makes "self indications." The person observes or notes objects and assesses their potential impact on the plan of action either being contemplated or carried out at the time. This reflexive process, this process of "self indication," causes human conduct to be constructed in the course of its execution instead of "merely being released from a pre-existing psychological structure by factors playing on the structure" (Blumer, 1966:535). The self, then, is an ongoing process of internal conversation. During the course of such internal conversations, new assessments and appraisals of oneself may emerge. The individual is, in fact, a self-changing being. Blumer's individual is the role maker, not the role player. His actors do not simply read whatever script society happens to hand them.

A good summary statement of Blumer's views, and hence in large part the views of many members of the Chicago school, is provided by Meltzer:

> Blumer commences with a depiction of human behavior and interaction as emergent, processual, and voluntaristic, entailing a dialogue between impulses and social definitions, in the course of which acts are constructed. He pauses, however, to recognize a level of human interaction devoid of social definitions and reflecting sheerly spontaneous behavior. Holding these two preceding ideas, he exhibits skepticism regarding the extent to which human behavior is predictable. And, finally, in light of the foregoing components of his imagery, he must insist upon a methodology that "respects the nature of the empirical world," relying upon a phenomenological approach, participant observation, and sensitizing concepts — all linked with a research "logic of discovery." (Meltzer, Petras and Reynolds, 1975:67)

Chapter 4 THE IOWA SCHOOL

As surely as Herbert Blumer's work best captures the flavor and spirit of the Chicago school of symbolic interactionism, the writings of the late Manford H. Kuhn best reflect the domain, or basic, assumptions and fundamental concerns of interactionism's Iowa school. Kuhn, in fact, was not only the founder of the Iowa school, but until his death in 1963 was also its principal architect and guiding force. The leading representatives of this approach today are, for the most part, either former students of Kuhn or students of sociologists directly trained by Kuhn. One may, in fact, say that many of the most illustrious representatives of the Chicago school were *taught by Blumer,* while many of the most capable proponents of the Iowa approach were *trained by Kuhn.* The *taught by Blumer* phrase reflects the Chicago school's conception of sociology as both social science and humane learning. The words *trained by Kuhn* are intended to reflect the Iowa school's view of sociology as a generalizing science meeting "the usual scientific criteria" in its search for a " standardized, objective, and dependable process of measurement . . . of significant variables" (Hickman and Kuhn, 1956:224–225). This emphasis on sociology as a *human social science* versus sociology as just another branch of *science proper* clearly sets the Chicago and Iowa schools apart. While the Iowa school is obviously more in line with the conventional, or orthodox, approaches to science, among symbolic interactionists the Iowa school's representatives stand out as being most distinct. The Chicago and Iowa schools have been characterized as being the two most divergent approaches within the larger symbolic interaction tradition, but one could just as readily argue that the major varieties of interactionism to be covered (Chicago, dramaturgy, and ethnomethodology) all share more in common with one another than any of them share with the Iowa school. Among interactionists, the Iowa school, in a sense, is an intellectual community unto itself, and the person who made it and kept it that way was Manford H. Kuhn.

Manford Kuhn was born in 1911 in Kennard, Indiana. Studying with Kimbal Young, whom Petras and Meltzer (1973:7) label "an eclectic proponent of the Median perspective," Kuhn took both his M.A. and Ph.D. degrees at the University of Wisconsin. Kuhn's teaching career saw him on the faculties at Wisconsin, Whittier College, Mount Holyoke, and finally in 1946 at the State University of Iowa, where he remained until his death. Graduate students at Iowa operated in an intellectual climate influenced not only by Kuhn's "rigorous, hard science" treatment of sociology but also by Bergson and Spence's positivistic approaches to psychology and the philosophy of science (Meltzer, Petras and Reynolds, 1975:56). In this setting, Kuhn and his students set out to make of symbolic interactionism something other than a "body of conjectural and deductive orientations." They sought to rid the Meadian tradition of its "nonempirical" content and to demonstrate that ". . . the key ideas of symbolic interaction could be operationalized and utilized successfully in empirical research" (Kuhn, 1964:72). Kuhn worked closely with many graduate students, and shortly before his death a major graduate training program was in the process of being established under the auspices of the National Institute of Mental Health. Had this major training program gotten off the ground under Kuhn's guidance, the Iowa approach to interactionism may well have come to exert a far larger influence than it exerts today. In speaking of this program and the influence Kuhn would have had on it, one observer notes that "if he had not died the year before it was to go into operation, the whole development of symbolic interaction since the early 1960s might well have been different" (Martindale, 1981:357). Nevertheless, with the exception of the Chicago school, the Iowa school is perhaps still one of the largest and most clearly identifiable of the remaining varieties of symbolic interactionism.

If one may say, as others have, that Blumer's image of people led him to his particular methodology and that, in his scheme of things, a rather large theoretical dog wags a less than awesome methodological tail, then we may say of Kuhn that his methodological predilections inexorably led to his particular image of people, and that in his scheme of things an awesome methodological tail wags a rather puny theoretical dog. Kuhn's methodology and, in turn, his image of human beings are products of the particular stand he takes with respect to the issue of the determinacy or indeterminacy of human conduct. According to Kuhn, contradictions and ambiguities in Mead's basic writings allow one to see people's behavior as either determined or largely unpredictable, depending on where and how one happens to read Mead. In Kuhn's view, this is a sad state of affairs, a state of affairs resulting in much confusion among, and lack of common purpose and cohesion between, symbolic interactionists. Just as Blumer came down hard on the side of the essential indeterminacy of human behavior, Kuhn comes down nearly as hard on the side of determinacy. He would appear to favor determinacy because presupposing it "preserves a premise that many consider indispensable to the scientific enterprise" (Meltzer, Petras and Reynolds, 1975:62). If behavior is not largely determined, patterned, regular, recurrent, and somewhat stable, then, given Kuhn's conception of science, it is neither predictable nor explainable—and, by implication, not controllable. One needs to keep in mind that Kuhn and the Iowa school spokespersons, unlike the Chicago representatives, are as much concerned, if not more so, with the prediction and control of behavior as they are with its explanation and understanding.

Kuhn's particular deterministic variant of symbolic interactionism he referred to as *self theory*. Self theory attempts to "codify the conceptions" of the Iowa school and "submit them to empirical test" (Martindale, 1981:356). As Manis and Meltzer (1967:vi) note, *self theory* "sought to operationalize symbolic interactionism by reconceptualizing the self in structural terms, by abandoning such nonempirical concepts as Mead's 'I,' and by developing paper and pencil measures of the self." While both Mead and Blumer dealt with the self as both "I" and "Me," Kuhn threw the "I" component out. By keeping the "I" component in, one always had a mechanism for "explaining the unpredictable." By either seeing the "I" as the real source of spontaneity or by viewing the dynamic interplay between the self's "I" and "Me" phases as a source of change-inducing conduct, the Chicago-style interactionists had a "built-in" potential explanation for novel and creative human behavior. By throwing the "I" component out, Kuhn preserved the deterministic image of people demanded by his positivistic methodology, but he did so at the price of sacrificing "the processual character of the self and the negotiated character of behavior" (Meltzer, Petras and Reynolds, 1975:62). A process image of the self and a negotiated conception of behavior characterize nearly all other varieties of symbolic interactionism and clearly sets them apart from the "scientism" of the Iowa school. Kuhn himself does not admit to seeing individual behavior as totally determined by the external environment, as opposed to self-determined and self-controlled. In Kuhn's own words, "The individual is not merely a passive agent automatically responding to the group-assigned meanings of objects" (Hickman and Kuhn, 1956:26). But as Meltzer points out, ". . . he [Kuhn] and his adherents are compelled by their methodological and deterministic commitments to deviate a bit from this disavowal" (Meltzer, Petras and Reynolds, 1975:64).

Kuhn's self theory offers a structural rather than processual image of both self and society. Without the "I" component, the self as "Me" simply "displays the influence of the generalized other of the groups within which an individual acts — at least those groups with which an individual identifies and takes as a reference in his or her various self-estimates" (Martindale, 1981:356). As Meltzer (1975:64) puts it, "Conceiving the self as a structure of attitudes derived from the individual's internalized statuses and roles, they [the Iowa school] assign causal significance in behavior to these somewhat fixed attributes . . . these elements are considered stable 'traits'. . . ." Hence, not only does Kuhn operate with a structural conception of self, he also assigns to the self a far more stable character than most interactionists assign to it. Among interactionists, Kuhn is one of the few who speaks of "a core self." The fact that he conceives of this relatively fixed and stable type of self as a mere reflection of the person's social anchoring is attested to in the following statement: "Central to an individual's conception of himself is his identity, that is, his generalized position in society" (Kuhn, n.d.:6). Kuhn's self theory, then, dispenses with the processual image of self. Within the individual there are no impulses, no "I," no nonsocial sources of spontaneity or change; there is only the "Me," only society's reflection. The actor is not a determining agent. The person's definitions, especially "self-definitions," are the socially determined antecedents of his or her actions.

The following statement by Meltzer summarizes Kuhn's position on this matter:

> For him . . . the self becomes a Me exclusively, and conduct is held to be wholly predictable (in principle) on the basis of internalized prescriptions and proscriptions. If we know the actor's reference groups, according to Kuhn, we can predict his/her self-attitudes, and, if we know these, we can predict his/her behavior. In short, antecedent conditions determine the human being's self; and his/her self determines his/her conduct. This view, of course, conveniently disposes of such "non-empirical" concepts as the I and Me impulses. (Meltzer, Petras and Reynolds, 1975:62)

That the above characterization of Kuhn's overall "explanation" of human behavior is, in fact, an accurate account can be clearly seen by comparing it with Kuhn's own words on this very point:

> As self theory views the individual, he derives his plans of action from roles he plays and statuses he occupies in the groups with which he feels identified — his reference groups. His attitudes toward himself as an object are the best indexes to these plans of action, and hence to the action itself, in that they are the anchoring points from which self-evaluations and other-evaluations are made. (Hickman and Kuhn, 1956:45).

Very much in line, then, with conventional role theory, Kuhn is arguing that the self is best seen as a structured group, or set, of self and other attitudes that, on inspection, turn out to coincide closely with the individual's prescribed role patterns. In short, people are not the role makers that Blumer and others conceive of them as being; like Goffman, Kuhn sees people as role players. Occupy a particular status, and you get a particular role, or script. You are, by Kuhn's reasoning, likely to read the script and play the role that society hands you, especially if the status you occupy you also identify with. Do people directly identify with the statuses they occupy? Are their self-definitions and self-concepts directly hooked in deterministic fashion to their social positions? Apparently Kuhn thinks so; his wording on this point is instructive in that it foreshadows the development of the "Twenty Statements" or "Who and I?" test, which later became the Iowa school's preferred methodological tool for the study of self-attitudes: "Social and cultural factors become determinants of personality factors only as the individual comes to internalize the roles he plays and the statuses he occupies. He asks 'Who am I?' and can answer this question of identity only in terms of his social position . . . ." (1954:60). The likely response to such a question as "Who am I?" would be, by Kuhn's reasoning, "I am a — — — — — — ," the blank representing a "social position" — for example, "I am a sociologist." One sociologist recently completed a "Who am I?" test by filling out one of the blanks with the words "an ass." While he thereby managed to avoid Kuhn's notion that the questions could be answered only with reference to social position, his response perhaps more accurately spoke to Kuhn's concern with "personality factors" than had he responded by noting that he was "a sociologist, a professor, a male, a husband," etc., etc. Kuhn, in spite of his previous statement, recognizes, of course, that people can and do characterize and define themselves in terms other than those directly referring to the social positions they occupy. Self attitudes are hierarchized in terms of a principle he terms "saliency." These attitudes are made up of "consensual" and "subconsensual" references. Consensual references are those such as mother, father, girl, boy, and the like, while subconsensual refences are those such as sad, happy, sympathetic, and so on. Hence, one could answer the question "Who am I?" by saying "I am happy, warm, friendly," and so forth. Consensual references require little in the way of interpretation, but much interpretation is required of subconsensual references if one wishes to use them as "clues" to self-conception and personality formation.

From the perspective of certain interactionists, Kuhn simply regards personality and/or self as an organization, or structure, of attitudes that, in turn, are merely internalizations of role recipes. Social roles become the norms in terms of which people both structure and respond to their environments and situations. Given this view, "Even idiosyncratic elements in role-performance are fully explainable, for Kuhn, in terms of composites or resultants of the role-expectations held by the actor's various reference groups" (Meltzer, Petras and Reynolds, 1975:65). Meltzer puts the matter as follows:

> Kuhn . . . characterizes both the self and human interaction as structured. The organized set of self-attitudes serves as a system of pre-established plans of action. And human association takes the form of fairly stable, ready-made patterns of role and counter-role prescriptions. For him, then, prescriptions of behavior and descriptions of behavior tend to coincide. Thus is social order maintained. (Meltzer, Petras and Reynolds, 1975:65-66).

At least in the phenomena of potentially conflicting expectations of one's various reference groups, Kuhn has a mechanism or device for possibly explaining change-inducing, novel, creative, and idiosyncratic behavior. One sociologist who is in general sympathy with Kuhn's approach acknowledges that Kuhn's image of people leaves "less room for creativity and innovation than there would otherwise be" in an individual's behavior (Stryker, 1980:103). As selves tend to be stable, in Kuhn's view, interaction itself tends to be stable, as it simply "follows the expectations that impinge on participants from one another" (Stryker, 1980:103). As Stryker points out, however, Kuhn's emphasis on stability is only relative. Stryker sees greater potential in Kuhn's framework when it comes to accounting for change and novelty than Kuhn's critics do.

> Some potential for volatility is introduced by recognizing the "slippage" between social structure and self attitudes, and there is some potential for creativity through the role-taking process . . . actors can use the perspective of others as a basis for adjusting and controlling their own responses — and, given multiple other perspectives, this can mean that the direction taken by self control may be away from simply meeting the expectations of others. (1980:103)

All of this, of course, is no different from what Kuhn's critics have said. The only difference lies in Stryker's willingness to see as basic sources of numerous and significant changes the same mechanisms others view as sources of infrequent and inconsequential change. Kuhn really has little room in his scheme for individual-generated change, but Blumer, given his grossly inadequate conception of social structure and social organization, has little room in his scheme for societal-generated change. Kuhn pays much more attention to both the structure of the self and the structure of society than do many Chicago school interactionists. Kuhn's own conception of social structure leaves much to be desired, but he realizes that it is not enough merely to say that the self is a social product; one must also say exactly where the self is produced. The Twenty Statements Test, or "Who am I?" test, developed by Kuhn is an attempt to locate "selves" in the most crucial roles they occupy. But given the hidden assumptions of stability built into the Twenty Statements Test, and given the fact that the Iowa school's own conceptions of social structure and social organization are hopelessly microscopic in nature, about the only real initial attempt to locate and deal with individuals in their most crucial social positions undertaken by the Iowa school was Kuhn's coauthored book, *Individuals, Groups, and Economic Behavior.* This book was a direct attempt to extend the scope of symbolic interactionism into an area seldom dealt with by those who preferred to take their examples from "game analogies" instead of from the "real nature of human life" they so frequently talk about. By demonstrating that ". . . interpersonal comparisons of utility or satisfaction are not universal events in the market place, but are substructured as events in smaller reference groups . . .," Hickman and Kuhn gave exchange theory a well-deserved slap in the face and simultaneously increased our understanding of the social psychology of economic behavior (Martindale, 1981:357). Although this study was far from being a complete investigation of economic conduct, it was nevertheless a step in the right direction, and few interactionists of any persuasion have taken such a step since.

Kuhn did not stop his attempt to systematically expand the scope of symbolic interactionism with his study of economic behavior. He and his students studied a wide range of intellectual problems such as role taking and self-formation, racial prejudice and the self, the self and social objects, attitudes and the self, communication systems and the self, mental illness and self-conception, the self and reference groups, and the self and social status — to name but a few of their areas of concern (Martindale, 1981:357).

By way of summary, one may note that Kuhn and other representatives of the Iowa school made major modifications in the original interactionist position espoused by Mead and others. Furthermore, these modifications were so basic and thoroughgoing that the label "self theory" is more frequently employed in describing the Iowa school than is the label symbolic interaction. Self theory weds to a symbolic interactionist orientation selected elements of both reference-group theory and role theory. In addition to the concept self, reference group and role taking become two of the key or indispensable concepts in the Iowa school's conceptual inventory. Such concepts as self, role playing, role taking, and reference group are not employed, as Stryker (1980:100) notes, for "conceptual reasons but to emphasize an interest in developing generalizations tested by theory."

In order to convert one's concepts to variables, that is, in order to submit them to empirical testing, the Iowa school came to define these concepts in ways differing from their treatment at the hands of other symbolic interactionists. Kuhn spoke of a "core self" as a *stable* group of meanings appending to oneself as an object and providing a "structure and comparative stability to personality and [giving] continuity and predictability to behavior" (Hickman and Kuhn, 1956:21). The "self" became simply an *organized* and *structured,* or ordered, set of self and other attitudes displaying a relatively *stable* quality. These attitudes were taken to coincide with the individual's prescribed role expectations. Process disappeared, and structure was substituted in its place. Self, roles, interaction, organizations, reference groups, and social structure were all redefined in terms that invested them with a relatively stable, rather than continuously shifting, quality. Such relative stability opens up the possibility of reliable measurement, and that is precisely what Kuhn and the Iowa school were after in the first place. Stryker puts the case both succinctly and well:

> Kuhn's methodological thrust is toward conventional science. He seeks general propositions from which specific hypotheses can be *deduced* and tested, the end result being

a theory that can predict and explain behavior and interaction. The strategy for developing such a theory is through
the utilization of concepts of a tentative theoretical statement in empirical research, and the key to the successful
use of concepts in research is proper measurement. . . .
The starting point of proper measurement is precise speci-
fication of theoretical concepts. (1980:103-104)

And as Stryker further notes, "Kuhn sees no contradiction between interactionism's concepts and meeting 'conventional
scientific criteria for standardized, objective, and dependable
measures" (1980:104). Indeed, as Kuhn and the Iowa school had
redefined interactionism's basic concepts, there were no conflicts
between them and the orthodox requirement for "scientific
measurement."

The Kuhnians assume that human behavior is both organized
and directed. The individual's self-attitudes are further assumed to
be the real source of both the organization and direction. Self-
attitudes largely reflect prescribed role patterns, but as self-
attitudes are the true keys to predicting and controlling
behavior, it becomes of paramount importance to acquire an instrument that will identify and measure them. To this end, the
Twenty Statements Test, or Who Am I? test, was developed. This
standardized attempt to measure self-attitudes simply asked
respondents to provide up to 20 answers to the question Who
am I?

The Twenty Statements Test is today perhaps the most widely
used instrument for the study of self-attitudes. It was no sooner
introduced than it became the favorite methodological tool of
interactionism's Iowa school. Like a small child with a new
hammer, the Iowa school employed the Twenty Statements Test
to "hit upon" all aspects of self-conception. As Tucker (1966)
has pointed out, Kuhn's methodology and the Twenty Statements Test could almost be said to be one and the same thing.
Kuhn even came to define, and operationally define at that, the
self as "answers which an individual gives to the question which
he directs to himself, 'who am I?' or to the question another
directs to him, such as 'what kind of person are you?' who are
you?', etc." (Kuhn, n.d.:6).

The school's method came to dictate its image of people instead of the other way around: "The members of this school focus more upon the necessity of obtaining empirical verification of the concepts of interactionism than upon compatibility with an abstract philosophical description of man" (Petras and Meltzer, 1973:3).

By way of a final summary of Kuhn's basic position, one offers the following brief statement by Meltzer:

> . . . Kuhn begins with a scientific concern, stressing operationalism, the TST (a paper-and-pencil instrument), and definitive concepts—all linked with a "logic of verification." Although conjoined with his symbolic-interactionist orientation, this concern brings him to an acceptance of a basically deterministic image of human behavior. Bound to the service of scientism and determinism, he must deny to the I any role whatsoever in conduct, thereby dismissing the possibilities of both emergence and true voluntarism, on the one hand, and nonsymbolic human interaction, on the other. In recognition of the magnitude of these modifications of symbolic interactionism, Kuhn relinquishes the customary name of that orientation in favor of "self theory." (Meltzer, Petras and Reynolds, 1975:67)

Perhaps those contemporary Iowa school types who insist on redefining the orientation in strict behavioristic terms, while giving us a "new reading" of Mead, will follow Kuhn's lead and start referring to themselves as self theorists instead of interactionists. But symbolic interactionism has always embraced a great deal of diversity; it will probably continue to do so, at least in the near future.

Chapter **5** THE DRAMATURGICAL
GENRE

The principal spokesperson for symbolic interactionism's dramaturgical approach was Canadian-born Erving Goffman. His undergraduate degree was from the University of Toronto, and he held both the M.A. and Ph.D. degrees from the University of Chicago. Until his recent death, he was on the faculty at the University of Pennsylvania, having previously been professor of sociology at the University of California at Berkeley. At the University of Chicago, Goffman became acquainted with the views of interactionists Herbert Blumer and Everett Cherrington Hughes and, probably through them, with the key ideas of George Herbert Mead, Georg Simmel, William Isaac Thomas, Emile Durkheim, William James, and very likely the dramaturgist Kenneth Burke. Goffman later joined his teacher Blumer as a fellow faculty member at Berkeley.

> From Mead, Durkheim, and Simmel, Goffman appears to have derived the inspiration for his views on the reality-constructing behavior of humans, the pervasive significance of ceremony and ritual in human social life, and the utility of a "formal" orientation that overlooks historical specificities in a quest for universal generalizations. (Meltzer, Petras and Reynolds, 1975:68)

Goffman further credits W. I. Thomas, Alfred Schutz, and William James with shaping his views on the nature of human nature and on the essence of elementary social life. In the main, Goffman's work combines elements of Schultz's and Gustave Ichheiser's phenomenologies and Blumer, James, Thomas, and Mead's interactionism with the dramaturgical approach of Hugh Dalziel Duncan and Kenneth Burke. Among symbolic interactionists, Goffman's work is much closer to the Chicago

95

and ethnomethodological varieties than it is to the Iowa school's brand.

Influenced by Burke's use of the dramaturgical metaphor, Goffman's early work is built on a single and simple premise: When people interact with each other, they do so through the use of symbolic devices that they employ in an attempt to "manage" the impressions others receive from them. The fact that Goffman prefers to treat life as a theater in which we stage, or "put on," shows for one another is made evident in his first major book. Writing in *The Presentation of Self in Everyday Life,* he informs us:

> The perspective employed in this report is that of the theatrical performance; the principles derived are dramaturgical ones. I shall consider the way . . . the individual . . . presents himself and his activity to others, the ways in which he guides and controls the impressions they form of him, and the kinds of things he may and may not do while sustaining his performance before them. (1959:xi)

Goffman reinforces this same essential point in the following manner:

> I assume that when an individual appears before others he will have many motives for trying to control the impressions they receive of the situation. This report is concerned with some of the common techniques that the person employs to sustain such impressions and with some of the common contingencies associated with the employment of these techniques . . . . I shall be concerned only with the participant's dramaturgical problems of presenting the activity before others. (1959:15)

An examination of Goffman's early work clearly reveals that he conceptualized human social behavior as a series of "performances" by "actors" who strive to present themselves (who "give" and "give off" "expressions" designed to create an "impression") as being exactly who and what they claim to be. Social behavior is a performance whose ultimate aim is to convince others of the authenticity of one's self. Operating either solo or in concert with their fellow actors and actresses as a team of players, people "stage shows" or "give performances" during which they "read social scripts," "enact routines," and "play parts" that utilize "props" and "settings." These performances are given in "front regions," which is to say before an "audience." The performances are "prepared" in society's "back regions." During these moments of preparation, when one is not "on stage," opportunities arise for anticipating whether one's performance will be well or ill received by the intended audience. The end product of a performance is the audience's "imputation" of a particular kind of self to the "character" being performed. Such imputation is a result of practical and substantive components in an actor's performance, but it is also, and perhaps more directly, a product of the ceremonial, expressive, and ritualistic elements displayed in the actor's behavior. (Meltzer, Petras and Reynolds, 1975:68).

Audiences have certain expectations, and one thing they always expect is a minimal coherence "among settings, appearance and manner" (1959:25). If such coherence is sustained, the audience may agree "tactfully" to accept the actor's appearance as sincere, believeable, or authentic. All of this interaction between actors and audience, between groups and between individuals, is a very delicate, temperamental, fussy business. Special techniques are needed to sustain a successful presentation of self: one personal slip, one faux pas, one misread cultural cue card, one social pratfall, and the self may have imputed to it an insincere, unbelievable, and unauthentic character. In the "life as theatre" world of Erving Goffman, boos are as easy to come by as cheers. We are all out, according to Goffman, to make a favorable impression on others through the use of elaborate symbolic devices. Hardly a new observation, and on the surface not an especially disturbing one. But, as Cuzzort points out, Goffman's writings present a view of humanity more disenchanting than that springing from either Freud's image of people as impulsive animals held in check by a repressive society or from Darwin's evolutionary theory. Cuzzort's reasoning on this point deserves to be presented in detail:

> Darwin leaves open the possibility that if man is an animal of low heritage, at least he is an intelligent one . . . capable

of building vast cultures [and] standing at the apex of an evolutionary process. . . . Darwin allows us to keep intact our view of man as something special and privileged in nature's realm. Freud, on the other hand, disenchantingly leaves us at the mercy of unconscious and devious impulses. Even so, the Freudian picture is a dramatic and . . . romantic one. Though Freudian man may be crushed by a repressive morality, he never admits defeat without a fight . . . it is an invigorating if not flattering conception of man. (1969:175)

How about Goffman? Well, according to Cuzzort, Goffman's image of people prohibits us from conceiving of ourselves as either special or privileged. His image of humans is neither flattering nor invigorating. People are nothing but an incorrigible pack of "con" artists engaged in a lifelong process of deceiving both self and others. Furthermore, we have no real choice in the matter as ". . . the same tricks that make a con game work are basically the devices used in the act of being 'human' " (Cuzzort, 1969:175). Cuzzort makes his case that Goffman's is the least flattering of all current conceptions of human nature as follows:

Goffman sees man as a manager of impressions. These impressions, grounded in the meanings we give to appearances, gestures, costumes, settings, and words, are all that man *is* as a social being. Strip these away and we have dehumanized man. Conversely, cloak man with those fragile devices that permit him to maintain an impression before others and we have given him the shaky essence of his humanity. This perspective reduces humanity to an act or performance; moreover, it is a performance based on dreadfully flimsy devices. . . . It is in this sense, then, that Goffman appears to leave man more naked and alone than did Darwin or Freud. the distinctive feature of human activity resides ultimately in something which is little more than a Santa Claus outfit. To be human is to perform, like an actor, before audiences whom we "con" into accepting us as being what we are trying to appear to be. And our humanity is the costume we wear, the staging on which we perform, and the way we read whatever script we are handed. (1969:175-176)

In the world of Erving Goffman the self becomes a mere object "about which the actor wishes to foster an impression" (Meltzer, Petras and Reynolds, 1975:69). The person has no basic integrity, no core essence, no real substance — all is a matter of style. We alter our performance depending on our audience; we present different selves to different persons, ever mindful of creating a good impression. William James's notion that we have as many selves as there are people about whose opinion we care is clearly a cornerstone in Goffman's conception of human nature. The Weberian nation of individuals as perpetual status seekers also informs much of his work. People who constantly engage in the "performance style" of behavior depicted by Goffman were given special names by other observers of the social scene. Arguing that such persons were products of specific socio-economic formations and the historical drift of the times, William H. Whyte (1956) labeled this "character" *the organization man;* David Reisman and his associates (1950) called such individuals *other directed persons.* But what others have carefully described as a special "personality type" both "in the making" and "on the make," Goffman, following Mead, attributes to human nature itself. Erving Goffman (1959:244) claims that he does " not mean to imply that the framework [dramaturgical] presented here is culture-free or applicable in the same areas of social life in non-Western societies as in our own." He also cautions that "we must not overlook areas of life in other societies in which other rules are apparently followed" (1959:244). He even provides us with the additional warning that ". . . we must be very cautious in any effort to characterize our own society as a whole with respect to dramaturgical practices" (1959:245). Such warnings aside, a reading of Goffman leaves one with the indelible and inescapable impression that he sees us all — rich and poor, black and white, citizens of the industrial nations and Third Worlders, capitalists and proletarians — as organization men, as other-directed persons, as a great, swarming herd of incorrigible and compulsive con artists. If Goffman's work is seen as being merely a series of descriptions of a new personality type both in the making and on the make, then we can conclude that Goffman is a splendid ethnographer. Some sociologists prefer to see Goffman in just this way. Only when Goffman is seen not only as an ethnographer but as a general theorist does his argument gain force and capture the attention of a large sociological audience. It is because he is generally viewed as a major spokesman for a perspective with something to say about humanity in general that he has been accorded his current high status in the profession. Good ethnographers are not exactly a dime a dozen, but the best of them in sociology do not enjoy reputations in any way comparable to Goffman's. Goffman is one of the last major figures out of the Chicago school; his work constitutes the real core of today's dramaturgical variety of interactionism, and his views have, in a sense, also provided a jumping-off point for many who consider themselves to be ethnomethodologists.

While much of Goffman's later writing is difficult and sometimes even impossible to classify as symbolic interactionism, for two decades his writings were basic to interactionism's dramaturgical variant, and the dramaturgical approach in the minds of most sociologists is still clearly identified with the works of Erving Goffman. It is therefore best to present a brief overview of some of those influential works.

As previously noted, Goffman's earliest major, and still best-known, statement of his particular dramaturgical theory appeared in book form in 1959. The manuscript was titled *The Presentation of Self in Everyday Life.* In this early work, Goffman draws a parallel between the acts we all engage in during the course of our everyday interaction with self and others and the kinds of acting that transpire during the course of theatrical performances. In a sense, Goffman spells out in great detail this analogy between social life and the theater, between human interaction and the stage. All the world's a stage in the very real sense that social performances maintain the interactional setting; and the interactional setting, in turn, maintains the social world. All is held in a delicate balance, all is a fussy business. One poor performance can upset the social apple cart, can disrupt the social world of the individual self as well as that of the rest of the cast of characters and even that of the audience. One has to be on one's toes when in the "front region," when performing before an audience where, through the use of social staging, props, costumes, and various other social and personal devices, one attempts to portray the character one wishes others to believe one to be. One's appearances and the imputation of character made by others in response to those appearances are central to both the theater and social life. Just as there is an "offstage" or "backstage" in the life of the theater, so too is there a "back region" in social life. In the backstage area the actor can ready himself or herself for the next performance; in the back region, partially shorn of social costuming, the individual can be more himself or herself. Goffman goes to great lengths to draw the analogy between social life and the theater, and in so doing he adds to the symbolic interactionist tradition a new dramaturgical metaphor capable of sharpening its traditional focus on the general process of human interaction.

The Presentation of Self in Everyday Life is not the only work in which one may catch the general flavor of Goffman's dramaturgical orientation. A fairly representative set of his ideas is contained in his book *Interaction Ritual: Essays in Face-to-Face Behavior* (1967). Here he deals with the fact that individuals interact so as to maintain both their own "face" and that of the other party(ies) involved in the interaction. In this work he also deals with the nature of deference and demeanor, with embarrassment, with alienation, with mental symptoms and tacit rules, and with the deliberate taking of avoidable risks in interaction. Other works of Goffman's in which at least elements of a dramaturgical approach may be glimpsed are *Encounters* (1961b), *Behavior in Public Places* (1963a), and *Strategic Interaction* (1969).

Goffman's contribution to sociological theory in general and symbolic interactionism in particular goes beyond the application of his dramaturgical framework. In *Asylums: Essays on the Social Situation of Mental Patients and Other Inmates* (1961a) and more directly in *Stigma: Notes on the Management of Spoiled Identity* (1963b) he also makes an important contribution to the "labeling perspective" favored by many interactionists. But while Goffman has indeed made a major contribution to symbolic interactionism, it should be noted that his later work has tended to move in a different direction. His book *Frame Analysis: An Essay on the Organization of Experience* (1974) clearly departs from the central concerns of most interactionists. In fact, feeling that Goffman's later work is best characterized as structuralism rather than interactionism, Gonos (1977:855) notes that "Goffman's work stands opposed to the central tenets and most basic assumptions of symbolic interactionism." In *Frame Analysis,* Goffman is out to examine not impression management but life's microstructures. He no longer feels bound by W. I. Thomas's dictum that situations defined as real may be real in their consequences. As Goffman (1974:1) sees things, "Defining situations as real certainly has consequences, but these may contribute very marginally to the events in progress." Furthermore, he apparently has come to think that people seldom come up with new definitions of the situation on their own. Instead, they simply avail themselves of the definitions that "society" has provided.

The main thrust of *Frame Analysis* is "to isolate some of the basic frameworks of understanding available in our society for making sense out of events and to analyze the special vulnerabilities to which these frames of reference are subject" (1974:10). Here Goffman has come to the position that sees human behavior as a product of simple adherence to society's rules and regulations. This view is, of course, anathema to most symbolic interactionists, as they favor a creative and less reactive picture of human action. This may, in part, account for the fact that while Goffman's works are indeed read by symbolic interactionists, he has, of late, attracted few interactionists to his banner. Furthermore, his later writings have come under fire by such well-known symbolic interactionists as Herbert Blumer and Norman K. Denzin. In fact, as very few interactionists would today identify themselves as dramaturgists, the dramaturgical approach may not remain a major variant of symbolic interactionism much longer.

Chapter **6** ETHNOMETHODOLOGY

Among the major variants of symbolic interaction theory, only the representatives of its Iowa variety seem to lack a general awareness of themselves as, for want of a better term, a "school of thought." The Chicago school interactionists and those favoring the dramaturgical approach seem to manifest a well-developed "sense of intellectual community"—perhaps because both coteries deviate more from orthodox sociology than do the Iowa school proponents. Among the ethnomethodologists, however, "consciousness of kind" is most manifest. They are the most tightly knit of the symbolic interactionists. Although there is considerable debate among sociologists regarding whether or not ethnomethodology is best categorized as a variety of symbolic interactionism, and while both the affinities and differences between interaction and ethnomethodology have been detailed, one could agree with Wallace (1969:34–36), who argues that "insofar as ethnomethodology embraces a theoretic (rather than methodologic) viewpoint, it is clearly interactionist." Therefore, ethnomethodology is treated as the last of the major varieties of symbolic interactionism, even though one realizes that fewer and fewer ethnomethodologists are now willing to class themselves as symbolic interactionists.

To date, the "ethnomethodological movement" lacks a definitive exposition of its principal views, but to the extent that it can be characterized as either a movement or a school of thought, it is led by sociologist Harold Garfinkel at the University of California–Los Angeles. Other ethnomethodologists either operate or have operated out of other branches of the University of California, most notably at the Santa Barbara and San Diego Campuses. In addition to the progenitors of symbolic interactionism proper, the intellectual precursors of the ethnomethodologists have included such phenomenologists as Gurwitsch, Merleau-Ponty, and most important, Husserl and Schutz—

Schutz, in turn, being greatly influenced by the *verstehen* concept of Max Weber. Modern logical and linguistic philosophy have also had an impact on ethnomethodology, and Goffman's sociology is likewise important in that some ethnomethodologists carry out the more radical implications of his particular style of sociology (Collins and Makowsky, 1972:204). With respect to Garfinkel himself, he studied with Talcott Parsons, which may, in part, account for his "convoluted, opaque prose" (Meltzer, Petras and Reynolds, 1975:75).

While ethnomethodology, then, can be said to have its precursors, its evolution is somewhat unlike that of most other theories. It really did not "take off" as a school of thought until it was given a name. Garfinkel named it, and his description of how he came by the name is instructive, for it tells us something about the common concerns of the ethnomethodologists:

> I will tell you about the origin of the term . . . I was interested in such things as jurors' uses of some kind of knowledge of the way in which the organized affairs of society operated — knowledge that they drew on easily, that they required of each other . . . they were concerned with such things as adequate accounts, adequate description, and adequate evidence. . . .
>
> When I was writing up these materials, I dreamed up the notion underlying the term "ethnomethodology." You want to know where I actually got the term? I was working with the Yale cross-cultural area files. I happened to be looking down the list without the intent of finding such a term. I was looking through their raglines, if you will permit that usage, and I came to a section: ethnobotany, ethnophysiology, ethnophysics. Here I am faced with jurors who are doing methodology in the "now you see it, now you don't" fashion. . . .
>
> Now, how to stick a label on that stuff, for the time being, to help me recall the burden of it? How to get a reminder of it? That is the way "ethnomethodology" was used to begin with. "Ethno" seemed to refer, somehow or other, to the availability to a member of common-sense knowledge of his society as common-sense knowledge of the "whatever." . . . It was that plain, and the notion of

"ethnomethodology" or the term "ethnomethodology" was taken in this sense. (Garfinkel, 1968:5-11).

The ethnomethodologist's position runs directly against the current of mainstream sociology, and, as Deutscher (1973:375) puts it, "They see themselves as a discipline — a radical perspective on human behavior and its study." The ethnomethodologists have not received kind treatment at the hands of their fellow sociologists, and their tight-knitness may, in large part, be explainable for the very reason Durkheim elucidates: "Of course, we always love the company of those who feel and think as we do, but it is with passion, and no longer solely with pleasure, that we seek it immediately after discussions where our common beliefs have been greatly combated" (1964:102).

The ethnomethodologists feel themselves to be "adherents of an embattled, 'encapsulated' speciality, targets of contemptuous rejection by "American sociology" (Meltzer, Petras, and Reynolds, 1975:75). They see themselves as put upon because they feel they offer a uniquely different framework for the analysis of sociological data. They have been characterized as "radical empiricists" (Collins and Makowsky, 1972:204), and this characterization of them as radical is, in one sense, correct — as long as one remembers that their radicalism is of an intellectual rather than a political or economic nature. Collins (1975:205) is quite correct when he notes: "The 'ethnos,' as they came to be called, were not necessarily revolutionary in a political sense; for most of them Marxism was just as much a part of the old way of thinking that had to be overthrown."

By the ethnomethodologists' reasoning, the assumptions of sociology are no different than the taken-for-granted assumptions made by nonsociologists in the course of carrying out their everyday activities. And ethnomethodology is, above all, concerned with, "the ways in which shared meanings . . . come to be taken for granted in human society" (Meltzer, Petras and Reynolds, 1975:79). As Filmer (1972:210) notes, ". . . sociology is, in an important sense, itself an everyday activity." Therefore, in approaching sociology as a form of everyday activity, and in seeking to explain that activity, the ethnomethodologists were led to look at sociology's own taken-for-granted assumptions.

Only by coming to grips with these assumptions, argue the ethnomethodologists, can we hope to come to grips with sociology itself. It is because of its insistence on analyzing the everyday assumptions, both conscious and taken-for-granted, of sociology that ethnomethodology stands apart from the other varieties of interactionism. It alone contributes to sociology's reflexive sociology of sociology movement. That in itself may be enough to occasion ethnomethodology's "contemptuous rejection" by orthodox sociology, but their questioning of one sociological assumption in particular is almost enough to guarantee it. That assumption is the assumption of order, and the way it is handled by the ethnomethodologists tells us something about ethnomethodology as a perspective.

The problem of order has always loomed large for conventional sociology, and the topic of order, or social order, has typically been approached in straightforward, "scientific" fashion, that is, order has always been assumed to exist naturally (Skidmore, 1975:259). Order is something that is simply taken "to be out there." Sociologists have long maintained that the assumption of order in the social world is no different than the parallel assumption that there is order in the physical universe. Both assumptions are felt to be necessary if physical and social science are to be a reality. Unless order could be assumed "to be out there," unless objects and events presented themselves in patterned, recurrent, regular, and "naturally occurring" form, both physical and social science were taken to be an impossiblity. Many ethnomethodologists make no such assumption. Those who do pay scant attention to it, preferring instead simply to bracket the genetic question. In fact, some ethnomethodologists argue that "the social order, including all its symbols and meanings exists not only precariously but has no existence at all independent of the members' accounting and describing practices" (Dreitzel, 1970:xv). As Mullins (1973:195) informs us, ethnomethodologists do not even directly examine the various manifestations of social order — such as social structure and social organization — they focus instead "on the process by which members manage to produce and sustain *a sense of social structure.*" For ethnomethodology "social order [is] a convenient fiction people allow each other to entertain so that mutual activity can proceed" (Skidmore, 1975:260).

In the case of sociology, the ethnomethodologists engage in a reflexive exercise designed to elucidate the very process(es) whereby *sociologists manage to produce and sustain their sense of social order.* The ethnomethodologists' posture with respect to this matter represents, of course, a case of extreme social idealism somewhat in line with a minority viewpoint among early interactionists but clearly out of line with the views of many past and present symbolic interactionists. Nonetheless, as the following statement reveals, the ethnomethodologists challenge the dominant "social facts" approach of Durkheimian functionalism:

> . . . in contrast to certain versions of Durkheim that teach that the objective reality of social facts is sociology's fundamental principle, the lesson is taken instead, and used as a study policy, that the objective reality of social facts as an ongoing accomplishment being by members known, used, and taken for granted, is for members doing sociology, a fundamental phenomenon. (Garfinkel, 1967:vii)

In a sense, one may take Garfinkel (1968:11) with a grain of salt here, for in discussing his own term, ethnomethodology, he notes: "I think the term may, in fact, be a mistake. *It has acquired a kind of life of its own.*" Durkheim could not have said it better, but he could have said it. Nevertheless, as Meltzer points out, in the writings of the ethnomethodologists ". . . we find depictions of the flimsy nature of social reality in general society, as well as indications of the way in which sociologists construct with each other an equally flimsy social reality" (Meltzer, Petras and Reynolds, 1975:79). The ethnomethodologists forcefully argue that the hidden, or taken-for-granted, assumptions of sociologists are the very things that hinder their efforts to understand the taken-for-granted assumptions of the nonsociologists whom they purport to investigate. The sociologist "is seen as imparting a distinctively arbitrary reification of those aspects of society he sets out to study" (Mitchell, 1978:135). Sociologists' own taken-for-granted assumptions often prevent them from understanding human conduct from the perspective of the actors engaged in it. Symbolic interactionists, of course, have always insisted on examining reality from one's subject's point of view. If your own taken-for-granted assumptions prevent you from doing this, you are in trouble. Assumptions conventionally made about social order, argue the ethnomethodologists, may cause sociologists more trouble than any other assumptions commonly made in the discipline. One more look at the ethnomethodologist's own conception of social order would therefore seem to be called for.

The ethnomethodologists argue that social order, or social reality, is not something that is simply "out there." Social realities "emerge relative to our particular position in social and cultural matrixes . . ." hence, ". . . exactly *what* system of reality is defined as warranting our trust varies." These assumed realities "come to define . . . the ways in which the relationships themselves are interpreted and carried out during interaction" (Meltzer, Petras and Reynolds, 1975:79). The ethnomethodologists, then, are concerned with the methods employed by both sociologists and nonsociologists, by the observer and the observed alike in constructing their everyday realities. If the sociologists' constructed realities differ too greatly from the constructed realities of their subjects, or if sociologists fail to realize that their realities too are simply constructions, or social products, the process of understanding will, the ethnomethodologists opine, be impeded. In the last analysis, it may be that establishment sociologists see ethnomethodologists as radical simply because the latter make this simple and apparently threatening observation: Sociologists are people, and sociological theorizing and research are themselves social activities; hence, sociologists and their behavior should be just as readily comprehendable in sociological terms as the behavior of any other collection of human beings. As Dreitzel (1970:x) expresses it, "Until we have understood how we . . . understand each other, all further sociological inquiry will be useless."

All of the foregoing is by way of illustrating the central idea of ethnomethodology:

> The ultimate reality is a puzzle, sometimes a myth, and the "realist" thing we can catch hold of is the behavior of people constructing reality . . . [we need to know] . . . how people go about constructing in their own mind and conversations a view of the social world around them . . . peo-

ple act as if reality were solid, given, and unambiguous, but the social world they communicate about is actually fluid, highly subject to interpretation, and not easily discoverable. (Collins and Makowsky, 1972:209)

As previously mentioned, the leading exponent of the ethnomethodological perspective in American sociology is Harold Garfinkel. Employing a bewildering array of esoteric concepts, Garfinkel, in his principal work to date, *Studies in Ethnomethodology*, provides us with an overview of his perspective's major concerns:

> Ethnomethodological studies analyze everyday activities as members' methods for making those same activities visibly rational-and-reportable-for-all-practical-purposes, i.e., "accountable," as organizations of commonplace everyday activities. . . .
> Their study is directed to the tasks of learning how members' actual, ordinary activities consist of methods to make practical actions, practical circumstances, common sense knowledge of social structures, and practical sociological reasoning analyzable. (1967:vii-viii)

In further describing the contents of his major work, Garfinkel notes:

> The following studies seek to treat practical activities, practical circumstances, and practical sociological reasoning as topics of empirical study, and by paying to the most commonplace activities of daily life the attention usually accorded extraordinary events, seek to learn about them as phenomena in their own right. Their central recommendation is that the activities whereby members produce and manage settings of organized everyday affairs are identical with members' procedures for making these settings "accountable" . . .
> I use the term "ethnomethodology" to refer to the investigation of the rational properties of indexical expressions and other practical actions as contingent ongoing accomplishments or organized artful practices of everyday life. (1967:i-ii)

In a different context, Garfinkel (1968:11) provided the same basic description of ethnomethodology in briefer terms: "It is an organizational study of a members' knowledge of his ordinary affairs, of his own organized enterprises, where that knowledge is treated by us as part of the same setting that it also makes orderable." Turner (1974:10) puts this matter in even more succinct fashion: "'Practical' actors make and find a reasonable world: Their doing so is topically available for the social scientist." Ethnomethodology, then, is the investigation of *all* phases (extraordinary and trivial) of practical activity transpiring in everyday life. In order to approach such "practical activity in everyday life," Garfinkel and other ethnomethodologists employ concepts such as the following: epoche, glossing, reflexivity, accounting, accountable, accounts, bracketing, practical reasoning, deep rules, et cetera clause, typification, talk, located practices, documentary interpretation, idealization, second order conceptions, reducting, utterance time, breaching experiments, indexical expression. These concepts are utilized by ethnomethodologists in general and Garfinkel in particular in an attempt to disclose

> (1) the nature of and extent to which various orders of meanings are *carried* in ordinary and common everyday exchanges of utterances, (2) the *underlying sense of meaning* tacitly accepted yet ordinarily unacknowledged by members involved in communication, (3) the *exchange* of intersubjectively meaningful *understanding* derived from communication, and (4) the nature of everyday exchanges as they constitute for members a sense of *rational, rule-like character* and thus are seen by members as making "sense." (Mitchell, 1978:133–134)

Among the numerous studies and works that employ concepts such as those just listed, and that attempt to deal with at least one of the four "intellectual problems" set out above, are the following:

1. Garfinkel's own works on bargaining for fixed-priced items, on suspected suicide, on sexuality, on breaching ex-

periments, on clinic records, on psychiatric outpatient clinics, and on fake counseling for personal problems
2. Pollner's 1979 work on the traffic court
3. Schegloff's 1979 work on conservations
4. Jefferson's 1979 work on laughter
5. Psathas' 1979 work on directional maps
6. McHugh's 1968 work on defining the situation
7. Cicourel's 1968 work on juvenile delinquency
8. Sudnow's 1967 work on death
9. Goodwin's 1979 work on the emergence of sentences
10. Sach's 1972 work on children's stories
11. Ryave and Schenkein's 1974 work on walking
12. Heritage and Watson's 1979 work on orderliness in conversations

An examination of the works cited indicates that Garfinkel and the ethnomethodologists wish to "make sense" of what is being said in the course of everyday activity. How does one set out to accomplish such a task: "How does one discover and make explicit what for Everyman is so taken for granted that he may not take notice of it? . . . How, in short, may one make the commonplace visible?" (Zeitlin, 1973:184). Garfinkel has a ready reply to such a question: "Procedurally it is my preference to start with familiar scenes and ask what can be done to make trouble" (1967:37).

The ethnomethodologists, and especially Garfinkel's long-suffering students, are troublemakers. Theirs is, Leon Warshay (1971:25) notes, a sociology of involvement, but it is also, and more profoundly, a sociology of instigation. Meltzer puts it as follows:

> Whereas Goffman appears content merely to study the drama of coping with the depersonalization and alienation prevalent in modern society, Garfinkel and his cohorts often deliberately inflict these conditions upon others. Demonstrations of the acquisition of power by disrupting taken-for-granted assumptions, e.g., not accepting statments at their face value, bargaining for fixed-value items in a store, and falsely purporting to help individuals with personal problems, all position the investigator as a superordinate

manipulator and his subjects as mystified dupes. Thus, Goffman's opportunist becomes Garfinkel's blundering fool, trusting in something that isn't there, willfully destroyed by those pretending to share his her/trust. (Meltzer, Petras and Reynolds, 1975:81)

Garfinkel's students are the intellectual agent provocateurs of sociology; they demand of those whom they attempt to study that they explain the obvious. Similarly, Garfinkel requires of his students that they come to view their own activities, as well as those activities unfolding around them, as if they themselves were but strangers in the social setting. He has required of his student experimenters that they view the goings-on in their own homes as if they were but boarders in their households. All of this is aimed at achieving a better understanding of common-sense knowledge and behavior by first rendering them problematic. Only by disrupting the "routine" are the very taken-for-granted assumptions that make of the social world a routine place more clearly revealed. By Garfinkel's reasoning, there is more than one objective world and more than one "correct" way of structuring it: "The question is not one of what is the objective world and what is objective knowledge, but what are the varieties of objective knowledge" (1952:383).

In simple terms, what Garfinkel seeks is to shake people up, to unsettle their daily routines and in the process of watching them putting their "lives back together" and "their houses back in order" to unearth and better understand the very processes by which social realities are constructed and social worlds rendered intelligible in the first place. In Garfinkel's words ". . . under the breach of the expectancies of everyday life, given the conditions for the optimal production of disturbance, persons should shift in exhibited confusion in an amount that is coordinate with the original extent of their grasp of the 'natural facts of life' " (1967:65).

It may be best here to look at one of Garfinkel's own studies as a "test" of the essential correctness of his statement on everyday life: ". . . persons should shift in exhibited confusion in an amount that is coordinate with the original extent of their grasp of the 'natural facts of life' " (1967:65). In an attempt to challenge the conventional sociological image of people as "cultural dopes," as uncritical puppets who simply comply with the official, "legitimate" patterns of culture, Garfinkel was led to examine the "institutionalized one-price rule," a rule Talcott Parsons deemed essential to the institution of the contract—a mechanism on whose existence the very foundation of Western civilization rests. Garfinkel gave his students the assignment of bargaining for standard, of fixed-price, merchandise. Under normal conditions, one simply does not bargain for fixed-price items—customers do not try it, and salespersons certainly do not expect it. As Garfinkel (1967:69) puts it, because of the internalized, or accepted, nature of standard priced merchandise ". . . the student-customers should have been fearful and shamed by the perspective assignment, and shamed by having done it. Reciprocally, anxiety and anger should have been commonly reported for sales persons." Sixty-eight of Garfinkel's students were given the task of offering much less than the asking price for an item valued at less than $2. An additional 67 students were given a more complex task: They were to bargain for three items costing less than $2 and for three items costing $50 or more. What were the results of this experiment? As might be expected, students experienced the greatest amount of anxiety and fear in both anticipating their assignment and approaching a salesperson for the first time. During the course of the experience itself, however, fear and anxiety decreased, and ". . . most of the students who bargained in two or more trials reported that by the third episode they were enjoying the assignment" (1967:69). More important, Garfinkel informs us that ". . . many students reported that they had learned to their 'surprise' that one could bargain in standard price settings with some realistic chance of an advantageous outcome, and planned to do so in the future, particularly for costly merchandise" (1967:69). This would seem to suggest that Garfinkel was right in assuming that disruption affords us a chance to see reality construction at work. It would also seem to imply that he should have stressed the fact that, as his own work demonstrates, once the challenging of taken-for-granted assumptions occurs, people many times do not, once the disruption has subsided, return to their original taken-for-granted worlds.

Now what does Garfinkel himself make of all this? First, he correctly concludes that people's adherence to society's rules "is not necessarily a product of their value commitments or belief in such rules. It may merely be . . . the anticipatory anxiety that prevents him from permitting a situation to develop, let alone confronting a situation, in which he has the alternative of acting or not with respect to a rule . . ." (1967:70). People may, then, fail to challenge rules, to break rules, to change rules, not because of a belief in the essential correctness of the rules, but because fear and anxiety prevent them from doing so. Much of our knowledge, sociologist and nonsociologist alike, of the "rules" confers on these selfsame rules a character that has never been submitted to any test, and as Garfinkel (1967:70) points out, ". . . the more important the rule, the greater is the likelihood that knowledge is based on avoided tests." The implication here being that "insofar as the sociologist ignores this—that fear, anxiety, and ignorance, not positive value-commitments, often account for compliance—he makes real persons in society into judgmental dopes" (Zeitlin, 1973:187). One does not have to agree with Garfinkel's implicit image of people being little more than "blundering fools" in order to see that he has touched bedrock with his critique of conventional sociology's "over-socialized conception" of human nature. But as Zeitlin notes, in speaking of the bargaining for standard merchandise study:

> This experiment [and the principle it illustrates] has more implications than Garfinkel explicitly draws out; it has critical and even revolutionary implications in that it points directly to the potential flexibility, contingency, and changeability of institutions. It brings out clearly that institutions often regarded as necessary are merely those whose necessity has not been tested. (1973:187)

Garfinkel's failure to spell out in detail the most radical implications of his findings is a characteristic shared by many ethnomethodologists. In some cases this reluctance may be a product of the belief that common-sense, everyday, knowledge, is "adequate and valid, with nothing more to be said about it" (Zeitlin, 1973:187). It may also, in part, be a result of the fact that much ethnomethodology focuses on those microscopic features of social reality whose radical implications for the larger social world are especially difficult to ascertain. Not all ethnomethodologists avoid explicitly facing up to the most radical implications of their own work, however, and not all of them dwell at the astructural, microscopic level of analysis. Much of Aaron Cicourel's work is of a more macroscopic character, and at least Mehan and Wood seem perfectly willing to deal with ethnomethodology's most far-reaching and potentially disruptive implications. For those interested in a more macroscopic approach to ethnomethodology, Aaron Cicourel's *Theory and Method in a Study of Argentine Fertility* (1974b) and *The Social Organization of Juvenile Justice* (1968) are representative. Hugh Mehan and Houston Wood's *the Reality of Ethnomethodology* (1975) is a serious attempt to deal with ethnomethodology's potentially critical implications. Nevertheless, as Harold Garfinkel has been the main exponent of ethnomethodology, and as his views are perhaps more representative, or at least representative of more of those diverse persons calling themselves ethnomethodologists than are Cicourel's or anybody else's, discussion here has been restricted to Garfinkel's style of ethnomethodology. But if ethnomethodology can be said to have more than one leading figure, then Aaron Cicourel is certainly a major spokesperson, and his major works are recommended to those who seek a better understanding of the ethnomethodological perspective. In referring readers to the works of more macroscopic and critical ethnomethodologists, I can now conclude this very brief discussion of this last major variety of symbolic interactionism.

By way of summarizing ethnomethodology, I note the following:

1. The methods, be they explicit or implicit, that human beings employ in generating a presumption or sense of social order are ethnomethodology's prime focus of attention and central intellectual concern.

2. The methods used in constructing social reality are far more interesting and important for ethnomethodologists than are the social worlds, or orders, those methods create. In Turner's words, the substance of social reality "is viewed as less interesting than the *methods* used by groups and persons, whether sociologists or laypersons, to construct, reaf-

firm, and alter a vision and image of what exists 'out there'"
(1978:405).

3. For most, but by no means all, ethnomethodologists, the
    question of whether a sovereign world exists independent of
    our senses is a moot one. The genetic question is bracketed,
    or suspended; it is taken to be largely irrelevant and not a
    topic of concern. What are important are the methods and
    interactive processes that allow society's members to sustain
    a sense of order, a sense that there is indeed "something out
    there." As Mehan and Wood put it: [Hobbes] was led to ask
    how order is possible. Contemporary theorists reject Hob-
    bes' answer, but retain his question. [We] have chosen to
    ask not how order is possible, but rather to ask how a sense
    of order is possible" (1975:190).

4. There are many interactive methods employed by human
    beings in the attempt to create or establish social realities.
    Among the interactive methods or procedures by which
    people both engage in interpersonal interaction and con-
    struct "their worlds" (their senses of social order), the
    following stand out as being of special significance:

    a. *The reciprocity of perspectives* refers to the practice of
        individuals conveying to each other that they would, in
        fact, experience the same things were their places switched.
    b. *Normal forms* indicates that if ambiguity and uncertainty
        arise in such a fashion that they make ongoing inter-
        action difficult, actors offer signals to one another that
        dictate that a return to "things as they normally are" is
        called for.
    c. *The et cetera principle* refers to the fact that much is left
        unsaid in normal conversation; individuals habitually
        either "fill in" or wait for the additional information
        needed to make sense out of what is being done or said.
    d. *Descriptive vocabularies as indexical expressions* refers
        to the fact that indexical expressions make up the very
        vocabularies that help men and women call up the ex-
        periences they desire to describe, while assuming that
        their expressions are apprehended by others in pretty
        much the same way that they themselves understand them;
        indexical expressions locate communication forms in

terms of time, place situation, intention, past experience, and biography (Cicourel, 1974a:85–88).

5. While ethnomethodology is more concerned with investigating the methods used to create and sustain realities than with reality itself, ethnomethodology nevertheless has a specific conception of what reality "is all about." In fact, ethnomethodology has itself been defined as "reality that investigates the common feature of all realities" (Mehan and Wood, 1975:6). From the ethnomethodological viewpoint, as expressed by Mehan and Wood, reality

a. involves reflexive activity
b. is organized into coherent bodies of knowledge
c. is a product of ceaseless interaction
d. is fragile
e. is permeable (1975:6)

In short, ethnomethodology sees social reality as a fragile and permeable *phenomenon* whose key elements are reflexivity, social knowledge, and social (which is to say, symbolic) interaction.

7 CONTEMPORARY
INTERACTIONISM:
SUMMARY
CHARACTERISTICS

Perhaps the first attempt to set forth in somewhat brief, but nevertheless detailed fashion the basic assumptions of contemporary symbolic interactionism occurred with the 1962 publication of *Human Behavior and Social Processes*. In the foreword to that work, Meyer F. Nimkoff could proclaim with genuine conviction:

> When one considers how important symbolic interactionism theory has been to social psychology, how great has been the number of students who have been exposed to its teaching over the years, and how abundant have been the scholarly contributions made to it, it is indeed surprising that so little should have been done up to now to consolidate our knowledge of this body of theory.

Arnold Rose, both the editor of *Human Behavior and Social Process* and the person actually to lay out the inventory of basic assumptions, put the matter as follows:

> Some scientific theories are systematically stated and empirically buttressed by their innovations. Others grow crescively, with an idea here, a magnificent but partial formulation there, a little study here, a program of specialized studies there. The interactionist theory in sociology and social psychology belongs in the latter category. (1962:vii)

Pointing out that interactionism, properly considered, does not even possess a name, Rose bemoaned this situation for many reasons—not the least of which was his estimate that "perhaps half the sociologists in the United States were nurtured, directly or indirectly, on its [interactionism's] conceptions and approaches to research" (1962:vii). There were no systematic collections of statements, propositions, and detailed analyses by the major proponents of symbolic interactionism in American Sociology when *Human Nature and Social Process* was published. More telling yet was the following pronouncement: For a theory which emphasizes the significance of self-consciousness, it has been unusually devoid of self-consciousness" (1962:vii).

As the foregoing section on varieties of contemporary interactionism makes abundantly clear, and as a swelling number of self-critical accounts by interactionists make even more manifest, the situation described by Rose (1962:vii) in the following statement has been markedly altered: ". . . nowhere within the confines of one volume has there been a systematic formulation of interaction theory, or a summary of empirical support for it or even a collection of related contributions by several exponents." The social protest and soul searching accompanying the antiwar and civil rights movements in the 1960s did not leave sociology untouched. Like many other sociologists, symbolic interactionists entered the "age of meta theory"; they, or at least some of them, became far more self-conscious. Rose's volume is no longer either the only collection of works by major interactionists or the only attempt to lay out in systematic fashion interactionism's basic assumptions and/or propositions. Interactionists, for the most part, have become both more self-conscious and self-critical. The very process by which interactionists gained additional self-consciousness, however, led them to focus as much on differences between and among themselves as it did to focus on those fundamental assumptions they shared in common. Today, while a number of attempts have been made to spell out interactionism's basic assumptions, the amount of agreement among contemporary interactionists concerning just what these fundamental assumptions really are is probably appreciably less than it would have been a decade or two ago. Nevertheless, a quick review of a few of the better-known efforts to lay out the perspectives' basic assumptions should serve as a useful conclusion to this section and as a jumping-off point for the book's ending.

In viewing these efforts to detail interactionism's assumptions, it should be noted immediately that not all persons who label themselves interactionists will agree with 100 percent of what is being presented as their perspective's "total" list of domain assumptions. Others will disagree with the very assumptions being posited. But the great majority of present-day interactionists may well find themselves in basic agreement with much of what is being said.

Two of the better-known attempts to set forward in very brief fashion interactionism's key assumptions were made by Herbert Blumer and Norman K. Denzin. As Blumer's and Denzin's sets of assumptions are not only well known, but fairly widely agreed upon, and very similar in nature, their views constitute a good starting point in the attempt to summarize the guiding assumptions of contemporary interactionism.

Herbert Blumer (1969:2–6), who coined the term "symbolic interactionism" and once referred to his label as a "barbaric neologism," argues that symbolic interactionism is a perspective that, at bottom, rests on three simple premises:

1. The action of a human being toward things is dependent upon the meanings those things have for him or her.
2. Meanings themselves are social products produced in the course of social interaction in human society.
3. Meanings are altered or modified and dealt with through an interpretive process used by the individual in handling the things he or she encounters.

Having laid out and detailed these three premises, Blumer (1969: 50) goes on to list and discuss what he refers to as "four central conceptions in symbolic interactionism." It is difficult to separate these "four conceptions" from his earlier "three premises"; so I present these conceptions here with the understanding that they too would be regarded by some as key assumptions of symbolic interactionsm:

1. People, individually and collectively, are prepared to act on the basis of the meanings of the objects that comprise their world.

2. The association of people is necessarily in the form of a process in which they are making indications to one another and interpreting each other's indications.
3. Social acts, whether individual or collective, are constructed through a process in which the actors note, interpret, and assess the situations confronting them.
4. The complex interlinkages of acts that comprise organizations, institutions, division of labor and networks of interdependency are moving and not static affairs. (1969:50)

It can be readily seen that this list of "four conceptions" looks a great deal like the initial list of "three premises." In fact, some premises and conceptions are identical, except that the conceptions are offered in a bit more elaborate detail. The list of "conceptions" may be the superior listing of symbolic interactionism's basic assumptions, however, in that it, in conception 4, affords us a glimpse not just of interactionism's image of people but also its image of society; the list of premises only implies, rather than states the latter. Conception 4, while very skimpy in terms of specifying the exact nature of human society, indicates that interactionism has a processual rather than static view of society. This view is spelled out in great detail in Blumer's article "Society as Symbolic Interaction" (1962), a strident rejection of the functionalist's equilibrium, or static, societal model.

Denzin agrees with Blumer in arguing that symbolic interactionism rests on three basic premises. Denzin refers to them as the three primitive assumptions. He reasons as follows:

> Theoretically symbolic interactionism rests on three primitive assumptions. Reality as it is sensed, known, and understood is a social production. As such it consists of social objects, the meanings of which arise out of the behaviors persons direct toward them. Humans are granted the capacity to engage in "minded," self-reflexive behavior. In the course of taking their own standpoint and fitting that standpoint to the behavior of others, humans interact with one another. Interaction is seen as an emergent, negotiated, oftentimes unpredictable concern. Interaction is symbolic simply because minded, self-reflexive behavior demands the manipulation of symbols, words, meanings, and diverse languages. (1974:269)

Like Blumer's list of three premises, with which it overlaps, Denzin has his implicit image of society. He tells us that interaction is "an emergent, negotiated, oftentimes unpredictable concern" (1974:269). Denzin could just as easily have said, and in all probability believes, that society is an emergent, negotiated, oftentimes unpredictable phenomena. He too has a processual, nonstatic, antifunctionalist image of society. It is often difficult to sort out certain interactionist's images of society from their conception of human beings. As Arnold Rose, for one, has argued, there are two major strains in interactionist theory: one social psychological and one sociological in focus. The distinction between these two strains is not always clear in the writing of the interactionists, and many interactionists reject distinctions between social psychology and sociology, just as they reject as artificial any distinctions between macroscopic and microscopic levels of social reality. As Rose (1962:vii–ix) notes, the refusal to distinguish between social psychology and sociology goes back a long way in the interactionist tradition: "Cooley and Mead implied this in insisting that the socialized individual and the society are two aspects of the same thing." It is of interest to note how closely the more thorough conceptions of symbolic interactionism's nature presented by both Blumer and Denzin parallel the definition of the perspective offered in the 1959 *Dictionary of Social Science* by John T. Zadrozny:

> *Symbolic Interactionism.* An approach to understanding human conduct which is based on the views that the human is primarily an active, goal-seeking person (not merely a responsive organism), that the stimuli toward which he acts are selected and interpreted by him, and that social interaction occurs in terms of these significant symbols. (1959:339)

It is somewhat unusual that both Blumer and Denzin discuss the basic theoretical assumptions, not in works devoted to social theory, but in articles given over to discussion of methods. The articles in which these basic assumptions appear are titled respectively "The Methodological Position of Symbolic Interactionism" (in Blumer, 1969) and "The Methodological Implications of Symbolic Interactionism for the Study of Deviance" (1974). I mention this here because the next attempt to set out the basic assumptions of symbolic interactionism that is presented was made by the late Arnold Rose, and Rose offers two different sets of interactionist assumptions: one theoretical, one methodological. In both sets of assumptions, commonalities with the Blumer and Denzin definitions emerge. The last two of Rose's three methodological assumptions fit nicely in with both Blumer's and Denzin's theoretical assumptions. However, Rose's list of theoretical assumptions is longer than Blumer's or Denzin's; so, one turns now to Rose's listing. Following this one needs to present Rose's listing of the methodological assumptions underpinning the symbolic interactionist framework. The theoretical assumptions offered by Rose are five in number; they are as follows:

ASSUMPTION 1. *Man lives in a symbolic environment as well as a physical environment* and can be "stimulated" to act by symbols as well as by physical stimuli. . . .

ASSUMPTION 2. *Through symbols, man has the capacity to stimulate others in ways other than those in which he is himself stimulated.*

ASSUMPTION 3. *Through communication of symbols, man can learn huge numbers of meanings, and values — and hence ways of acting — from other men.*

ASSUMPTION 4. *The symbols* — and the meanings and values to which they refer — *do not occur only in isolated bits, but often in clusters, sometimes large and complex.*

ASSUMPTION 5. *Thinking is the process by which possible symbolic solutions and other future courses of action are examined, assessed for their relative advantages and disadvantages in terms of the values of the individual, and one of them chosen for action.* (1962:5–12)

Working from this list of five basic theoretical assumptions, Rose feels he can deduce two additional statements, which he terms interactionism's "general propositions." They are as follows:

GENERAL PROPOSITIONS (DEDUCTION) 1. *Through the learning of a culture* (and subcultures, which are the specialized cultures found in particular segments of society), *men are*

*able to predict each other's behavior most of the time and
gauge their own behavior to the predicted behavior of
others.*

GENERAL PROPOSITIONS (DEDUCTION) 2. *The individual
defines, has a meaning for, himself as well as other objects,
actions, and characteristics. (1962:9–11)*

While Rose's list of assumptions and propositions is longer than
either Denzin's or Blumer's, probably fewer interactionists
would agree with all he says than would agree with the
Blumer–Denzin listing. This is not solely because Rose's listing
is longer, more detailed, and hence presents more points on
which to disagree. Rather, disagreement may arise at the very
point where Rose (1962:ix) chooses to argue that, apart from
assuming that social life is a process, symbolic interactionism
and functionalism "in practically all other respects . . . are very
similar or identical." Nevertheless, apart from possibly rejecting
Rose's assertion that physical stimuli as well as symbols can
stimulate people to act *(assumption 1)* and possibly rejecting
Rose's view of people as purely rational choice makers *(assumption 5)*, perhaps most interactionists would agree that he has
listed, if not all, at least some of interactionism's more salient
theoretical assumptions.

One can turn now to Rose's listing of the basic characteristics of interactionism that are of a methodological nature. It will
be seen immediately that characteristics 2 and 3 closely match
Blumer's and Denzin's notions of what interactionism's assumptions really are. Rose's list of methodological characteristics
reads as follows:

1. . . . the tendency to select behaviors, influences, structures, and
variables for study on the level of common experience with
them . . . empirical research tends to use observations from
a selected portion of "everyday" life . . . the research
technique tends to be observation in some form . . . .
2. . . . The assumption that human behavior and social life are
continually in flux. . . . Social life is assumed to be "in process" never "in equilibrium." . . .
3. . . . the assumption that all social objects of study (behaviors
influences, and the like) are "interpreted" by the individual

and have social meaning . . . they are never seen as "physical" stimuli but as "definitions of the situation.". . . (1962:ix–x)

Assumptions 2 and 3 are not of a methodological nature, as Rose assumes; they are, in fact, basic theoretical assumptions — the very assumptions Blumer and Denzin noted as characterizing symbolic interactionism as a theoretical perspective. In addition to Rose's work, a more recent and detailed attempt to spell out symbolic interactionism's basic assumptions is available.

In the third edition of *Symbolic Interaction: A Reader in Social Psychology* (1978), Jerome G. Manis and Bernard N. Meltzer list and discuss what they regard as being the seven "basic propositions" of symbolic interactionism. They state that these propositions or assumptions summarize the main features of modern symbolic interactionism. The propositions each identify a fundamental element of the perspective. Before discussing the seven basic propositions, perhaps it is best to list the elements identified in them:

1. The meaning component in human conduct
2. The social sources of humanness
3. Society as process
4. The voluntaristic component in human conduct
5. A dialectical conception of mind
6. The constructive, emergent nature of human conduct
7. The necessity of sympathetic introspection (1978:5)

One can turn now to a listing and brief discussion of the Manis and Meltzer propositions that embody the above-cited elements — keeping in mind that the first six propositions constitute theoretical assumptions, while proposition 7 relates to methodology. The Blumer and Denzin lists of assumptions are all contained in the Manis–Meltzer listing, and so too are most of Rose's. The Manis and Meltzer propositional inventory may well be the single best listing of interactionism's basic assumptions. Although fairly lengthy, it is apt to generate an appreciable amount of consensus on the part of present-day symbolic interactionists. The Manis and Meltzer propositions read as follows:

1. Distinctively human behavior and interaction are carried on through the medium of symbols and their meanings.
2. The individual becomes humanized through interaction with other persons.
3. Human society is most usefully conceived as consisting of people in interaction.
4. Human beings are active in shaping their own behavior.
5. Consciousness, or thinking, involves interaction with oneself.
6. Human beings construct their behavior in the course of its execution.
7. An understanding of human conduct requires study of the actor's covert behavior. (1978:6–8)

Drawing from the works of Rose, Blumer, Denzin, and others, but principally from the writing of Manis and Meltzer, a brief statement can be presented that I hope characterizes the views of many contemporary symbolic interactionists with respect to their basic theoretical assumptions. Such a summary statement would read as follows:

The most distinctive characteristic of humans is that they possess selves, and distinctively human conduct arises in the course of interaction, which is carried on through the use of symbols and their meanings. In addition to a self, the human also has a mind, and the mind and self are twin emergents from processes of human association. Neither is a biological given, hence society is essential in the formation of humanness. With the development of a self, the individual becomes capable of forming new meanings and engaging in new behavior through interaction with himself or herself. One is therefore not totally determined or coerced by antecedent events or experiences because one can induce changes in one's own conduct. Mental activity, or minded behavior, entails a dialectical process of interaction between the components of the self. In short, one carries on a dialogue with one's self as well as with others. The socialized person constructs his or her behavior in the course of its execution. Human beings do not simply and mechanically respond to external stimuli. Human behavior is not determined by antecedent conditions. Neither do people respond on the basis of preestablished drives, propensities, inclinations, or attitudes. Behavior that is distinctively human involves elaborate and complex processes of defining, interpreting, selecting, and rejecting alternative courses of action. A dialectical relationship exists between individuals and their environments; people and their environments are mutually determinative. The human being is highly selective in terms of which aspect of his or her environment is selected out, or perceived, interpreted, and ultimately acted toward. This selective process applies as much to the social world as it does to the physical. The social and physical environments in which the individual resides may set limits — sometimes very sharp limits — on the person's perceptions, interpretations, and actions, but they do not determine them.

If forced to provide a single sentence that captures the essence of the symbolic interactionist viewpoint, one could offer the following:

All meaningful human behavior consists of selves addressing action toward objects, including the self as that which can be an object to itself.

PART THREE

A PERSPECTIVE CRITIQUED

Over the past 15 years, the symbolic interactionist perspective has been subjected to a growing series of progressively intense criticisms. Unlike representatives of certain other sociological traditions, several interactionists have not only been "self-critical" of their approach, but have actively participated in the circulation of those major criticisms of interactionism offered by noninteractionists. A few (Hall, 1972: Denzin, 1969: Perinbanayagam, 1982; Maines, 1977; Stryker, 1980; Couch, 1984 and 1986), rather than "duck" or ignore their critics, as many functionalists have done, have attempted to meet their detractors head on. Hence, the criticisms to be catalogued below come from interactionists and noninteractionists alike. These criticisms are both numerous and diverse. The most general and sweeping of critiques that expose and chop up the philosophical roots of the general interactionist framework are presented, and so are the highly detailed and specific criticisms of the works of single interactionists. What follows is an attempt to present not an exhaustive but a representative set of criticisms of interactionism in general and of selected symbolic interactionists, largely contemporary ones, in particular. The only division imposed on the criticisms catalogued is the same classification utilized in a previous work by the present author (Meltzer, Petras, and Reynolds, 1975:83–117), namely, a distinction between criticisms originating within interactionism, on the one hand, and criticisms from "outsiders," on the other. I rely heavily here on this earlier and reasonably comprehensive compilation of criticisms of the interactionist tradition.

Chapter 8 INTERACTIONIST SELF-CRITICISM

The most detailed sets of "insider" criticisms of symbolic interactionism have been provided by Bernard N. Meltzer (1978) and Arthur Brittan (1973). Meltzer's criticisms apply to George H. Mead, the founder of the interactionist tradition; Brittan's critical remarks are directed at the general symbolic interactionist approach. As Mead has been the single most influential interactionist, however, much of what Meltzer criticizes in Mead's work also characterizes the work of many representatives of today's interactionist perspective.

Meltzer on Mead's "Sins of Omission"

A summary of Meltzer's (1959:24–26) criticisms of Mead reads as follows:

1. Mead's framework lacks much in terms of conceptual clarity. Many of his major concepts are either extremely fuzzy or lack the consistency demanded for sound, scientific explanation. Concepts in need of further clarity are object, gesture, mind, generalized other, self, role taking, symbol, image, meaning, the "I," self-consciousness, impulse, and attitude. Mead's emergent perspective on human action and the overall fragmentary nature of his ideas probably account for his lack of precision in defining and applying basic concepts.
2. Mead's framework suffers from certain sins of omission. Among the most "mortal" of these "sins" is his ignoring of both the unconscious and the emotional components in human behavior.
3. Mead's framework poses great difficulties of a method-ological nature. Not only does Mead provide little in terms

129

of empirical buttressing for his position, but the framework he proposes is very difficult to research. It gives us no clear procedures, no specific means by which to enhance its researchability.

Brittan on the Metaphysic of Meaning

Arthur Brittan's (1973:190–204) main criticisms of symbolic interactionism can be summarized as follows:

1. The perspective overemphasizes self-consciousness; it underestimates, downgrades, or outright ignores the impact exerted by emotive and unconscious factors on the process of interaction
2. Interactionists are obsessed with "meaning." Social structure and social change are slighted, and the whole social world is often seen as a mere accessory of or adjunct to symbolic analysis.
3. Interactionism has unduly demoted "the psychological" by "cheating" human aspirations, intentions, wants, needs, motives, and desires of their empirical reality by regarding them as but derivations, or worse yet, mere expressions, of socially constructed categories.
4. The framework's habitually relativistic analysis of human interaction leads to both overemphasizing "the situation" and being overly concerned with the shifting, episodic, and transient.
5. Symbolic interactionism both preaches and practices a "metaphysic of meaning" to the point that a fetish is made of everyday life.
6. Many interactionists see only the negative implications of a "fragmented self," and hence they mistakenly assume that multiple identities are solely the lamentable and dysfunctional end products of an equally fragmented system of social relations. Attention is seldom given to any positive adaptive aspects of a multiple identity.

These points, briefly stated, are the heart of Meltzer's and Brittan's "insider" critiques of symbolic interactionism. Although theirs are the major reflexive criticisms, they are not, of course, the only interactionists to critically examine the interactionist perspective. Herbert Blumer (1962:179), William Kolb (1944), Edward Stevens (1967), and Edwin Lemert (1974), to name but a few, have offered criticisms of selected aspects of George H. Mead's work; interactionists such as Manford Kuhn (1964), Norman K. Denzin (1969), John Lofland (1970), and Peter Hall (1972), again to name but a few, have provided insightful critical commentary on their perspective. Recent self-critical remarks by interactionists add either very little or nothing to the commentary provided by Meltzer, Brittan, Kuhn, Lofland, Denzin, and Hall. I therefore conclude this section on insider criticisms by briefly presenting the views of the latter four authors.

As Manford H. Kuhn's critical commentary is both older and more systematically stated than that of Denzin, Lofland, or Hall, I begin with him. Kuhn's own theory, self-theory, has been critiqued by Charles Tucker (1966).

Kuhn on the Evils of an Oral Tradition

Kuhn's (1965:61–84) criticisms are summarized as follows:

1. For far too long, symbolic interactionism has been handicapped by having its basic and best ideas passed around by word of mouth rather than systematically stated on the printed page. It has been too much an "oral tradition" and too little a published one.
2. Interactionism is beset with a whole host of partial or subtheories (i.e., role theory, reference-group theory, interpersonal theory, and self-theory) that contribute little to the overall perspective but much to the confusion of those attempting to gain greater familiarity with the general tenets of symbolic interactionism.
3. A goodly amount of ambiguity exists with respect to the question of the determinacy or indeterminacy of human behavior. Within the larger interactionist camp are to be found both fairly hard-line determinists and straightforward indeterminists.

4. Interactionists have failed to achieve an appreciable degree of consensus concerning the exact nature and proper definition of the concept *self*, perhaps the perspective's chief (along with *interaction*) working concept.
5. Interactionism lacks a base of empirical research focusing on the process by which self-conceptions change.
6. Symbolic interactionism has failed to make "appropriate conceptualization of the varieties of functional relations that regularly occur between self and other" (1964:78).
7. Traditional symbolic interactionism has utilized an individual, rather than sociological, model of the social act, and hence the perspective remains somewhat asociological.

Denzin on Methodological Difficulties

Norman K. Denzin's 1969 criticisms of interactionism are few in number and, for the most part, repeat the kinds of reservations voiced by Meltzer and Brittan. His criticisms are as follows:

1. It is difficult to make decent empirical observations of phenomena related to the concept *self* because the concept is so ambiguously and vaguely defined.
2. Interactionism provides us with far too small a number of concrete, researchable hypotheses.
3. The perspective is weakest when attempting to deal with large-scale forms of social organization.
4. The real sources of the definitions and meanings considered so crucial for understanding behavior are seldom pinpointed.
5. Firm strategies for the assessment and measurement of interaction processes are lacking.

Meltzer, Kuhn, and Denzin all speak to the issue of conceptual clarity. All three argue that conceptual clarity is not symbolic interactionism's strong suit. John Lofland (1970) too speaks to the issue of interactionism's conceptual inventory, but his criticisms are of a slightly different nature. Lofland is concerned with a dearth of mini-concepts and a surplus of analytic interruptus.

Lofland on Analytic Interruptus

John Lofland, it turns out, addresses himself not so much to the issue of conceptual clarity but to the issue of "conceptual poverty." It is not only a lack of concepts with clear and precise meanings that troubles symbolic interactionism, but, as Lofland sees it, certain critical concepts are simply absent, and one is confronted with "surplus sensitizing rhetoric as distinct from clear conceptual construction" (1970:37). In speaking of the general interactionism orientation, he notes that

> it seems sadly lacking in what one might call "mini-concepts" which are developed and treated with some care. There occur, certainly, encompassing conceptions such as "perspective," "negotiated social order," "impression management," and classic conceptions of the "act," the "self," "interaction," and the like, but there is very little attempt to develop limited and precise notions of microscopic social processes. (1970:37)

It may have been this situation of conceptual impoverishment that led Erving Goffman and a handful of other interactionists to "declare war on conceptual poverty," that is, to offer for consideration a whole range of concepts applicable to microscopic social analysis.

John Lofland has one other major criticism of many symbolic interactionists. They suffer from what he terms "analytic interruptus." They have many approaches but few arrivals. They find conception easy but delivery most difficult. Lofland puts the matter in the following terms:

> Interactionists of a strategic bent have been prone . . . to what might be called "analytic interruptus." This label is intended to denote the practice of starting out to perform a certain task but failing to follow through to the implied, logical, or entailed conclusion. . . . It is easier and takes less time to be vague than to be articulate. (1970:42)

Interactionists are still caught up with the characteristics one associates with an oral tradition. Furthermore, they like to talk, or more accurately, to interact. Less time spent engaging in the process of interaction and more time spent in the process of studying it may better serve their purposes.

Hall on Apolitical Interactionism

This brings us to Peter Hall (1972) and the last of the interactionist critiques of interactionism. Hall's criticism is brief and to the point: Until very recently symbolic interactionists have simply failed either to deal with the political system or to provide a detailed analysis of political behavior. With the exception of the writings of Richard S. Brooks (1969), Arnold M. Rose (1967), and Peter Hall himself, one is indeed hard put to find much in the way of interactionist writings on politics. Symbolic interactionism has long been an apolitical sociological tradition.

By way of a very brief summary of interactionist self-criticism, the main points seem to be that the perspective lacks sufficient concepts that are analytically rigrous and clearly defined; that it needlessly ignores politics, the unconscious, and "the emotive"; and that it is beset with serious problems of a methodological nature.

9 NONINTERACTIONIST
CRITIQUES

The noniteractionist criticisms of symbolic interactionism are greater in number, depth, and diversity than those offered by the interactionists themselves. Furthermore, the criticisms are frequently sharper and more direct. These critics, for the most part, have little by way of personal investment in the interactionist framework; emotionally, as opposed to practically, speaking, they have nothing to lose by being critical. The following constitute a list of fairly representative outsider criticisms of symbolic interactionism:

1. As Fred Block (1973:39–41), Dusky Lee Smith (1973), and Richard Ropers (1973) have all argued, symbolic interactionism has tended to be ahistorical and noneconomic in its analysis of society. Nowhere is this noneconomic, ahistorical approach as painfully evident as in the interactionist's treatment of social problems, although one well-known interactionist, Jerome G. Manis (1984) has recently tried to correct this state of affairs. Smith directs this criticism at two contemporary practitioners of the perspective:

> Symbolic interactionism as managed by the Loflands does not include social and historical conditions as relevant. . . . Focusing upon imputed definitions as autonomous from the social and historical conditions in which they exist results in a meaningless approach for people living in the closing decades of the twentieth century. . . . (1973:74–75)

2. Interactionism is loaded with certain philosophical and ideological biases that distort its image of life properly social (McNall and Johnson, 1975). As Joan Huber (1973:275) puts the matter:

> . . . the SI tradition shares with the philosophy of pragmatism from which it originates an epistemology which makes it reflect the social biases of the researcher and of the people whose behavior is observed. In a benignly liberal climate of opinion the outcome tends to go unnoticed; but in the long run, this kind of methodology is sensitive to the forces of social control.

Today's "climate of opinion" is not exactly "benignly liberal," and Huber's warning should be heeded by those who would practice the craft of interactionism.

3. Interactionism is culturally and temporally limited insofar as it "seems to work best" in those societies and or situations where individuals must constantly address themselves to a "multitude of others." The perspective is at its worst in analyzing those situations where the individual attempts "to be" or "to present" the "same self" consistently. Rather than provide us with a generic "theory" of human nature, interactionism may inadvertently be offering us nothing more than a description of a new personality type both in the making and "on the make," namely, the type Riesman and associates (1950) once dubbed "the other-directed person." Interactionism "works well" when analyzing the noncommittal, shifting encounter; it hardly works at all when the relationships in need of analysis are either emotionally binding or economically interested.

4. Symbolic interactionism lacks a proper appreciation of the role of social power in human affairs. Interactionists provide fairly useful analyses of social power when power is distributed on a roughly equal basis, but "under other circumstances . . . its utility is limited and its insight may even be biased" (Kanter, 1973:88). Needless to say, in contemporary industrial society, the "other circumstances" are the ones that usually prevail.

5. The interactionist framework offers up a far too quaint and/or exotic portrait of social reality (Shaskolsky, 1970: Horowitz, 1971).

6. Symbolic interactionism either ignores or has an improper understanding of both social organization and social structure (Gouldner, 1970a:370; Reynolds and Reynolds, 1973;

Turner, 1982). It manifests what Reynolds and Reynolds have termed an "astructural bias."

By way of summary here, we may say that the noninteractionists charge interactionism with ignoring economics and social power; with being ahistorical as well as culturally and temporally limited; with fostering an overly quaint, exotic, and unreal picture of the social world; with failing to deal with social organization and social structure; and lastly with possessing pronounced negative, idealist biases. Many of these criticisms can be collapsed into a single, more unifying one: Interactionism truly lacks a decent appreciation and adequate understanding of social structure and social organization. All of this is to say that symbolic interactionism manifests a marked astructural, or microscopic, bias, and any framework with such a bias is bound to be both ahistorical and noneconomic; with respect to power politics, it is also destined to be profoundly apolitical. When an individual's perspective is ahistorical, noneconomic, astructural, and apolitical, he or she may well wind up depicting (or constructing) a social reality that is overly quaint or exotic and that is devoid of transcultural applicability. One can best address such criticism by seriously discussing in some detail what has been termed (Reynolds and Reynolds, 1973) the "astructural bias."

In addition to the astructural bias, symbolic interactionism suffers from an "idealist" ideological bias that distorts its view of reality while preventing it from providing a sound, sociological analysis of the social world. Ultimately, the "idealist bias" blends with and shores up the "astructural bias," doing double damage to an interactionist framework with pretensions to sociological viability. A discussion of the biases of symbolic interactionism follows.

Interactionism's Biases: Idealist and Astructural

Until recently, symbolic interactionism has managed to avoid the scathing critiques of its ideological biases to which other minority perspectives have been subjected. This situation may have resulted from the fact that, as John Petras (1966) has suggested, symbolic interactionism has typically "fitted in" with American sociology's dominant orientation. Interactionists have long constituted what Mullins (1973:75) terms "the loyal opposition." Their reform proposals call for orderly reform within the confines of standard, academic sociology; there are no tigers here. All this is changing, however, and it has been for the past 15 years. Interactionists are no longer widely and benignly regarded as the "good folks in the white hats." Several sharp and sustained analyses of their alleged biases are now available to the student of sociology.

Here are to be briefly presented the views of a number of sociologists who have both detailed interactionism's idealist and astructural biases and attempted to assess their attendant human consequences. The views of Leon Shaskolsky (1970), Richard Lichtman (1970), Alvin Gouldner (1961; 1970a; 1970b), Joan Huber (1973), William Maryl (1973), Randall Collins (1975), and myself and my associates (1969, 1973, 1975) are examined.

Shaskolsky's comments deal with interactionism in the most sweeping of generalities, and as they appear in a single short article, they can be very briefly summarized. The same situation applies to Huber, Lichtman, Maryl, and Collins — the latter two direct their criticisms at ethnomethodology, but much of what they have to say applies to most major varieties of interactionism. Neither my comments nor Alvin Gouldner's are restricted to a single book or article, and hence they have to be presented in greater detail. We are both primarily concerned with the astructural bias. Gouldner, rather than deal with the general interactionist orientation, focuses his criticism on the works of leading representatives of the tradition. My associates and I do deal with symbolic interactionism proper, and in some cases we back up our criticisms with survey research data. I begin with the commentary of Shaskolsky, Lichtman, and Huber because all deal, in one fashion or another, with the larger, or general, interactionist perspective. Next I move to Maryl and Collins, who focus primarily on a single major school of interactionist thought, ethnomethodology. I then take up the still more specific commentary of Gouldner, who deals with major individual interactionists. Lastly, my criticisms and those of my coauthors are detailed. Where relevant, the comments of other noninteractionists are interspersed.

Shaskolsky on Americana and Interactionism

The quick overview of interactionism provided by Leon Shaskolsky opens on the following note: "Symbolic interactionism has its roots deeply imbedded in the cultural environment of American life, and its interpretation of society is, in a sense, a 'looking glass' image of what society purports to be" (1970:16). Bronislaw Malinowski (1944:53) long ago informed social scientists that they could never really hope to understand any society, institution, or collectivity merely by examining its "charter," its conceptions and pronouncements about itself. Shaskolsky alleges that interactionism has come uncritically to accept American society's pronouncements (that it is "free," "democratic," "open," "decent," "fair," "just," etc.) about itself at their face value. By making such pronouncements an integral part of its theoretical assumptions and conceptual constructs, interactionism has become just one more tired variety of what Jerome G. Manis (1972) dubbs "common sense sociology." Rather than constitute an accurate description of the larger features of American Society Inc., interactionism has sadly become little more than an intellectual manifestation of American society's charter. It is no longer part of the solution; it is part of the problem. Furthermore, by Shaskolsky's reasoning, interactionism's incorporation of American values is "an ethnocentric factor which has vitiated . . . its adoption into the academic thinking of other countries" (1970:16). With the exception of universities in Canada, Britain, and Japan, interactionism finds little favor in the academic circles of other countries.

Pressing on, Shaskolsky then characterizes symbolic interactionism as a refined and semirealistic variant of social Darwinism. It is a variant of social Darwinism out of line with a "rough-and-ready, robber baron" kind of laissez-faire capitalism, but it is sympathetic to and perfectly compatible with the early stages of corporate capitalism. Shaskolsky states his case in the following fashion:

... not for Mead a Summerian jungle society favoring the fittest, but a society undergoing gradual change and held together by the empathetic understanding of interacting individuals. . . . In society, the rough-and-ready capitalism of the halcyon days of the"robber barons" had been replaced by the philanthropic capitalism of their more sensitive [to scandal, government intervention, and popular revolt] descendants. The next step — welfare capitalism in the form of the New Deal legislation — was waiting off stage in history's wings. Symbolic interactionism reflected these subtle changes in American society. (1970:17)

Interactionism, then, is sensitive to shifts in the overall structure of the larger American state, but something about it also serves to make it "oblivious to the true nature of society" (1970:19). Shaskolsky addresses this point and wraps up his analysis of interactionism by raising the following chilling question:

What effect, for instance, does the fact of being a Negro have on the smooth interaction between individuals in "defining the situation" — would the possession of a black skin be merely to add one further factor into those of which account must be taken when defining the situation, or would the color of the skin be the sole or at least the decisive factor in determining the performance of the individuals involved? In brief, can symbolic interactionism retain its validity in a society in which some men are more equal, or more free, than others? (1970:19-20)

Remember Kanter's (1972:88) argument that interactionism applies best in situations where power is distributed on a near-equal basis and applies least where power is concentrated, shall we say, in white hands and not in black ones (Willhelm, 1983)? Clearly interactionism is deficient in this respect. It is utopian thinking written in the present tense. It sees the world, a world of "equal interactors," not as it is, but the way it wants the world to be. Such utopian thinking is not, of course, the exclusive property of the symbolic interactionists; the functionalists too share this proclivity.

Lichtman on the "Quaintness" Question

In a sense, Richard Lichtman (1970:75) opens with the same argument with which Leon Shaskolsky closed. He argues that interactionism typically fails to discover and reveal the real sources of people's "definitions of the situation." By ostensibly bracketing this genetic question, interactionism secretly assumes that definitions of the situation are either principally or even exclusively the mere result of individual's subjective constructs, which when taken in unison or added together produce an additional large-scale "socially constructed reality," *the* definition of the situation, as it were. In a highly stratified society where some command the media, and hence have the means with which to mold thousands, even millions of other people's "subjective realities," interactionism seems out of touch. You and I have our little definitions of the situation, and the Rockefellers have theirs, and a perspective that is either ignorant of or purposely ignores the difference between the two most assuredly has about it a "quaint" or "unreal" quality.

This quaint or unreal feature of symbolic interactionism results in Lichtman's labelling it a variety of social idealism. He attacks social idealism, and hence interactionism, in the following fashion: ". . . it is overly subjective and voluntaristic, lacks an awareness of historical concreteness, is naive in its account of mutual typification and ultimately abandons the sense of human beings in a struggle against an alien reality which they both master and to which they are subordinate" (1970:77).

Lastly, Lichtman provides a list of those general criticisms of social idealism that also apply to symbolic interactionism:

1. Human behavior is not to be understood either apart from or solely in terms of the interpretations of the actor. Such interpretations do not always reflect the real nature of things. As such interpretations are often "faulty," the phenomenon of false consciousness is also necessary to a proper appreciation of social acts. In short, action's objective structure may be at odds with its intended meaning, and this point is frequently overlooked by idealist theories.
2. The interpreted meanings of individuals are shaped and channeled by society's dominant institutions; these institu-

tions, in turn, both reflect a particular class structure and are class-dominated. Idealism conveniently forgets this point.

3. If we are all nothing more than what we believe each other to be, the self-fulfilling prophecy becomes the primary explanation of human behavior. While this prophecy holds true in many cases, it definitely does not in many others, regardless of what social idealism preaches on this point.

4. Human activities have a relationship with each other that is a certifiable and objective part of the real world. Whether or not they are part of our subjective reality, these relationships still exist. Social idealism needs to take note of them.

This same quaint or unreal quality appending to social idealism catches the eye of Irving Louis Horowitz. He focuses on it in critiquing the work of the well-known symbolic interactionist Howard S. Becker:

> . . . the amount of mechanical activity and behavioral response to organizational pressures and institutional constraints is either left out or reinterpreted into terms more amenable to personality, i.e., family problems, etc. In short, the philosophical bias of . . . voluntarism may create a more "wide open" and hence more exotic (albeit "deviant") universe than the one people live in every day. (1971:527)

Shaskolsky, Horowitz, and Lichtman, then, all regard interactionism as having a certain "unreal quality" about it. The quality stems either from the particular bias associated with voluntarism or from the more general philosophical biases appending to social idealism. They, of course, overlap because voluntarism itself is a key component of social idealism.

Huber on the Bias of Emergent Theory

The specific defect of symbolic interactionism capturing the attention of Joan Huber she labels "the bias of emergent theory." Huber (1973:274) warms up for her criticisms of interactionism by pointing out what many interactionists have themselves noted, namely, that the perspective is not systematically formulated, that theoretical and methodological postulates are not clearly articulated, at that specific directions for the conduct of qualitative research are not set down, that there are not means by which to convince others of the worthwhileness of one's results, and that many of interactionism's key printed works were never intended for publication. This all adds up to the larger observation that the basic relationship between theory and method is not spelled out in the majority of manuscripts that comprise the interactionist tradition. And now Huber is ready to state her fundamental criticism of the interactionist framework:

> When the place of theory is unclear, when the theoretical expectations are not explicated, then the social givens of the present serve as an implicit theoretical formulation. . . . All of these formulations have a *status quo* bias for, when no theoretical expectations are specified, and when truth is expected to emerge from interaction, then what is taken to be true tends to reflect the distribution of social power among the participants. (1973:276)

A paucity of concise theoretical formulation resulting in a status quo bias on the part of many interactionists may, in turn, be a product of their abiding by a domain assumption of American pragmatism. Unlike the Marxists, who believe that truth is discovered in practice, the pragmatists hold to the dictum that truth is created in practice. When this assumption holds sway, the best of all theories is seen as being "grounded theory," a theory that "emerges" from direct, preferably participant, observation. If grounded theory is your ideal, you will be little concerned with detailing in advance the theory construction procedures to be utilized. This approach, as Huber informs us, has negative consequences:

> When the theoretical formulation is primitive, when it "emerges" from the research, or when it is absent, then investigators will tend to use implicitly their own givens as a

theory. When the subjects studied by sociologists participate in the formulation of emerging theory, their own givens are added to the emerging theory. (1973:281)

This emergent bias on the part of interactionists has not been a terribly obvious one, and this, in turn, may be a product of the fact that the kinds of people typically studied by interactionists are those commanding little in terms of wealth or power. Because of this, Huber argues that "any lack of consensus among the participants in such situations can be settled by the researcher with little backtalk from the participants" (1973:281). Were interactionism's subjects the rich and powerful, the emergent bias of the theory would be more obvious, and perhaps painfully so. Huber's reasoning with respect to this crucial point is detailed as follows:

> The problem of scientific objectivity raised by lack of a prior theoretical formulation, by the absence of clearcut critieria for selecting creditable informants, would be highlighted were the researcher to inspect a group of top-dogs, say, the executives of a major corporation. In this situation, the researcher's colleagues might be uneasy if the researcher could not distinguish between theoretical concepts and observed behavior, if the hierarchy of credibility of the informants were arbitrary, and if other such judgmental procedures could hardly be replicated. Which of the participants in an interactive setting is to have most influence in determining the shape of an emerging theory is a question that the SI model has not confronted. The most important way to improve the practice of SI sociology would be for its adherents to confront the problems raised by their ambiguity toward the logico–theoretic components in their work. . . . Furthermore, nothing prevents a detailed observational account from being informed with notions from a stratification or any other theory. For the researcher to spell out in advance and in detail what is expected and why it is expected is more work than transcribing events with the atheoretical simplicity of a blank mind. (1973:281–282)

There is, of course, ample reason to detail one's logically interrelated theoretical propositions before engaging in direct research projects. Such advanced detailing forces the researcher not only to bet on a specific set of outcomes but to "explain" why these outcomes should be the expected ones. A failure to spell out expected, or likely, outcomes means that any and all results are acceptable: The interactionist always wins. But surely here Huber errs. She has just convincingly argued that interactionists use the folk wisdom of American society as the basis of their theoretical propositions. The folk wisdom of American society clearly does not accept all outcomes. It finds some more likely, or at least more desirable, and it "bets on them." Huber's main criticism, then, is not that interactionism hedges its theoretical bets, but that its emergent theory bias leads it to pander to the "conventional wisdoms" and "folk understandings" of American society; "common sense sociology" is, as previously mentioned, what Jerome Manis (1972) calls this tendency. Perhaps some sense can now be made of that variety of interactionism that spends its time making sense out of other people's attempts to make sense, namely, ethnomethodology.

Maryl on Sociology without Society

William Maryl (1973) provides us with a strongly worded critique of ethnomethodology, and Randall Collins (1975) offers up a powerful indictment of interpretive sociology, of which ethnomethodology is a highly visible variant. As Maryl sees it, ethnomethodology is symbolic interactionism's most unsociological and least useful variety; yet it is a perspective with some considerable appeal within the discipline. Its appeal is found in the fact that it purports to deal with that which is immediately human, but as Maryl is quick to note:

> . . . What is immediately human is not fully human. In fact, it is also ironic that while all social research must deal with abstractions, the ethnomethodologists, by focusing upon the consciousness of the solitary individual, have picked the one abstraction which is not justifiable. Unlike economic, political, religious and familial processes, it

cannot be concretized by being put back into a larger
structural context of which it is a part. . . . As Marx,
Mead, and more recently, Goffman among many others
have forcefully demonstrated, social relationships are
derivable (and explainable) from social relationships and
not individual consciousness. The only thing that can be
derived from the solitary ego is the solitary ego. (1973:28)

Maryl goes on to discuss those shortcomings of ethnomethodology (and interactionism) that he, like Lichtman, feels
spring from its larger social idealist stance. It turns out that
ethnomethodology suffers from many of the same disabilities
ascribed to symbolic interactionism proper; it too is ahistorical
and noneconomic, ignores social structure and social power,
and is apolitical and escapist by nature. Maryl concludes his
critique of ethnomethodology by focusing on its "escapist"
features. He argues that ethnomethodology,

like all idealism, is an exercise in avoidance. The assumption of the priority of individual consciousness over
history and the division of labor represents the feeble attempt to control these perplexing realities by substituting
them for something which seems more manageable. Dreitzel
is correct in pointing to fundamental similarities between the
hippie movement and ethnomethodology. The former's responses to crises in society is quite analogous to the latter's
solution to problems in sociology. (1973:28)

Collins on Interactionism as Common Sense

Randall Collins' reservations concerning ethnomethodology have to do with its lofty pretensions. Ethnomethodologists
see themselves as the pure, the brave, the beleaguered, the certifiable and courageous defenders of the faith. These are the
practitioners who would put sociology on a firmer scientific
footing by tightening up its methodology, but as Collins
(1975:30) notes:

A hidden rivalry to science comes to the surface in the
ethnomethodologist's more positive aim, which is to purify

research procedures. In this respect, ethnomethodology is reminiscent of a hypercritical positivist methodology taken as an end in itself. Some of the same rivalry is found in symbolic interactionism which, although extremely critical of positivist formulations, often puts itself forward as the basis for a truer scientific explanation of social behavior.

Have ethnomethodologists delivered on their promise to render sociology scientific? As the following statement makes clear, Collins does not think so:

> Since science must be about reality, interpretive sociologists claim to be the real basis for any scientific sociology, in contrast to theories derived from reified ideas about structure, attitudes, norms, and values. But this promise (or threat) is never really lived up to, for the interpretive sociologists do not develop and expand a body of testable generalizations. (1975:31)

Worse still, ethnomethodology, "Despite its occasional pretensions to develop a new science, . . . is bent on protecting a romantic version of human experience from science" (1975:33). Furthermore, ethnomethodologists have been both cultist and elitist in terms of their approach to building a viable "scientific" sociology. Collins (1975:32) puts this matter as follows:

> Even where it proposes to reorient the foundations of scientific sociology, ethnomethodology has jealously guarded its boundaries, refusing to allow generalizations from outside its own precincts even in tentative status. It has maintained an absolutist, nonpragmatist ideal of truth as a stick that only itself escapes being beaten with — and this only because it usually fails to attempt serious generalization.

Having pretty well worked over the ethnomethodologists, Collins raises two further criticisms of them and of other symbolic interactionists. We have seen both criticisms before; John Lofland (1970) called one "analytic interuptus," and Jerome Manis (1972) labeled the other mere "common sense sociology." On the first of these criticisms, Collins simply argues that ". . .

having performed both a critical and potentially reconstructive service for scientific sociology, the interpretive sociologists stop dead in their tracts" (1975:32). Collins's statement on interactionism as but one more variety of common-sense sociology, however, is particularly well crafted, and it provides a good concluding note to his larger set of criticisms:

> The flash of recognition, which hopeful sociology teachers have sought for decades to make their students experience when they are brought to see the very world they live in as enacted and interpreted, has been all too ephemeral. The symbolic interactionists, for all their self-image as proponents of freshness and life in sociology, are themselves largely responsible for the feeling that sociologists give other names to what everybody already knows. (1975:34)

Gouldner on Ahistorical, Noninstitutional Interactionism

Alvin Gouldner exposes the social origins and analyzes the political ramifications of those "definitions of the sociological situation" constructed by two of interactionism's leading lights, Howard S. Becker and the late Erving Goffman, past president of the American Sociological Association.

Gouldner begins his critique of Goffman's "all the world's a stage and life but a theater" theory of human conduct with the observation that Goffman's work ignores the binding constraints that society places on its individual members. As Gouldner sees it, Erving Goffman's approach "dwells upon the episodic and sees life only as it is lived in a narrow interpersonal circumference, ahistorical and noninstitutional, an existence beyond history and society, and one which comes alive only in the fluid, transient 'encounter' " (1970a:379). Such a view of social life has political consequences, and they are not benign: "Goffman's rejection of hierarchy often expresses itself as an *avoidance* of social stratification and of the importance of power differences, even for concerns that are central to him; thus, it entails an accommodation to existent power arrangements," (1970a:379). Gouldner's point here is simply that ignoring society's structure aids in its perpetuation. Goffman does not have a basic theory of human behavior good for all societies and all times; his is an exceedingly limited theory restricted to describing those individuals caught up within an apparently inflexible bureaucratic society whose victory over their hopes, desires, and aspirations both they and Goffman concede. Gouldner (1961) once pointed out just how quickly many sociologists accept the domination of flesh-and-blood men and women at the hands of an oppressive bureaucracy. These are the sociologists most enchanted with Erving Goffman's dramaturgical interactionism. Ironically, they see his theory as daring and unconventional, but as Gouldner (1970a:386) correctly notes, "A dramaturgical model is an accommodation congenial only to those who are willing to accept the basic allocations of existent master institutions, for it is an invitation to a 'side game.' " Better yet, it is an invitation to a play or performance.

Performance is the key word, for in the world of Erving Goffman, the value of people lies not in human abilities, intentions, energies, or deeds well done but in mere appearances. Goffman's image of people is most certainly not that of the Protestant Ethic character. He is no big admirer of the classical, or old bourgeois, but he has by no means given up on the bourgeois class. In fact, as Gouldner sees it, "Goffman's dramaturgy is an obituary for the old bourgeois virtues and a celebration of the new ones" (1970a:383). The world of the new bourgeoise is one in which style triumphs over substance, where "clothes make the man," and where cleverly staged performances, rather than real accomplishments, carry the day. The new middle class, whose interests Goffman caters to, no longer believes in the old success-through-hard-work formula. As Gouldner informs us, there is now "a keen sense of the irrationality of the relationship between individual achievement and the magnitude of reward, between actual contribution and social reputation" (1970a:381).

Goffman's work, then, contains an implicit but all-important distinction between exchange and production (including the production of symbols) as social processes. He further realizes that people are disproportionately rewarded not by their contribution to production but to exchange, but he applauds this state of affairs. His book, *The Presentation of Self in Everyday Life* is a license to deceive, to deceive self as well as others.

In capitalist society, people are accorded the status of commodities, and some must sell (package) themselves on the market (stage). Goffman apparently sees little wrong with this. In fact, Goffman is really telling us how to fit in and even succeed in a bureaucratic social order. What he is not telling us is how to dismantle this oppressive reality. *The Presentation of Self in Everyday Life* is a training manual for middle-level bureaucrats; it is a Dale Carnegie course for the incurably uptight. Goffman invites such folks to come on stage, to play the part, and to exist in life's little niches; he "invites us to carve a slice out of time, history, and society, rather than attempt to organize and make manageable the larger whole" (Gouldner, 1970a:385). Curtly put, the dramaturgical interactionists encourage us to do but two things: (1) put on the kind of performance that deceives both self and others; and (2) accommodate ourselves to the status quo of contemporary bureaucratic society.

Fletcher, et al. note that Goffman is not always open or honest in terms of his surrender to bureaucracy's dictates; he "fails to be explicit in his commitment to the bureaucratic model and all that such a model entails" (1974:16). One of the model's most pronounced characteristics is that it is nonchanging: "Goffman's organization lacks a dynamic that would allow for or bring about change. While the organization has the power to transform selves, it is apparently unaffected by those persons who constitute its basic fabric" (Fletcher et al., 1974:18). This model of bureaucracy produces in Goffman's work an overpowering concern with the "secondary adjustments" people make to society's larger institutional features. In Goffman's view, the bureaucracy is not to be dismantled or beaten; people must go along. Goffman's "people" are clearly not the type who could beat the bureaucracy even if the bureaucracy could be beaten. One dwells on Goffman's notion of bureaucracy because it, more than his dramaturgical metaphor, sets him and his fellow dramaturgists apart from symbolic interactionism's main thrust. He does not confront problems of social class and social structure, but takes them as nonchanging, immutable givens. As they are fixed and nonaltering, their influence is a constant. Consequently, Goffman's theory is totally absorbed by the mere secondary adjustments individuals make to inflexible structures. His concern is solely with a limited "going along," "game-playing," "making out" and "making do" variety of human action, which he incorrectly assumes represents the full range of human behavioral possibilities.

Goffman's microsociological bias differs somewhat from the astructural bias of other symbolic interactionists. Anselm Strauss (1963), for example, is committed to a model of organizations as "negotiated orders." He becomes so preoccupied with people as the active molders, changers, and creators of society that the essential coerciveness of social life simply slips from view. Unlike Erving Goffman, Strauss is not willing to see structure and organization as nonchanging, constant, taken-for-granted features of society. On the other hand, Strauss sometimes seems to assume that larger structural variables fail to exert a truly significant influence. Many, perhaps most, interactionists are closer to Strauss here than they are to Goffman. Both have different kinds of microscopic leanings, but both views are biased.

Let us leave Goffman now and move on to Alvin Gouldner's criticisms of Howard S. Becker. Not many interactionists purport to be value free or scientifically neutral. They tend to be value committed and ethically engaged. Howard Becker epitomizes a value-committed interactionism. He wants sociologists committed to society's underdogs, to those found on its underside.

What Gouldner finds objectionable in Becker's approach is that Becker, and numerous other interactionists, have selected a specific kind of underdog to be the object of their support. The underdogs to be supported are those already defeated by the system—mental patients, sexual nonconformists, prison inmates, small-time criminals, and so on. These underdogs in no way constitute a real threat to American society's "powers that be." In exclusively supporting this group of underdogs, however, the interests of another class of underdogs goes unnoticed. How many interactionists actively champion the aims and interests of underdogs who do indeed fight the system, and whose very existence poses a real threat to the larger American power structure? As Gouldner sees it, not many!

If one is to follow Becker and take sides, it pays to remember that, in taking sides with one group, one must also stand against another. In siding with Becker's underdog, one is forced to stand against middle-level bureaucrats and the caretakers of local mental institutions and prisons. What Gouldner wants to know is this: Which interactionists stand ready and willing not only actively to support status quo threatening underdogs but also forcefully to stand against persons more formidable than petty bureaucrats and local caretakers? Who among them is willing to stand up to fat-cat bureaucrats, the federal government, major corporations, and the ruling class? Furthermore, one could seriously question the extent to which interactionists' commitments to certain underdogs actually serve those underdogs' best interests. Gouldner has argued this very point in another context. Reviewing a book penned by noted members of the sociological establishment, he implicitly raises the issue of just whose side the interactionists are really on. In commenting on the book, Gouldner argues that it "reflects the development of an important new alliance within sociology itself: between the old style Chicago-type participant observers and the . . . high science researchers" (1970b:334). This alliance is the true "political meaning of the book's genuflections toward Becker and Goffman, toward participant observation, and toward the Chicago school more generally" (1970b:334).

This emerging alliance between structural functionalism and interactionism is, according to Gouldner, founded on

> the Welfare State's need for more Chicago-type informal research techniques, particularly when studying illicit or illegal behavior . . . the . . . alliance reflects the utility of "informal" research methods, and the helplessness of survey and experimental techniques, for the Welfare State's internal domestic, counter insurgency programs. (1970b:334)

Pursuing this point a bit further allows one to address again the question of whose side the interactionists are really on. Unlike today, with its reactionary political climate, structural functionalism faced a crisis in the late 1960s and early 1970s. It needed its basic conservatism reworked, retooled, and updated if it was to address the needs of the warfare–welfare, guns and butter, state. A good strategy would be to take on a "liberal partner," namely, the symbolic interactionists. Gouldner believes that the interactionists have been coopted; he sees functionalism and interactionism as but two sides of the same sociological coin, and so, as the following statement reveals, does Martin Nicolaus:

> Sociologists [structural functionalists] stand guard in the garrison and report to its masters on the movements of an occupied populace. The more adventurous sociologists [symbolic interactionists] don the guise of the people and go out to mix with the peasants in the "field," returning with the books and articles that break the protective secrecy in which a subjugated population wraps itself, and make it more accessible to manipulation and control (in Reynolds and Reynolds 1970:274)

This is exactly what was alluded to earlier when it was suggested that perhaps interactionism does no real service for those underdogs it allegedly sides with. Radical sociologists have been the ones critizing interactionism for crawling into bed with the sociological establishment; however, their charge finds some substantiation in the following statement by the late Talcott Parsons, the titular head of structural functionalism in American sociology: ". . . the underlying influence . . . of the 'social psychology' of C. H. Cooley, G. H. Mead, and W. I. Thomas . . . has fitted in closely with the more structural–functional movement" (1964:150).

The criticisms of Gouldner imply that both Goffman and Becker lack a decent appreciation of social structure and social organization. By suggesting that interactionism has a quaint or unreal picture of the social world, Horowitz, Shaskolsky, Lichtman, and Huber also imply the same thing.

It seems quite reasonable to set forth the argument that, if symbolic interactionism does not have an adequate conception of social structure and social organization, then it will not come to grips with those master institutions of market society that profoundly influence people's lives. It will be, in short, grossly inadequate as a sociological perspective (Turner, 1982). As this is perhaps the most damaging of all the criticisms directed at symbolic interactionism, it will not do to simply illustrate the presence of this "astructural bias" in the works of a mere handful of interactionists. If this criticism is to be taken seriously, then it must be demonstrated that an astructural bias characterizes the thinking of a sizable number of contemporary practitioners of symbolic interactionism.

A Note on the Astructural Bias

As part of a larger investigation of patterns of theoretical diversity within the camp of symbolic interactionism (Reynolds 1969; Reynolds et al., 1970; Reynolds and McCart, 1972; Reynolds and Meltzer, 1973; Reynolds and Reynolds, 1973; Reynolds and Reynolds, 1979; Reynolds, Reynolds, and Bowden, 1979), a questionnaire was constructed and mailed to 124 sociologists closely identified with the perspective. Eighty-four of these interactionists responded and hence constitute the sample of sociologists to whom the commentary that follows applies.

Respondents were presented with a set of four alternative definitions, all from the interactionist literature, of the concept *social organization*. They were asked to select the one they preferred, and if none of the four statements appealed to them, they were encouraged to write their own working definition. Furthermore, each interactionist was asked to provide, in order of importance, a list of concepts that he or she viewed as indispensable for solid sociological reasoning.

The following definitions of social organization were provided:

1. Social organization: *(a)* the structure of common meanings and values of a society (since meanings and values are often structured into institutions, the social organization is the totality of institutions); *(b)* a condition of society in which the members have most of their meanings in common.
2. The term *social organization* refers to a social relation in which the individuals so behave as to prevent the disruption of their mutual influences by extraneous events.
3. From a structural point of view, the framework of social organization consists in the members of the group and their cultural relationships. While the introduction of any new culture trait produces problems of readjustment and disorganization, it is also true that social organization is a result of cultural integration. That is, the attitudes, the folkways,

mores, laws, and institutions make up a system of social controls that the group imposes on its members. In a sense, the social structure seems to be synonymous with culture, since culture affects the framework of social organization. On the other hand, social organization is at once the product of the total culture and a part of it, rather than the sum total of man's achievements.

4. The unity of the social mind consists not in agreement but in organization, in the fact of reciprocal influence or causation among its parts, by virtue of which everything that takes place in it is connected with everything else, and so is an outcome of the whole . . . this differentiated unity of mental and social life, present in the simplest intercourse but capable of infinite growth and adaptation, is what I mean by social organization.

A comment or two concerning these definitions is called for before presenting the results of the survey. Definition 1 sees social organization as a system, or at least a condition, of shared meanings and values. This is a functionalist-style definition embraced by many, perhaps by most, members of the sociological establishment. Definition 3 actually equates social organization with culture, on the one hand, and views it as being merely a part of culture, on the other. Equating culture and social organization is commonplace among structural functionalists. Definition 4 also confuses culture with social organization by piling on an additional "mentalistic" component and by utilizing such terminology as "social mind" and "mental life." Definitions 1, 3, and 4, then, come far closer to being definitions of culture than of social organization.

Definition 2 differs significantly from the others. While flawed, it actually constitutes a potentially useful conception of human social organization. The concept social organization is best defined as the characteristic, principal, or most fundamental way in which people are related to people. Social organization is the principal form of human relationship in a society or collectivity. Utilizing such a definition, one could note that the basic form of social organization in Western Europe and North America is the depersonalized, atomistic, short-term contractual relationship. Only definition 2 sees social organization in terms of actual human relationships rather than in terms of cultural values and beliefs or mental states. Therefore, only definition 2 contains within it the potential for an adequate treatment of social organization and/or social structure (its big flaw lies in restricting "influence" to mutual influence).

The sample of symbolic interactionists replied to the four offered definitions of social organization in the following manner: Three persons failed either to write in their own definition or to select one of those provided; 64 chose from among the four definitions offered; and 17 provided definitions of their own. Of the 64 interactionists selecting an offered alternative, only 6 chose definition 2. As only definition 2 deals with social organization in social, as opposed to cultural, terms, fully 58 respondents favored definitions mirroring an astructural bias. The great majority of interactionists in the sample simply did not consider human relationships to be crucial to their conceptions of social organization.

A content analysis of the replies of the 17 interactionists electing to provide their own definitions revealed them to be diverse in nature. Nine turned out to be restatements of definitions 1, 3, or 4. Eight persons did, however, define social organization in terms similar to those found in definition 2. They referred to social organization as involving human relationships, binding relationships, or structured relationships. They had, in short, a decent grasp of what social organization is "essentially all about." Unfortunately, they constituted a small minority of the sample.

Again, results of the survey indicate that a large majority of the interactionists involved, including many of the perspective's most widely cited representatives, lack a proper understanding of social organization. They either confuse it with culture or assume it to be just one of culture's many parts. If the sample is at all representative, a very pronounced antimacroscopic tendency exists on the part of present-day symbolic interactionists. Responses to a request for a listing of "indispensable concepts" seems to bear this out.

The total number of "indispensable concepts" respondents were asked to provide was limited to seven. The average number of concepts listed was five. The most frequently mentioned concept was "role," being noted by 38 interactionists. The concepts "interaction" and "self" were each listed by 37 respondents. Twenty-nine interactionists considered "culture" to be an indispensable concept, and 25 accorded the same status to the concept "norm." *Role, interaction, self, culture,* and *norm,* then, were the five concepts most frequently noted. Role, interaction, and self are all concepts closely associated with the interactionist tradition, but culture and norm are concepts known to be identified with structural functionalism. Concepts identified with sociologists who manifest an abiding interest in society's larger features were seldom listed by the interactionists.

Only two respondents listed "social class," and only two mentioned "power." The concept "conflict" was noted only six times, and most important, the concept "relationships" or "human relationship" was listed by only three respondents. The concept "social structure" was all but absent from the listings.

Evidently the charge that modern interactionism has had an astructural bias is well founded. Again, as the following chapter by Prendergast and Knottnerus attests, symbolic interactionism still has its share of problems in dealing with society's larger features, but things are looking up.

10 THE NEW STUDIES IN
SOCIAL ORGANIZATION:
OVERCOMING THE
ASTRUCTURAL BIAS[1]

Christopher Prendergast and
J. David Knottnerus

For twenty-five years symbolic interactionism (SI) has been
accused of being incapable of developing or contributing to
macrosociology (Wagner, 1964; Vaughan and Reynolds, 1968). In
its most popular version, SI is said to be burdened by an "astructural
bias" (Reynolds and Reynolds, 1973) that operates as a permanent
epoche on structural analysis. By the 1980s the astructural bias
virtually defined the perspective (Alexander, 1988). To many observers, symbolic interactionism had become a voluntaristic social
psychology preoccupied with the processes of signification and
communication between self-reflective actors, whose freedom to
define the situation was limited chiefly by the constraints of mutual
understanding. Just as Parsonian theory disintegrated under the
rhetoric of the "over-integrated conception of society," so SI faces
increasing marginalization in sociology, unless it can demonstrate
progress in solving the astructural bias problem.

Unbeknownst to most sociologists, even those involved in the
micro-macro debate, progress has been made in solving the astructural
bias problem.[2] Indeed, interactionists began working on the problem
even before it had a name. It is often forgotten that the charges that
symbolic interactionism was "incapable of treating change at the
macro level" and "must learn to deal with the problem of social
structure before it can deal with the problem of social change"
(Vaughan and Reynolds, 1968:209) were made *by interactionists*
themselves. Fifteen years before Day and Day's influential critique
(1977), Arnold Rose complained of the "neglect of power relations

158

between persons and groups" in SI (1962:x). Responding to similar criticisms by Gouldner (1970), Zeitlin (1973), Turner (1974), and Kanter (1972), the astructural bias was the target of a number of agenda-setting pieces by Hall (1972), Meltzer, Petras, and Reynolds (1975), Manis and Meltzer (1978:438), and Maines (1977). The Society for the Study of Symbolic Interaction, founded in 1975, considered its solution one of its purposes (Farberman, 1975a).

From this ferment grew an impressive body of work addressing the very topics the perspective was purportedly incapable of treating: power (Hall, 1985; Luckenbill, 1979), social organization (Hall and Spencer, 1980; Stover, 1977), social stratification (Couch, 1984; Stryker, 1980:68–71), interorganizational relations (Strauss, 1982), and institutional change (Denzin, 1978). Given this redirection of effort—one of the few sustained efforts at presuppositional reform in contemporary social theory—it is little wonder SI spokespersons are ill-tempered with recent metatheoretical analyses defining the perspective by the astructural bias (Maines, 1988:45).

Even concerted effort does not guarantee success, however, if a problem is ambiguously defined and the criteria for correction unspecified. The apparent indifference of mainstream sociology to the new work suggests that this is the case. The purposes of this chapter are to clarify the nature of the problem, to provide criteria for the successful rehabilitation of the perspective, and to apply these criteria to the literature that has appeared so far.

Although we find much to commend, the new studies are often analytically weak, bereft of models of units and levels of social organization, and non-cumulative. What is more, they co-exist with voluntaristic and idealistic presuppositions about social order that seem to us incompatible and counter-productive. These shortcomings go unnoticed within SI, where the new literature has received extensive publicity (see Maines, 1977; Maines and Charlton, 1985; Fine, 1990; Hall, 1987). Dissatisfaction with that commentary prompts this evaluation. SI commentators underestimate the seriousness of the challenge. They attribute the problem to "benign neglect" (Maines, 1977:235), not to a systemic flaw in the perspective. As a result, they consider the new work prima facie proof that the astructural bias is now a "canard" (Fine, 1983:69) or a "myth" perpetrated by inter-paradigm rivalry (Maines, 1988:43). Some think the new studies vindicate the very presuppositions that produce the bias (Fine and Kleinman, 1983), while others uphold higher standards in their own work than they expect of the literature they review (Hall, 1987). Few address issues of concern for sociology as a whole.

If the discipline of sociology is to recognize the astructural bias as an accidental, rather than essential feature of the symbolic interactionist perspective, then an evaluative standpoint will have to be found that is both paradigm-neutral and robust. In our view theory integration is such a standpoint. It may be applied to any orienting strategy in contemporary theory. What counts is not the starting point, but the results: the models, explanations, or conceptual improvements. Accordingly, we ask what the new literature contributes to the theory of social structure. By the "theory of social structure" we mean the set of interrelated definitions and propositions, not yet axiomatically ordered, which attempts to map out a domain of phenomena consisting of social relationships, the opportunities for and constraints on joint action they entail, and their coalescence into complex systems of different types, which may be represented diagrammatically and described in models. We see the reconstruction of the theory of social structure as one of the foremost tasks of contemporary sociology, indeed, one of the two main by-products of the micro-macro project (the other being a theory of agency). One of the basic issues in this area is the question of how social organization emerges out of situated social action and interaction. Here SI is well-positioned to contribute, if it can put the astructural bias behind it. Thus, in asking what the new studies contribute to the theory of social structure, we are indirectly asking whether they indeed solve the astructural bias problem.

Our interests are quite different, therefore, from Hall's. In his "Interactionism and the Study of Social Organization" (1987), Hall selected from the new literature six analytical categories that could serve as "a paradigm for studying social organization" from an SI perspective. If interactionists accept Hall's suggestions, many of the complaints about the astructural bias would soon cease, but our criteria of evaluation would still stand. We will be at pains to spell out these criteria in order to show that they are indeed paradigm-neutral (although not presuppositionless).

We first define the astructural bias as a selection problem (choice of focus) and as a displacement problem (retaining the choice of focus inappropriately). We then explain what criteria we expect the new literature to meet. Finally, we turn to the individual studies and evaluate them according to these criteria.

The Astructural Bias

Everyone in sociology knows implicitly what the astructural bias refers to—the predominance of small-scale descriptive and phenomenological studies that try to put the reader "in the scene" through colorful language, often provided by the actors themselves. Any SI journal or annual will have a sample. *Studies in Symbolic Interaction* v.7 (Part A), to pick one at random, contains an informative ethnography on "Sociability in a Black Outdoor Drinking Place" (Roebuck, 1986), as well as two studies on body image, one among the aged (Hazen, 1986), and the other on breasts as "embodied identities" (Schmitt, 1986). The same issue contains two examples of what we call "structural reference" below (Clough, 1986; Bartlet, Hutter, and Bartlet, 1986). These studies acknowledge the role that socio-economic, legal-political, and institutional factors play in shaping a given setting, but they do so obliquely or through actors' reflections. Structural reference is first cousin to the astructural bias. It simply alludes to extra-local conditions before turning to the real task, the description of the emergent definitions of self, others, and situation.

If we use the expression "number of linkages" as an index of the "distance" in space and time covered by effective relationships, then we can define the astructural bias as a choice of analytical focus (interaction) plus a disregard for "system integration" (Giddens, 1984:89) or effective relationships more distant in space and time. Table 1 displays these choices.

Table 1 may suggest that it is a simple matter to adopt a system-centered focus. For SI it is difficult because it associates a system-centered focus with objectivism, determinism, and reification. To avoid these errors, it keeps interaction at the center of attention, with the consequence that structural analysis becomes problematic.

NUMBER OF LINKAGES

		Few	Many
Interaction-Centered	Astructural Bias	Structural Reference
System-Centered	Microstructural Analysis	Macrostructural Analysis

A N A L Y T I C   F O C U S

Table 1: The Astructural Bias as a Selection Problem.

Were symbolic interactionism merely an introspective social psychology or a phenomenology of interpersonal experience, there would be no legitimate grounds for complaint. But SI claims to be a general sociology, a perspective capable of comprehending social life in all its complexity (Blumer, 1969:57–60). That raises the issue of the epistemic status of objects and processes removed in space and time from the immediate setting. How can one maintain an interaction-centered focus and deal with such objects as markets and stratification systems?

The astructural bias in its more generalized or presuppositional sense stems from this dilemma. The classical solution is this: When it does not leave them in the background wholly or partially, SI treats them as micro phenomena. It maneuvers to find an insider's perspective on the object in question, thus converting it into a setting amenable to ethnographic or phenomenological analysis. In so doing it commits what Wagner called the "fallacy of displacement": It telescopes macro processes into micro processes (1964:583). The inappropriateness of this maneuver, and the rejection of analytical detachment that accompanies it, is what led Day and Day to conclude that it was "difficult to deal with macrosociological questions of structure and history from this perspective" (1977:127). Let us explore the dilemma and three versions of the classical solution more closely.

SI studies return again and again to a singular interpersonal drama—the process of role-taking and communication that results in a definition of the situation that permits interaction to proceed until joint action is terminated or a new definition of the situation is required. Studies that ignore, or take for granted, this drama are not considered studies in symbolic interaction. Consequently, researchers are under a paradigmatic obligation to be "interaction-centered" rather than "system-centered," to avoid reifying culture, social organization, or the self, and to examine the situational emergence of joint action in its full particularity, indeterminacy, and contingency.

When interactionists confront social structure so obligated, they are likely to tackle it in one of three ways: as context, meaning, or activity. Whichever strategy is adopted, social organization is treated as something emergent here and now (Alexander, 1988). Structure-as-context is preferred by negotiated order theory (Strauss, 1978a). Social organization is seen to provide resources, legitimacy, and symbols to interactants, who then reshape their relationships. Since this happens in every setting, social order "must be reconstituted continually" (Strauss et al., 1963:148). Interaction in "negotiation contexts" occurs up and down the organization and along its environments, producing an overall "negotiated order" which is temporarily stabilized in organizational charts, mission statements, and protocols. The focus of attention is necessarily drawn back to interaction, leaving social structure as the ever-receding horizon of negotiations, rather than an object of analysis itself. "Factors of power, resources, and skill may create imbalances in that contextualizing process," writes Maines, "but we need to know about those factors only to chart the particular trajectories of interaction sequences" (1982:275–76).[3]

Structure-as-meaning is preferred by the social worlds approach (Shibutani, 1955; Strauss, 1978b; 1984). Here the idealist tendencies of the perspective reach full bloom, as social structure is replaced by its shadow, members' "sense of social structure" (Law, 1984:174). A network, for example, is a "set of relationships that people imbue with meaning and use" (Fine and Kleinman, 1983:97). When people change the meanings relationships have for them, they change the relationships too. It follows that social worlds are fairly precarious, for "when members have discrepant conceptions of the structure of their networks, social order may break down" (Fine and Kleinman, 1983:102). Here social structure exists outside the setting, but only in the ideas members have of it.

Structure-as-activity is the third way of telescoping macro phenomena into micro phenomena. It starts from the incontrovertible idea that a power structure or art world is ultimately composed of "people doing things together" (Becker, 1986). Social organization then becomes the sum of the settings in which they actually meet face to face. As Couch puts it, "structure exists only in activity" (1984:10). When people are not acting together, social organization dissolves into the presumption that collective action can be reactivated by communication (Becker, 1982:34–5).[4]

The three strategies are not incompatible; some theorists use all three. No matter which strategy is employed, social structure is only a "metaphor" (Becker, 1982:370; Hall, 1987:15). Reality lies in the situation. Settings can be bridged in various ways: by signification (producing a "social world"), by overlapping "negotiated orders," or by a notion of latency. Macro-realities are secondary, provisional, and in effect someone else's micro-reality.[5]

John Law combines structure-as-meaning and structure-as-activity nicely when he writes, "it is not social structure that we observe. Rather we observe people playing out or representing versions of social structure. The central problem for sociologists is, therefore, to observe the communication of symbol systems" (1984:174). "[F]ollow the wash of the actors," he advises, "and observe how it is that they relate the various bits and pieces of action together to produce both a sense of social structure, and social structure itself—for there is nothing more basic lying behind the symbolic" (1984:174). If we take the "sense of social structure" to refer to the meanings of relationships near at hand, and "social worlds" to refer to those more distant in space and time, we can summarize these positions in Table 2.

In our view these strategies ask the wrong questions. The issue is not how one might conceptualize social structure so that it can be unfolded as interaction. The issue is (or should be) how the units and levels of social structure fit together. What is the *gestalt*, the arrangement of parts? Members' sense of social structure is data, not the thing itself. Social structure, those "reproduced relations between actors or collectivities" (Giddens, 1984:21) which bear the traffic of social transactions and interactions, must be assembled by the theorist from the evidence of recurrence. The concept of social structure is an *abstraction* from the infinity of events, transactions, and accommodations that transpire between individuals. (Reification is avoided by recognizing that fact, not by entering the participants' world). It is a construction, moreover, that greatly simplifies what actually transpires among actors, in order thereby to highlight processes of theoretical interest, for example, the exchange of influence and information. Models depicting systems of social relations tell us where the opportunities for interaction lie; they invite us to look at the recurrent practices that transpire at those locations. Knowing the pre-existing pattern "explains" the interaction, i.e. renders it normal. To "deal with" social structure, then, is to provide simplified descriptions of networks of relationships extending across time and space. For that one needs to adopt a system-centered focus—an observer's standpoint outside of the context of interaction.

NUMBER OF LINKAGES

		Few	Many
	Meaning	Sense of Social Structure	Social Worlds
TELE-SCOPING STRATEGIES	**Activity**	People Doing Things Together	Latent Networks
	Context	Negotiation Context	Negotiated Orders

Table 2: The Astructural Bias as a Displacement Problem

We may now define the problem concisely. By the astructural bias we mean the absence or underdevelopment of a coherent set of definitions and propositions describing, and accounting for, the interdependence of units of analysis beyond person-to-person interaction. The expression "beyond person-to-person interaction" means that structural analysis refers to emergent phenomena removed in space and time from the immediacy of face-to-face communication, and therefore not dependent upon signification for their continuance. The units of structural analysis are bounded sets of effective relationships, either between individuals, status positions, collectivities, communities, or social classes. The analysis aims to account for the origin and interdependence of such relationships in various social, cultural, and natural environments. To contribute to the theory of social structure is to add to this corpus of definitions and propositions. "Underdevelopment" is a relative term. It means that, relative to other schools of contemporary sociology, SI makes few contributions to the theory of social structure.

By virtue of this definition of the problem, a piece of SI research that overcomes the astructural bias will also contribute, however humbly, to the theory of social structure, either as microstructural or macrostructural analysis. We can thus evaluate such a contribution according to the same criteria we would use to evaluate research conducted from the premises of systems theory or network analysis.

Studies in Social Organization

The remainder of this chapter will have a different look and feel. With a few exceptions, we will have little to say about the fallacy of displacement and other metatheoretical matters. Instead, we will examine a sample of the new SI literature in social organization, and ask what each study contributes to the theory of social structure.

Before turning to the sample, three comments can be made about the new studies collectively. First, when these studies approach the domain of social structure, they refer to the same objects and processes that interest other sociologists: interorganizational fields, power elites, labor markets, and the like. What is more, they are perfectly willing to talk about "resources," "constraints," and "systems." If the astructural bias is defined as a problem of empirical reference (Zeitlin, 1973), then it is clearly a thing of the past.

Secondly, with varying degrees of success, the new studies adopt a "system-centered" view of these more remote objects and processes. To the extent that they do, they sidestep the telescoping strategies discussed above, and thereby overcome the astructural bias in its presuppositional form. The transition, however, is incomplete. Accompanying the empirical literature on social organization is a body of metatheoretical commentary that defends (or tries to patch up) structure-as-context (Maines and Charlton, 1985), structure-as-meaning (Fine, 1990), and structure-as-activity (Becker, 1986). This commentary has been highly influential within SI, so that the new studies often claim to be illustrating the validity of one or another telescoping strategy. In his study of the liquor industry in Illinois, for example, Denzin (1978) identified five levels of social organization: distillers, wholesalers, retailers, regulators, and customers. Denzin is mostly concerned to depict the exchange relations between groups and individuals across these levels and the institutional arrangements which support them. But he also wants to defend structure-as-meaning, claiming that the five tiers "resolve into distinct social worlds which constitute those collective realities that make up this particular industry" (1978:194). Even when they overcome the astructural bias in practice, SI theorists are reluctant to concede that social structure is something other than a situation writ large.

Thirdly, there is a new appreciation of the sociological imagination. As the new studies recognize, unless the larger structural contexts of action are incorporated into a sociological account, that account is inadequate, that is, it does not meet the goals of sociological explanation. To see the significance of this change, compare Denzin's analysis with Cavan's earlier (astructural) ethnography of public drinking places (1966). The former shows how legal and economic conditions affect the concentration of family holdings in the industry (Denzin, 1978:94–5), while the latter confines herself to the meanings of bar room behavior to participants.

A productive reformulation of the sociological imagination is Giddens' distinction between "social integration" (the reciprocity of practices executed in co-presence) and "system integration" (the reproduction of institutionalized practices over large expanses of time and space) (Giddens, 1984:89). Because large-scale institutional patterns can be implicated in micro settings, such as meetings, Giddens is skeptical of micro theorists such as Collins (1981), who see macro phenomena as the simple aggregation of micro processes (1984:139–142). So are Maines (1982:274) and Hall (1987:10). The concept of "mesostructure," as developed by Maines (1982), refers not to some intermediate level of social organization, but to "the ways societal and institutional forces mesh with human activity" (Hall, 1987:10). Here the structure-as-activity origins of the mesostructure concept, which elsewhere leads to voluntarism (Thomas, 1984), has been tempered by a system-centered focus. The sociological imagination is a powerful antidote to the astructural bias in SI.[6]

To see the extent to which the astructural bias has been overcome, we examine five studies in social organization. The order of presentation is not accidental, but represents degrees of success in overcoming the bias. Otherwise put, the five studies progressively contribute more to the theory of social structure.

Social Organization of TV Drama

In "Working for Television: The Social Organization of TV Drama," Sharon Mast is concerned with "the ways in which the prevailing perceptions of the aesthetic and technical requirements of TV drama production conventionalize and constrain TV work and the social relations arising from it" (1983:71). The aesthetic considerations are the cinematic factors that producers think a mass audience will find entertaining. Those judgments conventionalize the medium. Complexities of character and motivation are reduced to a narrower range of easily-recognized types, allowing predictable moral and cultural attributions (1983:73). Technical constraints include out-of-sequence acting, absence of an audience, positioning for the camera, rehearsals for the technicians, and the exaggerated naturalism induced by close-ups (1983:74–81). Social relations are affected in the following ways: All relations are subordinated to precise schedules; rehearsals are fewer and briefer; responsibility for the final product shifts from the actor to the director; actors ignore bystanders, invest less time in collegial relations, and practice "coordinated autism" before the camera; as the ratio of technicians to actors increases, technicians' functional importance increases and they experience the pre-taping stress that used to befall the cast; and directors attend less to actors than to technical matters (1983:74–81). The whole production may be seen as a "negotiated order" resting upon the "consensually defined ways of working at a particular point in time" (1983:81).

The essay has many virtues, some of which stem from Mast's experience as an actor, others from her knowledge of the profession and its evolution. Here we are only concerned with its contributions to the understanding of social organization. We note, first of all, that social organization is here the dependent variable. The research question is, how do the technical factors of production affect the actor's occupational role, given the commercial nature of TV drama? The usual problem of generalization (Mast examines a single six-episode production) is not severe, since the technical facilities are common throughout the industry. But to see how social organization has changed, we need to know what it was like before its technical environment changed. This Mast tries to provide through a comparison with the theatrical stage. There the actor's role had more autonomy and bore more responsibility for the success of the production (1983:7). The comparison is a fertile one, as we have seen, but it rests upon a romantic idealization of the past. The article succeeds rhetorically. What it lacks is a depiction of the relationships between the respective settings (stage and studio) and the alignment of associations upon which they depend.

Two features of social structure omitted here seem relevant to an analysis of the changing occupational role of the actor in the two media: (1) the interstitial positions that control the flow of resources in and out of each system, be they publicity, personnel, or capital; and (2) the social class composition of their respective audiences. Mast's structural analysis amounts to an informal, first-hand description of the relations between actors and their immediate consociates.[7] The essay succeeds in showing the effects of TV production technologies on various positions in the social system, with the actor's on-set autonomy as the main dependent variable. But the social system is described incompletely, and severed from its wider structural context and history. The analysis is system-centered, but a larger-scale system is required to explain the phenomenon of interest.

Criminogenic Market Structures

One of the first studies to look beyond shared meanings for an understanding of joint action was Harvey Farberman's "A

Criminogenic Market Structure: The Automobile Industry" (1975b). Farberman, long interested in political economy from a SI perspective, was studying the front-stage tactics of low-income car buyers when he observed a pattern of "short sales." In a short sale, a customer would pay roughly twenty-five percent of the sales price in cash, saving an equivalent twenty-five percent in sales tax. As Farberman inquired into the economic rationality of such transactions, his focus shifted to the external pressures on the seller. His interviews uncovered a pattern of economic coercion leading back to Detroit. At the center of his analysis was the financial squeeze imposed on car dealers by the high-volume/low margin-of-profit policy of the manufacturer (1975b:452–54). The manufacturer, seeking economies of scale in production, forced car dealers to maintain large inventories. That in turn forced dealers to maintain large lots and staff, to borrow extensively, and to clear inventory through price reductions. The cash collected in short sales financed kickbacks to used-car managers, who wholesaled trade-ins to local dealers needing compensatory profits to meet overhead. From his "home base" in a single car dealership, Farberman tracked a chain of relationships extending across time and space to the top of the Fortune 500. As he summarized his findings, "a limited number of oligopolist manufacturers who sit at the pinnacle of an economically concentrated industry can establish economic policy which creates a market structure that causes lower level dependent industry participants to engage in patterns of illegal activity" (1975b:456).[8]

The essay brilliantly employs pre-established structural conditions (oligopoly, dependency relations, and market pressures) to account for the economic choices of actors. As such, it is an exemplar of the sociological imagination. The causal argument, depicted in a notation suggested by Coleman (1987), is summarized in Figure 1.

Farberman's essay succeeds in depicting social organization as a causal system. We see clearly how joint action is shaped by resource contingencies. While actors possess shared meanings that enable them to negotiate these illicit transactions, the causal accent is on the pattern of relationships between positions in the system, and not on occupational socialization or "role-making." Actors are self-reflective, and exercise their options for "exit, voice or loyalty" (Hirshmann, 1970) as they wrestle with identity and moral issues, to be sure. But recognizing that does not prohibit Farberman from depicting the system of relationships as an object in its own right.

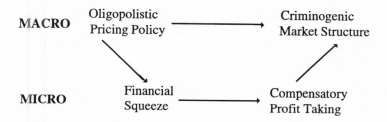

Figure 1: Farberman's Causal Argument

Mast sought to understand changes in the relative autonomy of various positions in a small-scale social system. Taking the actor as the focal point, she confined herself to single-linkage ties radiating outward from this center. Farberman envisions a whole vertical order of relationships many links deep. This is a significant focal shift. Instead of being the background reference for foreground interaction, social structure is interrogated directly. Nevertheless, the linkages become more speculative the further Farberman recedes from home base. Although aware of the literature on the automobile industry, Farberman does not sketch its overall structure. He depicts the economic rationality of local dealers realistically, but substitutes populist imagery of anonymous executives gathered around boardroom wall-charts at the far end. Farberman portrays "system integration" (Giddens, 1984) superbly, but his social organization is ultimately concrete and local, shading off into populist typifications just when one wants to see how power/dependency relations operate at the other end of the market.

Reproductive Sciences

Adele E. Clarke studies the emergence, evolution, and products of the reproductive sciences (embryology, endocrinology, and other disciplines dealing with the sexual reproduction of mammals) (Clarke, 1991a; 1990a; 1987). Her historically-oriented sociology of science ably represents the social worlds perspective of her teacher, Anselm Strauss. Clarke's skills as a writer, theorist, and historian of science are exceptional. No contemporary interactionist has provided a more persuasive defense of the Straussian perspective (Clarke, 1991b; 1990b; Clarke and Gerson, 1990). For Clarke social worlds are "groups with shared commitments to certain *activities* sharing resources of many kinds to achieve their goals" (1990b:18). Following Gerson (1983), she distinguishes between communal, social movement, and production worlds. A scientific specialty is a production world committed to doable problems under the guidance of a paradigm (1990b:20). A fundamental term in her lexicon is "commitment" (Becker, 1960). Structures, she writes, "are ultimately based in the commitments of individual actors to collective action—to work of some kind" (1991b:129). Social worlds are themselves "structural units" within the overall social order (1990b:20). Because their respective commitments differ, processes of negotiation, conflict, and exchange are found wherever social worlds intersect (1990b:20). In Clarke's hands the social worlds perspective becomes "an open but strongly structural framework for conceptualizing scientific work and its organization" (1990b:33). We shall examine, first, her study of "the infrastructural organization" of early twentieth-century physiology (Clarke, 1987), and secondly, her explanation of the "late" emergence of the reproductive sciences (Clarke, 1990a; 1991a).

Between 1890 and 1920 experimental physiology overtook descriptive morphology as the primary research activity of American physiologists. Anatomy and morphology required extensive collections of preserved specimens, but only a few of each type. These materials were acquired episodically, through expeditions and transactions among networks of collectors and scientists; some networks were maintained through several generations of researchers and students (1987:326). Acquiring specimens was "a major investment in terms of time and energy as well as money" (1987:326). The shift to experimental work altered physiologists' needs for specimens and equipment and created new research questions and specialties. Experimental embryology sought to chart the entire development of a species from ovum to embryo to sexually mature adult, while the emerging discipline of endocrinology traced the chemical mechanisms of such development. These enterprises required live specimens or fresh cadavers in large quantities of the same species. While scientists first sought to increase the flow of materials from their existing networks, they soon emulated the agricultural sciences and created "biological farms" or near-site colonies of laboratory animals ranging from mice to opossum to primates (Clarke, 1987:329–40). As colony management techniques evolved to cope with unforeseen problems and as the demand for more exotic specimens grew, a new institutional form was created, the multi-purpose, multi-user biological colony (1987:328). Gradually, the old networks were replaced by a national market composed of biological supply houses, equipment suppliers, animal providers, and zoos, each with their own specialized personnel, commitments, and demands.

Scientific research, Clarke points out, is "constrained or enhanced by the accessibility, cost, organization, and pacing associated with specific materials, instruments, and techniques" (1987:324). Among other things, the availability of research materials influences the content of research, as scientists seek to maximize their infrastructural investments, generating research problems in light of sunk costs. The expenses associated with experimental work soon led scientific teams into dependency relations with government, private capital, and foundations (a.k.a. "Big Science") (1987:340–41).

Two brief comments on the structural analysis here before turning to the essays on the "lateness" of the reproductive sciences. First, the essay explains the transition from one structural form to another (network to market) by examining the changing goals, needs, and practices of research scientists. It is a story of innovation under constraint, rational problem-solving, and "path dependence" (the ways in which prior commitments structure the alternatives available to actors at the next juncture). Although she speaks of "commitments" rather than "choices," Clarke's story could be appreciated as readily by rational choice theorists as by symbolic interactionists. Secondly, Clarke surpasses Mast and Farberman by putting structural change at the center of analysis and by using historical rather than ethnographic methods to reconstruct the social system. If there is any shortcoming, it stems from the legitimate desire to keep close to the historical data (mainly memoirs and grant proposals). Although the study clearly contributes to the theory of social structure, the structural analysis is thin and familiar. Neither network nor market are explored in any detail as to their form and operation; the accent is on the emergence of the research colony as an institution.

If the infrastructure essay gives a micro-to-macro explanation of structural change, the lateness essays are system-centered throughout. Clarke's reputation as a sociologist of science rests on her answer to the question, "Why were the reproductive sciences so late [to emerge]?" (1991a:107). Clark 1991a provides an "internalist" answer: In America (though not elsewhere) genetics and developmental embryology had to develop sufficiently before the reproductive sciences could emerge as "doable" lines of work with their own "problem structure." Clark 1990a provides an "externalist" answer: Where they broached issues of human sexuality, the reproductive sciences faced problems of legitimacy and support. It is to Clarke's credit that she integrates both answers into one differentiated explanation. "Doability," a term Clarke attributes to her collaborator Joan Fujimura (1987), refers to the feasibility of a line of research, its costs relative to expected utility (1991a:116). The "problem structure" of a discipline refers to the research questions generated by a line of work. Disciplines with manageable questions which promise cumulativity, external support, and technological application emerge more readily as legitimate specialties. As Clarke points out, the development of the Pap Smear in 1917, and its application to human females in the 1930s, made reproductive science "doable" as a specialty, especially relative to embryology, which required expensive and hard-to-obtain ova and embryos (1991a:118). As embryology slumped during the 1920s, the reproductive sciences (and genetics) attracted new talent, funds, and prestige (1991a:121).

But the internalist account would be incomplete without an analysis of social conditions that make some subset of potential research questions "important" and "doable" in a given window of time. Those conditions are partly economic, so Clarke attends to the flow of research funds and their sources. But external funding is often dampened by controversy, so Clarke attends to issues of legitimacy and the social movement sources of controversy. Under her broad definition, all of the organized participants in scientific controversies are "social worlds." When worlds collide, their boundaries are drawn more sharply. Commitments are given fresh justification, norms are reformulated and reweighed, and individuals step forward as representatives of their world before publics and opponents alike. Participants rehearse these arguments in an "arena": a "conceptual location where all the groups that care about a given phenomena (sic) meet" (Clarke, 1990b:19). All sciences insofar as they modify the life-world find themselves in arenas wherein their representatives must justify at least the consequences of their products, if not research activities themselves.

Reproductive sciences, Clarke notes, are inherently controversial since they tamper with human sexuality. This was the main external reason for their late appearance in the United States. Two others were their association with quackery (due to the use of testicular extracts from other species to improve fertility) and popular Faustian tropes about a race of "test-tube babies" (1990b:21–26). As Clarke points out, reproductive biologists overcame these problems of legitimacy by attaching themselves to clinical medicine, infertility research, and especially the "pure science" of endocrinology. These strategies, plus the slump in embryology, allowed the specialty to thrive through the inter-war years. Its heyday came in the 1960s with the discovery of the "population bomb." Funding increased ten-fold over the decade, mostly from foundations concerned with population control. Since then abortion and the pill earned reproductive biology the opprobrium of the social movement worlds of the New Right; since 1980 external funding fell twenty-five percent from its 1972 peak (1990b:28). Clarke carefully weaves her way through these ups and downs, sometimes allocating causal weight to internal factors (such as the rise of molecular biology as the flagship discipline in the 1960s, which pulled talent and funds from the reproductive sciences, making them more dependent on the population-control movements), other times to external factors (such as the much-publicized cases of sterilization abuse, which brought feminist and civil rights groups into the arena).

These essays herald the arrival of a strong new voice in SI, someone who embodies what Sheldon Stryker recently called "the vitalization of symbolic interactionism" (Stryker, 1987). While some in SI take social worlds to be free-floating communities of discourse, Clarke hues to the system-centered or "social wholes" orientation of the Park-Hughes tradition (Clarke, 1990b:16). Her use of the term "commitment" also avoids the voluntarism that accompanied Becker's usage. On the other hand, we have reservations about the metaphorical looseness of the terms "world" and "arena." The potential for telescoping is also present when Clarke writes, "Analytically, a social world or arena is merely an extended situation" (1990b:136). And Clarke could focus more explicitly on the structures she identifies. Her diagram of the social worlds intersecting the reproductive sciences (1990b:29) is more of a topical outline than a model. Nevertheless, hers is clearly a social structural approach to science studies.

Agricultural Sciences

Two papers by Lawrence Busch (Busch, 1980; 1982) are frequently cited as exemplars of SI's new approach to social organization (Maines, 1982; Hall, 1987; Clarke and Gerson, 1990). Busch is concerned with a complex social object: the set of institutions and associations linking farmers, agribusinesses, the agricultural sciences, State Agricultural Experiment Stations (SAES), lawmakers, the Department of Agriculture, local government agencies, and various publics. His empirical work lies in an area between the sociology of science and rural sociology, while his theoretical interests are catholic.[9] The two papers use Anselm Strauss' negotiated order perspective to account for the rise, organization, and research questions of the agricultural sciences. Busch 1980 highlights the conflicts and accommodations between researchers, administrators, and clients (consumers of agricultural research) in a typical State Agricultural Experiment Station (SAES). Under the aphorism "history *is* negotiation," Busch 1982 retells the story of the origin, evolution, and institutionalization of the SAES. The theoretical message of both papers is straightforward: Negotiations "resolve certain structural problems and in so doing modify social structure" (1982:368).

The extent to which these papers overcome the astructural bias hinges on Busch's use of the negotiated order perspective. When recurrent social relations are described as "fleeting working arrangements" (Strauss 1978a:6) that are "reconstituted continually" (Strauss et al 1963:148) or dissolved into tenuous definitions of the situation in the temporal present, the astructural bias reigns. There is none of that in Busch. Indeed, there is little of it in Strauss, despite the fact that his metaphor of the "negotiated order" became *the* counterpoint to social structural analysis, seen by some to be reifying by definition (e.g. Frank, 1979). Nevertheless, there are inherent limitations in the negotiation perspective, as we shall now show. To the extent that he follows Strauss' footsteps, Busch's conquest of the astructural bias is incomplete.

According to Strauss (1978a), any theory of social structure requires a theory of negotiation. This is a simple corollary of the SI maxim that social structure arises from interaction. Strauss' originality lay in the identification of eight variables which affect negotiation outcomes. They are: the number of negotiating parties; their respective stakes in the outcome; the visibility (or relative secrecy) of the negotiations; whether the negotiations are episodic, sequential or linked; the number and complexity of the issues on the table; the legitimate bounds of the negotiable; and the alternatives to negotiation that may be available. Many of these variables are well-known to students of bargaining (Bacharach and Lawler, 1981). More importantly, many are *structural* variables. Their contingent, combined, and variable presence yields a *negotiation context*. The persistent environmental conditions which structure the negotiation context (by fixing the stakes, etc.) constitute the *structural context*. Strauss' negotiated order perspective examines the transactions between actors (including clans, organizations, and states) in a given negotiation context. It instructs the analyst to focus on the trade-offs, agendas, decision rules, reorganizations, alliances, rhetorical appeals, weak links, logrolling, and tacit agreements of all kinds. Anything subject to collective action or distribution may become an object of negotiation at one time or another, sometimes at "inappropriate" times. Its relevance to structural analysis is manifest.

But so are its shortcomings. Unless complemented by counter-instructions, it pulls the analyst into the immediate setting, invites her or him to overlook recurrent patterns over longer time-spans, and downplays system integration. These concerns can be overstated, as Strauss (1978a:247–59) and Maines (1982) have shown. Nevertheless, ours is a version of the standard complaint. The negotiated order perspective takes us *up to* the structural context, but does not penetrate it. Structure is like the vanishing point in a perspectivist painting. It makes the foreground possible, it provides depth, but it is always on the horizon, receding from view. To analyze structure, one needs to step outside of the setting by the formulation of *models* of on-going systems of relations. How well does Busch meet this criterion?

The two papers cited earlier fall short of the mark, but in subsequent work with sociologist William B. Lacy, Busch surpasses it. Busch 1980 briefly lists the major players in the typical SAES (administrators, clients, etc.), then using hypothetical cases shows how research projects are chosen or funded. Cotton growers, for example, may successfully lobby the state legislature to increase funds for cotton research. While researchers quickly respond with proposals, the SAES administrator may find them wanting relative to other projects. In the main body of the paper, Busch walks through Strauss' list of context variables (visibility, etc.) and confirms their salience. The client's political and economic clout, the balance of power between researchers and administrator, precedent, and the arguments brought to bear at the choice point, he suggests, are the key factors which tip the scales toward some subset of projects (1980:41). Busch knows the production process at the typical SAES well. The analysis is entirely convincing. It is limited only by its purpose, which is to show "the dynamics that occur within [the] structure" (1980:31), rather than to reveal the structure itself, which is sketched in broad, ideal-typical strokes.

Busch 1982 is more ambitious. Here he retells the story of the rise of the agricultural sciences (see also Busch and Lacy, 1983:5–36). Among the key events were the Land Grant College Act of 1862, the Hatch Act of 1887, which established the SAES as a research institution independent of the U.S. Department of Agriculture, and the founding of the Cooperative Extension Program in 1914 (which is under USDA control). The last institution, which arose during the era of Progressivism and Taylorism, sought nothing less than "an organized rural society" and a "new farmer." It brought agricultural economists and rural sociologists into the SAES. At each of these pivotal points Busch pauses to underscore the conflicts and accommodations between the increasingly-urbane and well-organized interest groups. This story has been told before (Hadwiger, 1982; Peterson, 1980). But Busch tells it sociologically, using the same ideal types as in 1980, and draws a similar moral from it: Systems of social relations can be brought into existence by law, but social structure emerges as a "sediment" of the negotiations between interest groups along the seams. The lesson is a valuable one, which we ignore at our peril. Nevertheless, the focus on emergent relations is self-limiting. Although this complex social system was fully institutionalized by 1930, and persisted for more than forty years, Busch does not provide as much as a diagram of it. In calling 1930–1970 the "period of silence" (1982:379), he suggests that only evolving social systems are theoretically interesting.

In these studies Busch identifies a complex social system, sketches the categories of actor that operate within it, draws attention to stratification and power processes, and provides a reprise of its negotiation history. Busch surpasses Mast in depicting the institutional order as an interdependent system, using ideal types to represent recurrent relations. He surpasses Farberman in dispensing with the residual ethnographic "home base" from which Farberman proceeds by "progressive contextualization" (1975a:436). He surpasses Clarke in his dedication to macro-level associations and institutions. But the object under scrutiny is too complex to be depicted so informally, and the history of negotiations angle distracts from the attempt.

Since 1982 Busch published two books, two edited volumes, and several articles with William B. Lacy (Busch and Lacy, 1983; 1984; Lacy and Busch, 1988; Busch, Lacy, Burkhardt, and Lacy, 1991) and other co-workers. Collectively they have emerged as one of the most productive teams in rural sociology. This collaborative work overcomes the astructural bias completely, but in a way that calls Busch's adherence to SI into question. We note three adjustments. First, negotiation plays a diminished role. One hears echoes of the negotiated order in discussions of the "politics of research" (Busch and Lacy, 1983) and in the conflicting definitions of the "quality of flour" to farmers, millers, and bakers (Busch et al, 1991:121). But the term itself virtually disappears (but see Bush and Lacy, 1983:22 and Busch et al, 1991:49). In the later work the basic structure-producing factor is supply and demand, not negotiations. Accordingly, Busch now calls his approach an "'economic' model of science" (Busch et al., 1991:95). The reader unaware of the commentary on Busch's work by Maines, Hall, and us would identify his position as political economy, not symbolic interaction. That raises the thorny question of whether SI has not become a residual element in Busch's theorizing. (This dilemma compels us to ignore Busch and Lacy's important recent work on the biotechnology industry [Busch et al., 1991].) Secondly, the focus has shifted to the structuration of social systems over larger expanses of space and time. Earlier references to world system theory (Busch and Sachs, 1981) are now realized in empirical studies of the impact of biotechnologies on third world agriculture and in comparative histories of the wheat and tomato industries (Busch et al., 1991). Finally, Busch et al. now provide diagrammatic models of the U.S. wheat and tomato industries (1991:112, 148), although they remain informal and schematic. Clearly, since 1982 Busch has become "more structural." But did he do so as a symbolic interactionist? We think not.

The Hollywood Film Industry

The relationship between Robert Faulkner's *Music on Demand* (1983) and the previous papers is depicted in Figure 2. Each study moves progressively outward from settings to more complex social systems, and each adopts a more system-centered perspective in getting there. With Faulkner, the astructural bias is completely extinguished.

Faulkner's goal is to explain the career development pattern of Hollywood composers. In particular, he wants to account for the unequal distribution of rewards and access to big-budget films. In so doing, he draws upon the Hughes occupational careers tradition. But a natural history of careers cannot reveal why ten percent of composers scored forty percent of the top-grossing films over a ten-year period, while fifty-one percent scored only one film (1983:43, 101).

Faulkner retains an ethnographic component, observing the negotiations between composers, directors, and editors. But he combines it with a "transactional approach" and network analysis. The transactional analysis focuses on the buying and selling of talent on a project-to-project basis. Talent is a marketable commodity, but an unpredictable one. To protect themselves against unconventional and erratic work, producers rely on a handful of composers of known quality. The success of the few reduces access to creative, reputation-enhancing work for the majority. Overworked, the "inner circle" subcontracts projects to colleagues on the periphery. These recurrent transactions establish a network of collaboration, which constitutes the labor market in a given period of time.

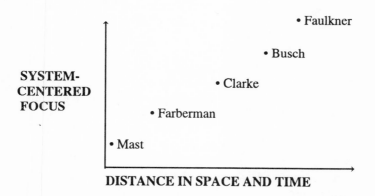

SYSTEM-
CENTERED
FOCUS

• Faulkner

• Busch

• Clarke

• Farberman

• Mast

DISTANCE IN SPACE AND TIME

Figure 2:   Degrees of Success in Overcoming the Astructural Bias

Faulkner supplements the transactional analysis with network analysis. He uses Harrison White's blockmodel techniques and a 62 X 40 matrix to represent the links between producers and top freelancers. The result is a "morphology of Big Hollywood" (1983:193). This "escalon social structure" (1983:193) is remarkably resilient, given craft production and the open market for talent. "Big Hollywood," Faulkner writes, "narrows the range of collective action so that participation is permanently restricted to a chosen few. The people who form the networks may change from decade to decade, but the centralized social structure itself persists" (1983:170).

Faulkner's formula for overcoming the astructural bias has several elements, the absence of which we noted in the previous papers. Faulkner (1) examines the whole system of relationships that comprise the labor market from top to bottom, not just the slice of it he could observe from home base; (2) flawlessly blends micro and macro levels of analysis, without a trace of either voluntarism or determinism, or the fallacy of displacement; (3) mixes symbolic interactionism with other theoretical approaches, such as bounded rationality theory; (4) recognizes constraints upon actors stemming from resource contingencies, supply and demand, network position, career stage, and class interest; (5) provides a causal analysis which explains patterns of dependency, while leaving the actor capable of judgment and self-reflectivity within these parameters; and finally (6) formalizes the relationships using the techniques of network analysis.

Conclusion

Beginning in 1975 a body of substantive research and metatheoretical commentary devoted to solving the astructural bias problem began to appear in SI journals and annuals. The metatheoretical work legitimated (to some extent) system-centered analyses and issues of system integration, but it also defended presuppositions that drew attention back to interaction or warranted one of the telescoping strategies depicted in Table 2. Neither branch of the literature stated explicitly what the sources of the astructural bias were, or what had to be done in order to rehabilitate the perspective.

In our view the astructural bias is a theoretical problem. It can not be solved by making reference to pre-existing social phenomena outside the interaction setting, unless those phenomena are also analyzed theoretically. Empirical or ethnographic studies that merely refer to a "structural context" or "history of negotiations" while keeping their analytical focus on the interaction-at-hand can not be considered solutions to the astructural bias problem. At minimum, such studies must (a) focus analytically on a system of relationships, demonstrating their interdependence, and (b) leave behind some description or analysis of this object that is relevant to the rest of sociology.

The five studies reviewed here progressively resist the temptation to treat social organization as the framework for interaction, until with Faulkner the astructural bias is completely extinguished.

Mast cannot account for changes in the actor's status without incorporating the larger institutional context of TV drama. Farberman understands local interaction in terms of system integration, but the self-imposed limitation to interview data foreshortens his structural analysis. Clarke uses structural analysis to supplement her historical and transactional account of developments in reproductive biology. Busch provides a decentered analysis throughout, but his models are too primitive to account for much that transpires within the complex object under investigation. Faulkner puts it all together: system-centeredness, many-linked relationships, causal (transactional) analysis, system integration, and formalization of the units and levels of social organization. The more successful the studies are in overcoming the astructural bias, the more they contribute to the theory of social structure.

But we may also say: the more successful they are, the less they depend on intellectual resources unique to SI, and the greater their debts to other orienting strategies. That finding contradicts the premise that inspired the new studies in social organization—that SI merely needed to apply an unreformed paradigm to macro-level phenomena (Denzin, 1969:929; Hall, 1972:35). Our evaluation has shown that premise to be mistaken. The astructural bias is the consequence of a set of instructions telling adherents of the perspective what to look for in the study of social life (the definition of the situation) and what to avoid (reification). Overcoming the bias means adopting an alternative set of instructions. The good news is, the new instructions need not supplant the first, only supplement them. Presuppositional reform along the lines suggested by Faulkner and Hall (1985, 1987) will be sufficient, instead of a Kuhnian paradigm shift. The bad news is, SI metatheory remains wedded to a three-fold dualism in which the only viable alternatives to objectivism, determinism, and materialism appear to be subjectivism, voluntarism, and idealism, with the consequence that social organization becomes telescoped as context, activity, or meaning. When SI metatheory has legitimated the new system-centered instructions, the astructural bias will be no more.

Notes

1. A shorter version of this paper appeared in the second edition of this volume under the title, "The Astructural Bias and Presuppositional Reform in Symbolic Interactionism: A Non-Interactionist Evaluation of the New Studies in Social Organization." We again thank Harvey Farberman, David Maines, Gary Alan Fine, and Clark MacPhail for their comments. This version retains the analysis of the sources and consequences of the astructural bias. It adds one new study to the four studies on social organization previously reviewed and significantly revises another.

2. The recent collection of essays by German and American theorists on the micro-macro problem completely ignores the literature reviewed in this paper. As a result, it portrays the perspective as permanently bound to the astructural bias (see Alexander et al., 1987:366–67). In his contribution to the new *Handbook of Sociology*, Smelser introduces symbolic interactionism under the rubric, "Structure Rejected" (Smelser, 1988:121).

3. Despite this remark, in the same essay Maines spells out three ways in which social structure impinges on social interaction. First, it segments social settings. Social structure differentiates populations and collectivities into segmental units, thus creating "multiple social worlds" as lines of communication are restricted and reinforced (see also Stryker [1981:22] and Strauss [1984]). Secondly, resources are distributed unequally across the units, so that the capacities of actors in negotiation contexts are unequal at the onset (1982:271), a point also noted by Strauss (1978a:238). Finally, social structure persists over long periods of time, and this historicity affects negotiations in numerous ways (Maines, 1982:277). These remarks overtake the structure-as-context strategy without providing a clear analytical alternative to it.

4. This strategy is clearly the most receptive to social structural analysis, at least descriptively. Social relationships are indeed opportunities for interaction, and thus latent in Becker's sense. It is equally true that if all actors in a network suddenly lost their memories, or were permanently barred from communicating with one another, the network would cease to exist. Memory, communication, and shared culture are preconditions for social organization. That provides no justification, however, for directing attention away from systems of relationships as emergent realities toward signification or communication in here-and-now settings.

5. Although some SI metatheorists consider these strategies to be solutions to the astructural bias problem, they are the essence of it. Thus, the astructural bias is more than merely "benign neglect" (Maines, 1977:235). It is the consequence of a set of instructions (an "orienting strategy") that tells SI researchers what to look for in the study of social life (the definition of the situation), as well as what to avoid (reifying social relationships). The fear of reification is taken to the point where it places an epoche on theoretical abstraction itself. Any model of a system of relationships detached from an insider's view is put under a ban. Perhaps Coser was right to call this an "atheoretical bias" (1976:156). Its effect is severe. One can not adequately depict systems of relationships phenomenologically or ethnographically, and one can not avoid projecting the contingency of interaction unto them when one tries.

6. Because the sociological imagination is so important for overcoming the astructural bias, it is distressing to hear Denzin recently accuse C. Wright Mills of bad

faith for his "totalizing theory" that tried to "wed the micro and macro levels" (1990:4). Denzin rejects the sociological imagination in favor of "thick interpretive descriptions" that are "written from the point of view of what the situated individuals see, feel, hear and say" (1990:5). Were symbolic interactionists to accept Denzin's council, the movement we have been applauding here would come to an abrupt halt.

7. Mast is explicit about the selectivity of her perspective. "As a participant observer, I acquired my view of the social organization of TV drama by taking the role of the actor, rather than any other organizational employee. I therefore focus on the social relations among the TV workers who *directly* interact with the actors (e.g., the director, technicians, co-actors) excluding from examination the numerous participants whose contribution to the production either precedes or follows the rehearsal period" (1983:72, emphasis in the original).

8. The concept of a criminogenic market structure had earlier been applied to the auto industry by Leonard and Weber (1970). Farberman's accomplishment was to obtain the car dealers' own candid understandings of the mechanisms involved.

9. The theorists Busch seeks to integrate include Habermas, Latour, Saussure, Wallerstein, Maulkey, and Berger and Luckmann.

11 HUMAN EMOTION,
SOCIAL STRUCTURE,
AND SYMBOLIC
INTERACTIONISM

Bernard N. Meltzer and
Nancy J. Herman

Chapters 8, 9, and 10 have described various strictures relating
to symbolic interactionism. Chief among these has been the claim
that the perspective scants the emotional facets of human conduct
and the social-structural facets of social life. More specifically,
critics have asserted that the perspective views human conduct as
unrelievedly rational, or devoid of emotion, and social structure as
simply an adventitious concern of interactionists when dealing with
individual acts and joint actions.

Are these adverse judgments well founded ones, or mere
canards? This chapter will consider that question. As part of
such consideration, we shall discuss how emotions and social
structure have been treated in each of three periods marking the
history of symbolic interaction: (1) the early period, beginning
around the turn of the century and ending in the mid-1930s with
the posthumous publication of the four books credited to George
Herbert Mead; (2) the middle period, ending around 1970, in
which Herbert Blumer, Manford Kuhn, and their students
brought about the flowering of the perspective (notwithstand-
ing Nicholas Mullins's [1973:78] premature reference to symbolic interaction's *demise*); and (3) the current period, in which
the numerous recent responses to the critics have brought a revi-
talization of the perspective.

In the pages that follow, we shall pick up the gauntlet flung by critics both within and outside symbolic interactionism. We shall do so, first, by describing and evaluating interactionist theoretical and research work on emotion; secondly, by doing the same for social structure; and, finally, by presenting an overall assessment of the extent to which the perspective has effectively answered its critics.

Emotion

Given the ubiquity of emotion in human conduct and social life, the criticism that symbolic interactionism slights the emotions is indeed of crucial importance. In the following pages, however, it will be shown that this criticism is not fully warranted. True, among most early interactionists the affective side of life has been assigned an adjunct, or secondary, role. This fact has led some critics to consider the interactionist perspective to be dominated by an overcognitized conception of humans. But a careful reading of the progenitors of the perspective, the middle-generation contributors to it, and, especially, recent contributors challenges the claims of these critics.

Mead, for example, devoted a fair amount of attention to emotion — albeit incidentally to other, primary concerns — in several of his published works (e.g., Mead, 1895, 1909, 1934:18-40, 348-349, 1936:386-404, and 1938:271-300). As Franks (1985) and Baldwin (1985) point out in some detail, his treatments of the subject include a number of penetrating insights, many of which anticipate modern analyses, particularly (according to Baldwin) those of modern behaviorism.

Another early interactionist, James, dealt with emotion in his classic textbook, *The Principles of Psychology* (1890). Here he enunciated the often-quoted assertion, "We do not cry because we feel sorry, we feel sorry because we cry," which conceptualizes emotion as the simultaneous occurrence of cognitive and visceral responses. Franks (1987:228) views this formulation as the original statement of the specificity theory of emotions, which holds that each emotion entails a specific set of physiological responses.

Dewey, another founder of symbolic interactionism, viewed emotion in a fashion congruent with his views on cognitive behavior. For him, both the cognitive and the emotional components of conduct serve adaptive functions. Each arises in situations of blocked action, emotion manifesting itself chiefly when various impulses and tendencies contend for expression, thereby creating tension of some sort and issuing in emotion (Dewey, 1926).

Among the early interactionists, Cooley is, by far, the one most committed to a concern with human feelings. Students of introductory courses in sociology become familiar with the concept of "the looking-glass self," which emphasizes self-feelings. Less familiar, but equally important, is his affect-emphasizing conception of human nature, summarized in the following statement:

> By human nature...we may understand those sentiments and impulses that...belong to mankind at large, and not to any particular race or time. It means, particularly, sympathy and the innumerable sentiments into which sympathy enters, such as love, resentment, ambition, vanity, hero-worship, and the feeling of social right and wrong (Cooley, 1909:28, 1902:32).

It is this common human nature, of course, that provides the basis for the major method advocated by Cooley for the study of human conduct, namely, sympathetic introspection.

The chief successor to the early interactionists, Herbert Blumer, has, also, concerned himself with emotion. Readers of his work on collective behavior (Blumer, 1939) have encountered his analyses of such affective mechanisms of elementary collective behavior as circular reaction, social unrest, collective excitement, and social contagion, as well as of such aspects of social movements as *esprit de corps* and religious ecstasy. Moreover, his article on "Social Attitudes and Nonsymbolic Interaction" (1936) focuses on the affective nature of attitudes, sees feeling as being intrinsic to every social attitude, and asserts that feelings are "regularized by social codes much as is language or conduct" (522). This latter view, repeated in the statement, "These affective rules, demands, and expectations form a code, etiquette, or ritual..." (Blumer, 1936:522-523), clearly anticipates current ideas on "feeling rules" (to be considered later in this chapter).

Other middle-generation interactionists have, also, shown interest in emotion. The earliest textbook using the perspective of symbolic interactionism, Krueger and Reckless (1934), gives the subject passing attention. Another early textbook (Coutu, 1949) makes possibly the first reference to the current idea of "vocabularies of emotion":"Love, hate, fear, and courage are vocabularies which explain and justify personic behavior in socially defined situations" (Coutu:278)[1]. Similarly, Gerth and Mills (1954:57 and 62) refer to "vocabularies for feelings" and "conventions" for feelings. And, finally, a textbook by Shibutani (1961) devotes two chapters to the emotions, including one titled "Conventional Norms and Sentiments," again noting the constructed character of emotions. The middle period of symbolic interactionism is marked, also, by the publication of two articles on embarrassment, one by Goffman (1956) and the other by Gross and Stone (1964). Both analyses consider the social sources and consequences of a specific emotion, a subject to be discussed later in this chapter.

Stung by the censures relating to interactionism's purported slighting of the emotions, modern interactionists have instituted a profusion of interest in the subject. Recently, an Annual Symposium of the Society for the Study of Symbolic Interaction has been devoted to emotion; a section of the American Sociological Association has been established for the Sociology of Emotion, in part through the efforts of interactionists; an issue of *Symbolic Interaction* (published by the Society for the Study of Symbolic Interaction) has focused upon emotion; and numerous works have begun to address the subject.

The following pages of material on emotion will present the main features of recent interactionist works on the subject. Our presentation will cover the following topics: (1) the nature of emotion, (2) types of emotions, (3) social sources of emotions, (4) social consequences of emotions, and (5) unresolved or neglected issues. The works covered under each rubric will include both those by known interactionists and those by theorists or researchers whose ideas on emotion are compatible with an interactionist perspective. It should be borne in mind that, in view of the presence of several paradigms within the perspective (e.g., the Chicago School, the Iowa School, and more recently, the highly positivistic Illinois School), the designation "symbolic interactionism" does not comprise a clear-cut, unitary set of consensual concepts and propositions.

The Nature of Emotion

Several controversial issues relate to the topic of the nature of emotion, most of them involving the relative importance of the biological and the social components of emotion. Symbolic interactionists, of course, typically (but not always) stress the primacy of the social component.

Hochschild (1938:201-222) considers this issue by differentiating the *organismic* model (used by Charles Darwin, William James, and the early Sigmund Freud) from the *interactionist* model (used by John Dewey, Hans Gerth and C. Wright Mills, and Erving Goffman). Let us briefly characterize these models. First, the organismic model defines emotion as primarily physiological in nature; the interactionist model, in contrast, focuses upon the *meaning* taken on by the biological process. One implication of this feature of the organismic view, of course, is a basic fixity of emotion and its basic similarity across human groups. Secondly, the organismic model views the manner in which people label, assess, manage, or express an emotion as *extrinsic* to the emotion; interactionists, on the other hand, *emphasize* these very things. Thirdly, the organismic model assumes a prior existence for emotion apart from introspection and views introspection as epiphenomenal, lacking in the power to evoke emotion; by contrast, interactionists hold that focusing attention on a feeling helps to shape the feeling itself, as does the act of endeavoring to manage one's feeling. Finally, the organismic model directs interest to the origins of emotion; the interactionist model focuses instead on those aspects of emotion that uniquely differentiate social groups of normal adult human beings. These differences imply that the organismic model sees social factors as merely "triggering" biological reactions and helping to steer the expression of these reactions into customary channels, while the interactional model sees social factors as entering into the actual *creation* of emotions.

A somewhat similar differentiation between models is made by Theodore Kemper (1981), who contrasts social constructionists (chiefly interactionists) with positivists (chiefly organicists). Kemper's labels for these models are more widely employed in the literature of emotion than are Hochschild's.

Illustrative of the positivist (or organismic) approach is the work of Thomas Scheff (1983, 1985, 1988), which we present here primarily to provide a contrast with more clearly interactionist approaches. Scheff, adopting what we consider an outmoded "needs psychology," places emphasis upon "expressive needs common to all human beings, which grow out of [certain] biologically based...emotions: grief, fear, anger, joy, and love-attachment" (1985:241). In Scheff's view, "the evidence does not support the exclusion of *cultural universals* [in emotions] from research designs" (1983:333; emphasis added). In fact, according to Scheff (drawing upon Darwin, William McDougall, and early instinct psychologists), the arousal of, even, *shame*—usually considered a social-derived sentiment—is largely biological(1988).

The work of Sue Shott is almost diametrically opposed to Scheff's. Shott begins by pointing out that the actor's experience of emotion comprises two essential elements, physiological arousal and cognitive labeling as affect (1979a:1318). She goes on "to analyze the emergent, constructed character of the actor's experience of emotion and the importance of both definitions and internal stimuli for the construction of feelings" (Shott 1979a:1317). In further contrast to Scheff's position, Shott points to the variability in emotional experience and expression across cultures, which she deems inexplicable without the application of a perspective stressing social and cultural influences (1979b). Such influences produce distinct "vocabularies of emotion" in different societies, which designate the feelings one can expect to experience in given situations. We can best summarize Shott's ideas on the foregoing matters in her own words:

> Within the limits set by social norms and internal stimuli, individuals construct their emotions; and their definitions and interpretations are critical to this often emergent process. Internal states and cues, necessary as they are for affective experience,

do not in themselves establish feeling, for it is the actor's definitions and interpretations that give physiological states their emotional significance or nonsignificance...Symbolic interactionism is well suited for bringing out the interplay of impulse, definition, and socialization that is central to construction of feeling (1979a:1323).

Probably the foremost contributor to the social constructionist frame of reference is Arlie R. Hochschild, who, in a number of articles and a book, has spelled out constituent elements of "emotion work" and "feeling rules." By "emotion work," she refers to "the act of trying to change in degree or quality an emotion or feeling" (Hochschild 1979:561). Two broad types of emotion work can be distinguished: *evocation*, in which the actor's cognitive focus is on a desired feeling that is initially absent, and *suppression*, in which the actor's cognitive focus is on an undesired feeling that is initially present (Hochschild 1979:561). Using a content analysis of 261 protocols given by university students, she illustrates various more specific types of emotion work (Hochschild 1979:562): (1) *cognitive* emotion work, in which the actor attempts to change images, ideas, or thoughts in order to change the feelings associated with them; (2) *bodily* emotions work, in which the actor attempts to change somatic or other physical signs of emotion (e.g., trying to breathe slower, trying not to shake); (3) *expressive* emotion work, that is, attempting to change expressive gestures in order to change inner feeling (e.g., trying to smile or to cry).

"Feeling rules," or "feeling norms," tie in with emotion work. It is when people endeavor to experience the feelings dictated by social norms for given situations that they are likely to engage in emotion work. Hochschild discusses these feeling rules, which reflect how culture influences what we feel and how we name what we feel, in various of her works. She gives some examples of the constructionist concepts of "vocabularies of emotion" (in a very specific sense) in the following passage:

...certain terms came into use in English only after the 18th century (e.g., depression, ennui, chagrin, apathy), and the modern sense of some older terms has become more subjective (e.g., constraint, embarrassment, disappointment). Labels [for emotions] are not univocal symbols corresponding through the ages to fixed varieties of human disposition (Hochschild, 1975: 300).

It is in her book, *The Managed Heart* (1983), that Hochschild presents one of the major empirical studies of feeling rules and emotion work. This highly influential monograph reports her study of 30 flight attendants and five bill collectors, which examines the "commoditization," or commercialization, of feelings in these occupations. (Who among us has escaped the forced smile and cheery "Have a nice day" of salesclerks and other service workers?) While flight attendants are trained to ingratiate themselves with passengers by constant smiling and helpfulness regardless of their actual emotional impulses and inclinations, bill collectors must learn to intimidate and unsympathetically coerce their clients despite any actual compassionate inclinations. The effects of such disjunctions between their "natural" emotional inclinations and the corporately-required emotion work are commented upon in a later section of this chapter.

Other constructionist treatments of the nature of emotion include, among many others: J.R. Averill's analysis of types of feeling norms relating to anger (1982); Lyn Lofland's challenge to the universality of the grief experience, which examines the issue of how deeply social arrangements penetrate into private emotion, just how molded by culture and history even intimate internal experience may be (1985:172); and D.D. Frank's attempt to resolve the issue of how interactionists can "address the bodily component of emotion without falling into psychological reductionism..." (1985:220).

Types of Emotions

Everyone recognizes that emotional experiences may vary in level of intensity, situations of arousal, social and cultural sources, and the extent to which physiological concomitants occur. Building upon the last of these characteristics particularly, several writers have drawn upon James's distinction between "coarse emotions" and "subtle emotions" (1890). Coarse emotions, such as grief, fear, rage, and love, are held to have powerful organic accompaniments, while subtle emotions, such as the sentiments of patriotism, pride, and contempt, are, it is held, not readily defined by distinct organic accompaniments. Franks (1987:231), referring to the distinction by such paired opposites as "primary" and "secondary" emotions and "emotions" and "sentiments," maintains that the coarse emotions are simple, innate, and universally shared, while the subtle emotions are complex, learned, culturally relative, and developed later in life.

Using the same categories, Kemper (1987:263) identifies the primary, or primordial, emotions as fear, anger, depression, and satisfaction. These "physiologically grounded" emotions, he holds, are of evolutionary value, are cross-culturally universal, emerge early ontogenetically, and link up with important outcomes of social relations. For Kemper, the secondary emotions (such as guilt, shame, pride, gratitude, love, nostalgia, and ennui) "are acquired through socializing agents who define and label such emotions while the individual is experiencing the autonomic reactions of one of the *'primaries'*" (emphasis added). Thus, according to Kemper (1987:263), guilt is "a socialized response" to arousal of the physiological concomitants of fear; shame to those of anger; pride to those of satisfaction.[2]

We consider it necessary at this point to reject the false dichotomy described above. Employing an Aristotelian, two-valued logic (namely, that things are either A or not-A), the advocates of the dichotomy into coarse and subtle emotions conveniently overlook the fact that *intensity* of feeling may influence the level of physiological arousal. Hence, actors may experience significant organic reverberations as part of, for example, intense patriotic fervor, while undergoing only subtle organic accompaniments with, for example, mild anger.

From the standpoint of sociology in general and symbolic interactionism in particular, Shott's classification of feelings is of greater utility than the above differentiation between presumably elemental, or fundamental, emotions, on the one hand, and their presumed social derivatives, on the other. Shott (1979a:1323) first distinguishes between "role-taking emotions,"

which require the actor to place him/herself in another's position
and to take that person's standpoint, and other emotions, which
do not require role-taking for their evocation. She further
divides the role-taking emotions, or sentiments, into two types:
reflexive role-taking emotions, which the actor directs toward
him/herself (e.g., guilt, shame, embarrassment, pride, and
vanity) and *empathic role-taking emotions*, which are evoked
when actors mentally place themselves in another's position and
feel what the other person feels or what one would feel in similar
circumstances (Shott, 1979a:1324).

Denzin (1984) provides still another typology of feelings:
(a) "sensible feelings," (b) "lived feelings," (c) "intentional value
feelings," and (d) "self-and-moral feelings." Sensible feelings include bodily sensations like pain and hunger that may lack
meaningful, self-directed sources; lived feelings (e.g., hap-
piness, depression, and exhaustion) have human action and its
outcomes as their referent and, often, their source; intentional
value feelings (e.g., anger, fear, resentment, and love) are moral
judgments of other feelings; and self-and-moral feelings (e.g.,
despair, bliss, serenity, and awe) reflect the actor's evaluation of
his/her total life situation.[3] In an interesting application of this
typology, Denzin (1985) examines an account offered by James
Joyce, the novelist, of the emotional experiences felt by a character in one of his works of fiction.

We conclude this brief discussion of types of emotions by
referring to Hochschild's (1983:230-233) classification of
specific emotions in terms of, among various other dimensions,
"the relation of the self to the causal agent." Thus, for example,
she sees the individual's momentary focus in the feeling of contempt as, in part, involving the underlying cognition "X is
beneath me"; in guilt, "I am the cause"; in shame, "I see the audience of this [act], and they are better than I"; and so on.[4]

Social Sources of Emotions

Treatment of the social sources, or antecedents, of emotions
necessitates concern with, on the one hand, social norms (more
specifically, feeling rules), and, on the other hand, social structure
(more specifically, certain kinds of social relationships).
Although these two facets of the sociocultural matrix of emo-

tions are actually complementary, symbolic interactionists in the social constructionist camp have tended to emphasize the influence of social norms upon the elicitation and shaping of emotions, while others have tended toward emphasis on aspects of social structure.

The work of Kemper epitomizes the social structure emphasis. Kemper, in a series of articles (1978b; 1979; 1981; and 1987) and a monograph (1978a), asserts emotions very frequently result from real, imagined, anticipated, or recollected outcomes of social relationships (1978b.) He selects two dimensions of social relationships, *status* and *power*, as his foci of attention, proposing that each one importantly impinges upon the evocation of specific emotions. For Kemper (1979:435), power encompasses such acts as "coercing, forcing, threatening, punishing, dominating, and so on," and status "accounts for the voluntary, uncoerced giving of benefits, rewards, and privileges" (1979:435). Looking chiefly at distressful, or "negative," emotions, he describes such connections between power or status and specific emotions as the following: (1) *guilt* - experienced when an individual senses that s/he has used excessive power against another person or persons (Kemper, 1979:436); (2) *shame* - experienced when an actor thinks s/he has claimed and or received more status than s/he deserves (Kemper, 1979:437); (3) *anxiety* (or *fear*) - experienced when, given an imbalance in the power relationship between actors, the one with less power is both vulnerable to the encroachments of the other's use of power and anticipates such use (Kemper, 1979:438); *depression* - experienced when the actor undergoes a deficit of status, i.e., an insufficiency of reward and gratification given voluntarily by others (Kemper 1979:439). In his book (1978a), Kemper adds such other connections between the power-status dimensions and specific feelings as the following: *anger* - resulting from interaction outcomes in which expected, customary, or deserved status has been denied or withdrawn by another actor who is perceived to be responsible for the reduced status (1978a:128); *satisfaction* - resulting from interactions in which the power outcome is nonthreatening and the status outcome is in accordance with what the actor desired and expected (1987a:chapters 12 and 13).

Careful consideration of the foregoing material should make it evident that the designated linkages may be sufficient, but not necessary, ones. That is, the indicated interpersonal power or status relationships may *suffice* to evoke the specified emotions; however, none of the relationships is a *necessity* for the occurrence of the linked emotion. Thus, as Kemper recognizes, other situations and antecedents may elicit any of these emotions.

Although Hochschild's works are generally viewed as exemplars of the social constructionist approach, emphasizing feeling rules and emotion work, she has also paid passing attention to the linkage between social structure and emotions. For example, she points out what everyday experience makes clear to us:

> ...anger is most likely to be aimed at people with less power, and least likely to be aimed at people with more power. ...[T]here is both the downward tendency of negative feelings and an upward tendency of positive ones. ...As a consequence, powerful and powerless people live in different emotional as well as social and physical worlds (Hochschild, 1975:295-296).[5]

In another comment on social class, this time in the context of subcultural class differences in feeling rules, Hochschild (1979:571) cites research suggesting that middle-class children are more likely to be punished for "feeling the wrong way, or seeing things in the wrong light," whereas working-class children are more likely to be punished for wrong behavior and its consequences. This class difference in socialization, she asserts, amounts to different degrees of training for the commoditization of feelings. Thus, "in this way, each class prepares its children to psychologically reproduce the class structure" (Hochschild, 1979:551).

Hochschild (1983:227) also comments on changes in the occurrence of *pity* over time. She claims that pity became a common occurrence with the establishment of the Christian church, which came to power in a period marked by both extreme differences in wealth and widespread brutalizing conditions of life. In addition, there were communal ties between people in dire need and people who could "take pity" and provide for them. In her speculative view, with the bureaucratization and impersonal almsgiving that mark modern societies, pity may be less common today.

Turning more directly now to the impact of feeling rules upon emotions, we can cite several illustrative studies. Louis A. Zurcher, for example, has examined a war game (a military Reserve exercise) as a participant observer and through informal interviews (1985). He finds that the top military officers were able, within limits, to "script" the emotional experiences of the participants. Included in the "script" were such feelings as pride, patriotism, courage, aggressiveness (in competition), and joy (in comradeship), as well as high morale (Zurcher, 1985:194). Zurcher concludes that various organizational levels influenced the construction of the Reservists' actual emotions: the organizational scripting, which constitutes the macroscopic level; the specifics of the changing situation, the meso-structural level; and interactions among the actors, the microstructural level (Zurcher, 1985:191).

Lofland (whose study we have previously cited) describes four social components of the grief experience that significantly shape the experience during bereavement mourning. Varying by culture, these components include: (1) the level of significance of the deceased other; (2) the actor's definition of the situation of death; (3) the character of the self experiencing a loss through death; and (4) the interactional situation or setting in which the foregoing three components occur (Lofland, 1985:173). In modern, Western societies, Lofland suggests, the grief experience is shaped by the following modalities of these components:

> (1) a relational pattern that links individuals to a small number of highly significant others; (2) a definition of death as personal annihilation and as unusual and tragic except among the aged; (3) selves that take very seriously their emotional states; and (4) interactional settings [such as households that are relatively spacious and contain only a few others] that provide rich opportunities to contemplate loss (Lofland, 1985:181).

Cheryl and Daniel Albas provide still another example of studies of emotion rules, as well as emotion work (Albas and Albas, 1988). Their study builds on Hochschild's work to examine how approximately 300 students manage their feelings during examination periods. The findings of the study are interesting, if not surprising. As we are well aware, the student culture includes rules concerning the emotions appropriate at exam time, and students learn these rules from others in the subculture. The Albases find that when students believe that their own emotions "are not appropriate as to duration, intensity, or direction they will do [emotion] work to enhance or suppress them to conform to ...rules" (Albas and Albas, 1988:260). One final note on this study relates to variations in the feelings students initially experience at exam time. The authors draw upon their version of symbolic interaction theory to explain this: when students perceive their self-conceptions to be at great risk, they experience an emotional pitch *higher* than the feeling rules prescribe, whereas when students perceive minimal risk to their self-conceptions, they experience an emotional pitch *lower* than that prescribed by the feeling rules.

Another empirical inquiry into emotion work is that by C.P. Gallmeir (1987), who conducted a participant-observation study of the emotional behavior of professional hockey players before, during, and after games. His focus was on the mental and emotional preparation the players undergo in getting "psyched up" and "putting on the game face" of determination and toughness. Directing the staging of emotions are the coach, the trainer, and team-mates, who evoke genuine feelings and not merely superficial displays.

Social Consequences of Emotions

Having given a brief overview of social antecedents of various emotions, we now find it appropriate to look at the other side of the picture: the effects of emotional experience upon social arrangements. As with the other topics we have considered, symbolic interactionists have made a number of contributions to this topic. Shott (1979a: 1317-1318) has shown that certain types of emotions are of such critical importance to social control that "society as we know it could not exist without them." The emotions most clearly involved in this function are the role-taking sentiments. Starting from a fundamental proposition of symbolic interactionism, namely, that social control is, in large measure, self-control, Shott points out that such *reflexive* role-taking sentiments as guilt, shame, and embarrassment, each of which is evoked by different circumstances, restrain and punish one's own deviant behavior (Shott, 1979a: 1325). The *empathic* role-taking sentiments, too, enter into the maintenance of social order and control, prompting moral conduct. Such sentiments, Shott(1979a: 1328) claims, have been shown by several experiments to encourage altruistic conduct.

In another study, Shott (1979b) examines Durkheim's analysis of the powerful collective emotions often evoked by collective rituals, which are an important mechanism for increasing social solidarity. Drawing upon Mead's thinking, she points out that the sort of emotional exaltation Durkheim describes results, according to Mead, from a fusion within the individual of the "I" and the "me." That is, this intense collective sentiment arises when the actor ceases to have the usual awareness of social control because s/he feels that his/her "interest is the interest of all" (Shott, 1979b: 455; quoting Mead, 1934: 274). The main point of this formulation for our present purposes, however, is the importance of the diffusion of collective emotion for the existence of social cohesion.

What happens to people whose emotions have been *commoditized* by their jobs? Hochschild's book (1983) presents data that demonstrate certain consequences for many airline attendants and bill collectors. She suggests that while laborers doing manual work may become alienated from what they produce, laborers doing emotional work may become estranged from their own emotional expressions and what they actually feel (Hochschild, 1983: 187-90). Thus, the individuals studied by Hochschild often found themselves doubting the authenticity of their feelings in everyday, off-the-job situations and relationships. Given the growing proportion of service occupations in modern, post-industrial economies — occupations in which emotion work is typically a constituent ingredient — the broad implications of such alienation for the nature of interpersonal relationships should be obvious.

Patricia L. Wasielewski (1985) addresses, through content analyses of speeches by Martin Luther King Jr. and Malcolm X, the emotional bases of charisma. Charisma, she states, is usually considered a personal characteristic of dynamic leaders; in contrast, she proposes that knowledge of, and ability to manipulate, emotions are the wellsprings of charismatic authority (Wasielewski, 1985: 208). Thus, she conceives of charisma as "an understandable outcome of certain types of emotional interaction, not as a mysterious power possessed by charmed individuals" (Wasielewski, 1985: 218). Specifically, the charismatic's appeal derives from his/her ability to manipulate both the emotions and logic in redefining, or producing a new perspective on, the social order for followers (Wasielewski, 1985: 211).

Seeking professional help with mental or emotional problems is widespread in our society. Peggy A. Thoits (1985) inquires into the conditions under which many people undertake such seeking. Viewing mental illness as deviation from feeling or expression norms, she goes on to outline the circumstances in which individuals' feeling management efforts are likely both to fail and to result in self-labeling as mentally disturbed. Her chief finding, then, is that "self-observed emotional deviance can lead to psychiatric treatment seeking" (Thoits, 1985: 226). In view of the large aggregate of persons involved, the impact of self-attributions of serious violations of feeling rules is, clearly, a significant one.

Another study in the genre under consideration is Scheff's use of Asch's study of conformity to reveal the role of shame in compelling such behavior (1988). Asch's classic 1956 study involved the use of groups of confederates who endeavored to persuade single, naive subjects to give obviously erroneous estimates of the relative lengths of lines; a majority of the subjects were swayed by the false "estimates" of the confederates. Scheff (1988: 403) interprets these findings (along with post-experimental interviews with subjects) as demonstrating that subjects who complied with judgments of the majority (i.e., the confederates) were trying to avoid the embarrassment or shame of appearing different from the group . Conversely, the subjects who maintained their independent judgments, *despite* the pressures exerted by the fallacious majority estimates, may have had sufficiently high self-esteem (a form of pride) to cling to their estimates despite feelings of shame (Scheff, 1988: 404). Here we see, then, the impact of reflexive role-taking sentiments (embarrassment and self-esteem) on conforming behavior, a basic element of social order. In this study, as in the others reviewed in this section, we gain insights into the ways in which the emotions of individuals "ultimately work upward to reconfirm, maintain, and change society and social structure" (Adler, Adler, and Fontana 1987: 224).

Unresolved or Neglected Issues

That symbolic interactionists have, largely, refuted criticisms as to the inherent difficulty of their perspective in dealing with affective phenomena, is attested by their prolific response to such criticisms, particularly in the past dozen or so years. As we have seen, interactionist writings now abound on the nature, types, social sources, and social effects of emotion. These writings should serve to lay to rest further critical comments in this genre.

And, yet, much remains to be done if symbolic interactionism is to bring its treatment of human feelings up to the level of its treatment of the non-affective side of social life. In the paragraphs that follow, we shall briefly indicate some of the gaps in the current interactionist literature on emotions. We do not pretend to present a comprehensive inventory of such needed research and/or theory; rather, we shall select for mention only one broad, fundamental need, plus one representative specific need falling under each of the topics previously discussed.

Still lacking is a systematic framework for the interactionist analysis of emotions. At the present time, we find, chiefly, on both the theoretical and research levels, discrete, atomistic treatments of various aspects of the human passions, rather than attempts to form a general and well-rounded perspective. We find nothing comparable in scope to Mead's *Mind, Self and Society* (1934) or Blumer's essays in *Symbolic Interactionism* (1969), or to various textbooks, each of which does for the cognitive aspects of behavior what needs to be done for the emotional aspects. This broad, general desideratum brings us to a closely related neglect in the area of the nature of emotions.

A number of interactionists have contended that emotions are active ingredients in *rational* behavior (e.g., Hochschild, 1975:285), which are separable only analytically from reason. Still, other than recognizing that emotions have a cognitive component, current interactionists have ignored the ways in which emotions and cognitions work together in the construction of the act (including joint actions).[6] This oversight is all the more inexplicable because Mead is known to have dealt with emotion as rooted in the preparatory stages of the act, that is, in impulse and perception (see Franks, 1985:163).

With respect to types of emotions, an unresolved issue concerns the validity, utility, and heuristic value of viewing specific emotions as having specific physiological concomitants or, oppositely, lacking them. Most social constructionists, of course, take the latter position, identifying emotions on the basis of the actor's *definition* of whatever organic reverberations may be present. True, some efforts have been made to resolve this issue (e.g., Franks, 1987; Kemper, 1987; Scheff, 1983); but these efforts have not proven, in our judgment, to be very successful.

Another area in need of further thinking is that of the social antecedents of emotions. Both feeling rules and social-structural features have tended to be regarded as *determinants*, rather than influences merely, of emotional experience. Chicago School adherents (e.g., Shott, 1979a:1320) have sometimes challenged this view; but the more typical position taken in the literature has been less critical than it should be. After all, a fundamental assumption of symbolic interactionism (at least of its Chicago School) is that of the *active* nature of humans and, correspondingly, the *constructed* and indeterminate character of the actor's conduct!

In the sphere of the social consequences of emotional experiences, we point to a need that relates closely to the topic to be dealt with by subsequent sections of this chapter: social organization. Most of the social consequences studied thus far have been either global social psychological phenomena (e.g., social control, social solidarity, alienation, and charisma) or aggregate social psychological phenomena (e.g., self-labeling as mentally disturbed). More work is clearly needed on *social-organizational* consequences, especially on the macroscopic level (e.g., the various social institutions). This comment applies, also, although to a lesser extent, to the social sources of emotions.

Readers should not interpret the foregoing problems as unique to symbolic interactionism. Even a few moments of reflection by those familiar with the various frames of reference in sociology and social psychology should make it clear that the indicated unresolved and neglected issues are common among not only the different paradigms in sociology and social psychology but also the various other disciplines that study human emotion. The tasks confronting symbolic interactionism, then, are those confronting *all* students of human behavior.

Having reviewed and assessed the interactionist approach to emotions, we now direct attention to the perspective's approach to social structure, or social organization. (For our present purposes, we find it unnecessary to make any fine distinctions between social structure and social organization, although some sociologists insist upon them.) We shall follow this section with a brief summary of our conclusions about both criticisms.

Social Structure

It will be recalled that some commentators have charged that symbolic interactionists tend to overlook social structure, particularly on the macro-level and with reference to history and power. As in the case of emotion, we shall now show that the "astructural bias" censure is, also, not entirely warranted.[7] We are constrained to respond to the allegation by admitting that it is not entirely without foundation; however, it reflects, to some degree, a rather cursory reading of the vast range of relevant works found within this tradition. It is our contention that symbolic interactionism has never completely ignored social structural considerations. In fact, there is nothing inherent in the tradition that precludes an analysis of organizational features of social life, or of problems of historical, economic, and political import. The astructural bias criticism must be tempered by the fact that some of the early and later interactionists were indeed studying social structure, although not in systematic fashion. We contend that such textual materials have been missed, overlooked, disregarded, or perhaps even misinterpreted by the detractors.

The very title of Charles Horton Cooley's work, *Human Nature and Social Order* (1902), clearly illustrates his concern with macrosociological matters. Moreover, in his work, *Social Organization* (1909), Part Four is devoted to an in-depth discussion of castes, social classes and their nature, class consciousness, the ascendancy of a capitalist class, the nature and sources of capitalist power, poverty, and class antagonisms. Speaking of the capitalist class, for example, Cooley (1909:256) writes:

> Since in our age commerce and industry absorb most of the practical energy of the people, the men that are foremost in these activities have a certain ascendancy, similar to that of warriors in a military age...It is well enough indicated by the term capitalist or capitalist-manager class...Like everything else that has power in human life, the money-strong represent...the survival of the fittest...The political power of wealth is due only in part to direct corruption, but is even more an indirect and perfectly legal pressure in the shape of inducements... Newspapers are generally owned by men of wealth, which has no doubt an important influence upon the sentiments expressed in them...

Further, in Part Five of this same work, Cooley turns his attention to social institutions, their nature and their relationship to the individual; to social disorganization in the family; and to religious institutions, the economic system, education, the fine arts, and government.

We turn next to George Herbert Mead, the prime exemplar of symbolic interactionism. As John D. Baldwin (1986) points out, it is true that the macro components of Mead's theoretical system are developed in noticeably less detail and precision than are the micro components. Yet, we find in his works discussions of social evolution, ecology, and social organization. One of the worthwhile ideas Mead presents, reflecting the fundamental interactionist assumption of the social construction of social life, is summarized by Baldwin (1986:132) as follows:

> The continuous emergence of social institutions and problems requires frequent readjustment of social institutions and practices along with our theories about them. Thus, we need...flexible methods for understanding and guiding social changes...

Another idea expressed by Mead on social organization relates to caste systems. In such systems, he suggests, the scope of the generalized other of individuals is limited by the taboos on interaction between members of different castes (Mead 1934:327; also see Wood and Wardell, 1983:90). As a result, mutual understanding of how actors affect, and are affected by, those in another caste is precluded. Speaking on the manner by which social organization enters and affects the experience of human beings, Mead (1932: 86-87) states:

> A society is a systematic order of individuals in which each has a more or less differentiated activity. The structure is really there in nature, whether we find it in the society of bees or that of human beings. And it is in varying degrees reflected in each individual ...It is due to the structural organization of society that the individual, in successively taking the roles of others in some organized activity, finds himself selecting what is common in their interrelated acts, and so assumes what I have called the role of the generalized other.

Just as in the case of emotion, Blumer[8] contravenes the allegation of astructural bias quite thoroughly. To begin with, his intensive concern with collective behavior entails, of necessity, a parallel concern with social organization, or social order, for he defines the field of collective behavior as the study of the ways by which the social order comes into existence (Blumer, 1939). Further, his analysis of the fashion industry (Blumer,

1969b) details the place of fashion (conceived as occurring in all spheres of life) in contemporary society. Challenging Georg Simmel's earlier view that the prestige of the social elite *determines* the direction of fashion, Blumer points out that fashion is now an effective mechanism for enabling people to adjust in an orderly and unified way, through collective definitions, to a changing world, thereby forming a new social order in the modern type of society.

Blumer's macrostructural view is also revealed in his "Suggestions for the Study of Mass-Media Effects" (1959), in which he urges study of the *historical* dimension in order to trace the lines along which people become sensitized to respond to media-influences. Similarly, he rejects the microstructural approach in maintaining, in another article (Blumer, 1948b), that the formation of public opinion does not occur through the interaction of disparate individuals but, instead, reflects the composition and organization of society, for it occurs in large measure through the interaction of groups.

Moreover, in a number of papers and essays, Blumer adopts a clearly macro-level standpoint when discussing sociological theory in industrial relations.[9] For example, he asserts (Blumer, 1948a: 277-278):

> A proper orientation to the study of industrial relations in our society must be based...on the recognition that such relations are a moving pattern of accommodative adjustments largely between organized parties...It must further visualize their collective character—as arranged in diverse ways and incorporated in [an] intricate and indirect network of relations. It must embrace the complicated behavior of these collectivities...

Also, in still another series of articles and essays, this time on race relations, Blumer, as Lewis Killian points out, "viewed race prejudice as a reflection of social structure, not of individual predispositions" (Killian, 1970 : 180). Favoring a group-interests point of view, Blumer saw racial prejudice and discrimination as weapons employed by groups in social conflict over rights and opportunities attaching to a superordinate position (1958). As in other writings cited above, he here drew attention to the *historical* process through which a sense of group position is formed. Implicit in his treatments of both industrial relations and race relations, of course, was a concern with power relationships, with group hierarchy in human affairs.

Finally, Blumer's writings include theoretical treatments of such macro-level topics as: group tensions and interest organizations (1950), social structure and power conflict (1954), desegregation (1956), early industrialization and the working class (1960), and developing nations (1966). Surely, these studies, along with the others cited in the foregoing paragraphs (as well as subsequent ones), give the lie to those critics who charge early and middle-period interactionists with an astructural bias.

Manford H. Kuhn, progenitor of the Iowa School of symbolic interactionism, has, also, contributed to the analysis of social structure. In *Individuals, Groups, and Economic Behavior* (Hickman and Kuhn, 1956), he analyzes the motivation of business managers—important to the theory of the business firm—examining the interplay between managerial actors and economic organizations. It should also be pointed out that both Kuhn's "self theory" and his preferred research technique (the Twenty Statements Test) emphasized the importance of self components that are anchored in social groups and organizations. Despite the foregoing, however, it is evident that Kuhn gave much less direct attention to social structure than did Blumer.

Beginning in the late 1950's, Anselm Strauss (another member of the middle-period cohort), and his colleagues began to develop a perspective on organizations, the *"negotiated order perspective,"* which differed radically from the (then) dominant structural-functionalist and Weberian rational-bureaucratic orientations. In their landmark study, "The Hospital as Negotiated Order" (Strauss et al., *1963*:15), these scholars portrayed organizations as in the process of being acted out, with their norms constantly subject to change: "The rules that govern the actions of various professionals, as they perform their tasks, are far from being extensive, clearly stated, or even clearly binding. This fact leads to necessary and continual negotiation."

Their study pointed to the *fluidity* of organizational life. Rules were more akin to shared understandings than absolute dictates, more often broken or stretched than followed. People in these organizations were conceived not as robots, acting in response to predetermined structures, but rather, as having minds and selves, having the ability to engage in conscious reasoning. Thus, in order to obtain desired outcomes, hospital personnel develop negotiative stratagems. Hence, for Strauss and his colleagues, social order was negotiated order; there could exist no organizational relationships without concomitant negotiations. The specific forms of negotiations were dependent upon specific structural conditions, such as: who negotiated with whom, when, and about what. Further, the results of negotiations would hold for a certain period of time, but certainly not indefinitely; the shared rules and understandings would at some point be re-evaluated, reviewed, revoked, or otherwise handled.

No discussion of the middle-period interactionist perspective on structure can afford to overlook the labeling theory of deviance. Howard Becker (1963), especially, has shown the importance of *power* differentials in the definition and punishment (or treatment) of deviant behavior. The role of powerful groups (e.g., the elite social classes) and individuals, particularly persons holding authority, or legitimate power (e.g., the police, judges and lawyers), in deciding what acts are to be considered "wrong" and which "wrongful" acts will actually be punished continues to be studied by interactionists and other researchers alike.[10]

Let us conclude this section by noting that, following the lead of Blumer, three additional books have dealt with power (and status) relations between dominant and subordinate ethnic groups. Shibutani and Kwan (1965) have written a textbook on the subject; Killian's monograph (1968) is a prescient and pessimistic review of the history of black protest in the United States; and Braroe (1975) has done an ethnographic study of Indians and whites in a Canadian Plains community. These works draw upon Blumer's rich storehouse of insights about the role of a sense of position in racial and ethnic group conflict.[11]

We turn now to the recent responses of interactionists to the astructural bias critique. As we shall see, such responses more directly and systematically treat social structure than did the work of most of the early interactionists. Unlike our discussion of emotion, which dealt with substantive topics, our discussion of social structure will emphasize the various theoretical *approaches* to the subject. These approaches, the first two of which dominate in symbolic interactionism, are: (1) *role theory*, which conceives of social structure as configurations of social positions and roles; (2) *negotiated order theory*, which (more than any other approach) stresses the accomplished character of social organization, that is, its constructed, emergent nature — as opposed to its reification, or what has been called "the fallacy of misplaced concreteness"; and (3) *network analysis* (which stresses the linkages among participants in both simple and complex organizations) *and other less frequently employed approaches*. A final section, as in the previous section on emotion, will briefly consider unresolved or neglected issues.

Role Theory

Since the charges of deficient treatment of social structure were laid in the 1970's, symbolic interactionists have made a number of self-conscious attempts to remedy past shortcomings in the treatment of social structure — one of the few concerted efforts at reform in modern sociological theory. According to Gary A. Fine (1983:69), systematic examination of structure has, all of a sudden, become "one of the *new frontiers* of symbolic interaction and has put the perspective on the 'cutting edge of' sociology." We would argue, also, however, that middle-period symbolic interactionism gave a measure of systematic study to social structure, as we have shown above.

A number of scholars have contributed to the development of role theory, including Sheldon Stryker (1980, 1982), Peter Burke (1977), Ralph H. Turner (1962; 1978), and George McCall and J.S. Simmons (1978). However, profound differences exist among their respective versions of role theory. Stryker and Burke can best be described as *"structural role theorists,"* while Turner and McCall and Simmons can be referred to as *"processual role theorists."*

Adopting a neo-positivist, social behaviorist orientation, structural role theorists, Stryker in particular, have much in common with Manford Kuhn and the Iowa School, as well as the later "Behavioral Sociology" camp of that school (Couch and Hintz, 1975). Presenting his orientation in several general principles, Stryker (1980:52-55) stresses the relationships among: (1) social structure, which he defines as positions or socially-recognized categories; (2) roles, which are behavioral expectations attached to positions; (3) the naming process, wherein people define the situation by applying names to it, to the other actors, to themselves, and to the specific characteristics of the situation; and (4) role-making and role-taking processes, the possibilities of engaging in which are dependent upon the openness of the social structures. For Stryker, then, as well as for other structural symbolic interactionists, the social world is organized with respect to various status networks and concomitant clusterings of expectations. Social structures, which encompass social statuses and social roles, shape social interaction. Such structures constrain the opportunities for the making of roles. They do so by determining which actors come together, for what reasons, in what social settings, with what resources, etc. In this conceptualization, then, the individual is portrayed less as a creative entrepreneur than as one who adjusts to the "script" of other actors, and who enacts roles, thereby responding primarily, to a set of expectations inherent within the social structure.

While we can credit Stryker and the structural role theorists for attempting to move symbolic interactionism to a structural level, their orientation possesses a number of serious shortcomings. As critics (e.g., Turner, 1986), charge, this version of symbolic interactionism presents an *overly-structural* conception of the social world with its focus on status positions or networks, norms, and the enactment of expectations. While it is conceived that expectations are mediated by role-playing and self, the major emphasis of this orientation is on how individuals *adapt* to the demands of an overpowering structure, to other individuals, etc. True, while some behavior may be structured in the aforementioned manner, a great deal is not. Much social interaction is *fluid* and *negotiated* with each new social encounter. A second problem concerns the influence of role enactments on the social structure. As Turner (1986:370) correctly notes, Stryker and the structural role theorists examine, primarily, the manner by which changes in behavior affect self-images and self-concepts, while virtually ignoring how changes in behavior effect changes in the organization of status networks, reference groups, organizations, and other aspects of social structure. Granted, social structures do exist, associated with them are normative expectations, and they do order individuals' access to various types of social groups. However, in our view, the structural role theorists have painted a far too deterministic picture of social reality.

Further, this orientation can be criticized (Turner, 1986) for its over-emphasis on such "abnormal" social processes as *role strain* and *role conflict* almost to the exclusion of more "normal," everyday processes of interaction. Fourthly, critics maintain that structural role theory fails to utilize the concept of role-taking adequately. We shall expand upon this criticism in our presentation of Turner's views (which follows this paragraph). Finally, this theory can be taken to task for failing to deal adequately with larger-scale social structures. While Stryker (1980:69) himself recognizes this as a deficiency in his work, he claims, in extenuation, that a "full-fledged development of how such incorporation could proceed is beyond the scope of the present work."

Partly in response to the shortcomings of structural role theory, especially its over-structured bias, others have developed an alternative version — one with the underlying assumption of flexibility and fluidity in organizations. This processual version of role theory stresses interpretation, negotiation, and emergence. Reworking role theory, Turner seeks to bring in an appreciation for Mead's concept of "role-taking." Role-taking, asserts this scholar, is the *basic* process of social interaction. It involves standing outside of oneself by placing oneself in another's place, and adjusting one's behavior in the course of interaction through the use of significant symbols — gestures that stimulate implicitly in one person the same response that they stimulate in others explicitly. As indicated in previous chapters, humans role-take in an effort to identify others' roles. Gestures and cues are interpreted to discover what these roles are. They role-take in order to make sense out of others' actions and, thus, facilitate their own responses to others in the context of the social situation.

Extending Mead's concept, Turner goes on to assert that such societal definitions of roles are not always clear-cut; in fact, they are not only often vague, but sometimes even contradictory in nature. They merely represent a general framework within which individuals construct their behavior. Therefore, individuals will not only create their social roles, but also then communicate such roles to others in order to enable effective interaction with others.

Turner further asserts that humans behave as though others are playing identifiable social roles. Operating upon the folk assumption that others are playing social roles provides any given social encounter with a shared foundation. Persons become able to interpret verbal and non-verbal gestures in order to define what roles others are playing. In short, for Turner and other processual role theorists, the *role-taking* process is also conceived as a *role-making* process. Following Blumer, Turner views social interaction as tentative in nature, dependent upon shared assumptions about others' social roles. Individuals engaging in interaction, he argues, continuously test or assess others' behavior to ascertain whether the linguistic symbols and the objects being utilized validate the occupancy of a status and the playing of a social role. If so, effective interaction continues; if not, it becomes problematic.

While these role theorists reject an overly-structural conception of social roles *á la* Stryker, they nevertheless recognize that most social roles are enacted within structural contexts. When roles are embedded within organizations and institutions, important personnel and institutional goals are influential in the role-making process. It is largely within such structural constraints that role and status may merge. Moreover, Turner contends that social roles in structured environments emerge as ways of adapting to other roles that are assigned by organizational members. Further, institutional or organizational roles become formalized in written statements that have the power to exert much control over certain role systems, as well as to shape certain norm expectations.

Two representative studies should suffice to illustrate empirical investigations of the role concept. Karp and Yoels (1979) report inquiries into the "micro-politics of interaction"—how power affects everyday interaction. Focusing on the links between power and role-playing, they demonstrate (Karp and Yoels, 1979:154) the innumerable ways in which elites and males, respectively, exert power over members of minorities and lower classes and women, respectively. Some of the devices used by those in dominant positions include: unilaterally frowning, looking stern, using names of familiarity, and staring. We see here how class, ethnic group, and gender roles establish frameworks within which pervasive asymmetrical power relationships are acted out.

One of the studies cited by Karp and Yoels is especially worthy of summary. Thomas, Franks, and Calonico (1972), studying over 200 families, test hypotheses to the effect that role-taking accuracy is *inversely* related to power within families. The major findings of the research are that fathers are significantly less accurate role-takers than mothers, and mothers significantly less accurate role-takers than their children. The general proposition exemplified by these findings is that persons in higher positions do not need to be as sensitive to the ideas and feelings of subordinates as do the latter to the former. Thus, this study strongly suggests that characteristics of social structure (e.g., positions of higher or lower power) are probably more predictive of role-taking ability in given situations than are individual characteristics.

We conclude our review of role theory by reminding the reader that analyses employing this frame of reference rarely rise much above the micro-structural level of interpersonal (or inter-role) patterns. The larger social structures that help to perpetuate these patterns tend to be taken for granted, rather than considered explicitly. Thus, this approach does not constitute a compelling counter-attack upon the allegation of an astructural bias in symbolic interactionism.

Negotiated Order

Of the various approaches to social structure, the negotiated order approach most closely epitomizes the interactionist frame of reference. The great volume of recent studies, both theoretical and empirical, spawned by this approach attests to its accord with basic interactionist premises. These premises include, as we have previously indicated, a view of social organization as constructed, emergent, and processual. Anselm Strauss's book, *Negotiations: Varieties, Contexts and Social Order* (1978), is an excellent illustration of the applicability of negotiated order theory to a number of diverse topics. These topics range from micro- to macrostructural issues, such as negotiations between a corrupt judge and his victims, between an insurance agent and his client, intraorganizational negotiations between individuals in psychiatric and geriatric wards, international negotiations between the U.S.S.R. and the United States over the Balkans, power struggles among various ethnic groups in Kenya, and the bargaining structure of NATO. Throughout this book, Strauss illustrates the conditions under which negotiated orders come into being and that structured negotiated orders occur within a social world when commonly shared understandings break down or are in need of reworking, occurring even in the most repressive settings.

Some treatments of the conditions under which negotiation orders or social realities come into being are those by Altheide (1988), Hosticka (1979) and Mesler (1989). Altheide's study of the persistence of non-profit organizations demonstrates that such organizations can continue to exist if they are successfully able to negotiate new conceptions of reality through their clients, mission statements, funding sources, methods of securing payment for services rendered, conceptions of appropriate board members, and other conditions. In terms of the latter, Altheide points out that a factor crucial for the successful renegotiation of a new reality was the recruitment of powerful board members, individuals with ties to governmental officials, funding agencies, and politicians.

In a similar vein, Hosticka (1979), exploring the relationships between attorneys and their clients, describes the power of the former in determining social realities for the latter. Specifically, the data reveal that in the course of their social interchanges the major concern was *not* what actually happened to the client *nor* the type of trouble he/she was in; rather, at issue was the lawyer's power to define, through the use of leading questions, control of topics of conversation, and interruption control, what happened and the type of trouble the client was in.

Studying clinical pharmacy within the framework of negotiated order theory, Mark Mesler (1989) analyzes the larger structural constraints within which behaviors were being realigned, pointing specifically to the negotiations in which pharmacists engage in an effort to establish a social order in which they are accepted as clinical practitioners. Pharmacists employ three general strategies in their negotiations: tact and diplomacy, role-taking, and tactical socialization. As a major strategy, tact and diplomacy, a product of the pharmacists' professional socialization, was employed when they (as subordinates) were required to provide their input to the medical team (those with superior status). Pharmacists also engaged in role-taking, that is, attempting to view themselves as others (in this case, physicians and nurses) saw them, and then aligning their responses in a situationally-appropriate manner. Upon taking the role of each individual physician, for example, the pharmacists made efforts to enhance the physician's acceptance of their input. Tactical socialization was a strategy employed to educate specific doctors and nurses to a level of therapeutic knowledge that could be provided only with the help of the pharmacist.

The following summaries of additional reports in the negotiated order mode may appear to be redundant as they cover ground already treated. Just as in the summaries previously given, they treat the various facets of the negotiation process, namely, the recurrent construction and re-construction of structure in a variety of social settings.

Turning now to other social contexts within which negotiation is found, we can summarize several studies. Jim Thomas's (1984) research on maximum security prisons is an apt illustration of the fact that even in "total," or custodial, institutions, negotiations among social actors relocate social power in such a way as to de-couple formal elements of authority within such structures. Both inmates and institutional staff frequently reject formalized norms and techniques of social control. Negotiating their own interpretations of social order, both parties develop their own rules and behavioral stratagems that are dependent upon, but apart from, the formal structures. Thomas shows that the staff need information about the inmate population, and this becomes a bargaining tool between themselves and the inmates. Various forms of negotiation strategies, such as hassling, intimidation, compromise, exchange, conning, and corruption, have the effect of dramatically altering the formal power structure. Even those at the bottom of the hierarchical system possess the mechanisms for transforming the asymmetrical power relations.

While Thomas's study centers on the modification of formal structure to enable the maintenance of social order, Peter Manning (1977), in his study of the police, focuses on how social power and social structure lead to a negotiated order that enables work procedures to be carried out in an effective manner. This study indicates how the social constraints of organizational rules lead the police operating in a narcotics division to alter or redefine the social meaning of the goals of the organization. Manning's study suggests that, because the rules are not shared by all members of the organization, there is a great deal of tacit understanding that develops in order to allow the everyday work to be carried out efficiently.

We shall summarize only a few more works that reflect the outpouring and range of studies in the negotiation genre. In an excellent analysis of two school districts, Hall and Spencer-Hall (1982) detail the social conditions that both impede and facilitate contract negotiations between school employees and administrators. The findings indicate that the distribution of power, the daily life of the school building, the environment, the unit of operational focus, and the role of tradition and history functioned to limit intra-organizational negotiations and to affect behavior. Interestingly, however, Hall and Spencer-Hall discovered the presence of great variability in negotiative activities among school districts, between the general classroom and special education classrooms, and among levels of organization. Specifically, their study points out how the following things contribute to differences in negotiating success among school districts: (1) differences in the interest, knowledge, and interaction among boards of education, (2) differences in the status positions and leadership styles of school superintendents, (3) the career aspirations, age, level of commitment, and ideology of principals, (4) the ideology, pride, social change, and militancy of the teachers, (5) the number and level of interactions by directors of education, and

(6) the involvement of the community. We can commend Hall and Spencer-Hall for developing their ideas in terms of testable propositions concerning the structural and social conditions that either facilitate or circumscribe negotiation.

As in the Hall and Spencer-Hall study, O'Toole and O'Toole (1981) successfully document the manner by which social structural constraints impede negotiations between organizations. Examining negotiation processes among eleven rehabilitation social agencies, O'Toole and O'Toole document such structural impediments as: lack of a central unifying technology, dependence upon external resources, political control, funding, fragmentation, types of disease and disabilities treated, professional dominance, religion, ethnicity, and client affiliations — all of which affected each agency's attempt to negotiate interorganizational goals. Once again, we see evidence that, in order to understand negotiations fully, one must examine not only the negotiation process *per se* but also the *structural* contexts within which it occurs.

Similar studies, by Regan (1980,1985) and Wallace (1988) merit mention. Regan provides an analysis of the responses of three Canadian health-care agencies to a directive from the provincial government requiring integration of their mental-health programs. Wallace's paper presents an examination of situational and structural conditions affecting the negotiation of the role of manager of a not-for-profit hotel. While these papers are worthwhile, we give them short shrift because we have already touched upon comparable researches.

One more inquiry in the same vein as those presented above is Mast's (1983) examination of the social organization of television drama production. Mast (1983:81) convincingly shows that television "represents a setting in which the balance between aesthetic and commercial goals is renegotiated each time that actors, directors, and production staff join together to mount a dramatic production." She further demonstrates that the social organization of such enterprises involves the strained intersection of the distinct occupational cultures of bureaucratically-oriented and artistically-oriented participants (recognizing, however, the frequent presence of ambivalence in individuals).

Before continuing our survey of negotiated order studies, it may be useful at this point to review for readers three levels of social structure: the micro-, meso-, and macro- structural levels. Although some interactionists eschew this differentiation, we have found it worthwhile. The micro-structure includes recurrent or patterned *interpersonal relationships*. Its polar opposite, the macro-structure, includes *larger-scale social phenomena*, such as complex organizations, social institutions, and interorganizational relationships. As for the meso-structure, a concept formulated by Maines (1977,1978,1979,1982), it includes the *mutual relations between interacting individuals and the environing social organization*. We have introduced these terms in order to point to a difference between negotiated order studies surveyed thus far and those we shall survey in the following paragraphs. Putting the matter briefly, while the previous studies have dealt chiefly with micro-level and meso-level structures, the following studies focus chiefly on macro-level structures.

One of the few recent interactionist efforts to address the macro-structure is Hall's (1972) analysis of certain power aspects of the American political system. His paper discusses several mechanisms of political power, such as: bargaining over material resources; political talk, impression management, and definitions of the situation; control of information flow; and symbolic mobilization of support. He lays especial emphasis on the last two of these mechanisms, control of the flow of information through behind-the-scenes machinations of politicians and symbolic mobilization of support through public persuasion.

Moving from the political sphere to the economic, we look now at Denzin's (1977) excellent historical analysis of the liquor industry, in which he deals with the ways in which certain economic structures constrain the behavior of other collectivities. Describing different spheres of organization (distillers, retailers, customers, wholesalers, tavern owners, enforcement agencies), Denzin points out the complex network of shifting relationships among them. He (1976:23-24) states that these levels:

> intersect along moving and shifting lines of accommodation, acceptance, cooperation, tolerance, at times rejection, and open hostility. Various tiers

may band together as when the brewers cooperated
with Temperance forces during prohibition. Sub-
groupings of the public may be co-opted into pro-
paganda campaigns to further the sales of a new
product just released by a distiller...Corruption,
payoffs, and deals can arise when new liquor
licenses are under consideration...blocks of votes
can be purchased when local, state and national
politicians take a stand on temperance, prohibition,
expanded liquor licensing, or increases in federal or
state tax of alcohol products.

Negotiation is, thus, evident throughout the entire system.
This study reveals how laws at the state and federal levels set
conditions under which liquor distributors and retailers have to
negotiate the prices at each level. Further, this study points to
how differences in market conditions allow for coercion and
manipulation and how large corporations manipulate the legal
structure. In short, just as Farberman (1975, to be summarized
in the next section) discovered organizationally-induced illegal
actions, so too did Denzin document such actions in the form of
violation of anti-trust laws, territorial violations, bribery,
kickbacks, and so forth. Both of these studies illustrate the complexity of networks across both time and spatial dimensions. As
Hall (1987:6) points out in his assessment of them, "they ground
these substantial collectivities in the capitalist political economy,
historically and contemporaneously. They recognize that the
social organization exists throughout the transactions... but only
make sense in the context of the overall system."

In his study of the history of publicly supported agricultural
research, Lawrence Busch (1982), also, shows the link between
inter-organizational negotiations and their larger structural
contexts. This study examines the historical processes through
which certain structural conditions are produced by negotiation; once they are created, they affect further negotiations. As
Hall (1987:7) notes, a number of important observations result
from Busch's study: (1) negotiations may result in alterations in
social structures that provide little or no opportunity for subsequent negotiations; (2) once an organization comes into being,

it enters into the process of negotiation itself in manners often quite different than initially intended; (3) dominant social groups may constrict the range of topics to be negotiated; and (4) the creation of an organization may transfer the location of some negotiations from the outside to the inside.

We can summarize the voluminous literature falling within the negotiated order approach by indicating that, despite their vast range of foci, they have shown a penchant for micro-level and, especially, meso-level analysis. That the relative paucity of macro-level analyses is not intrinsic to the approach is strongly suggested by such studies as those by Hall (1972), Denzin (1978), and Busch (1982).

Network Analysis and Other Approaches

The studies to be reviewed in this section represent a variety of approaches or, in some instances, no explicit, clear-cut approach other than symbolic interactionism itself. That they are not inspired by widely-used approaches should not be construed as detracting from their value.

We begin our survey of studies employing these approaches by commenting upon two studies, one theoretical and the other empirical, employing the network concept. Fine and Kleinman (1983), who build their ideas upon the formulations of several British social anthropologists, present a brief for the use of the social network approach, which they view as a variant of the negotiated order approach. Conceiving the network "as a set of relationships that people imbue with meaning and use for personal or collective purposes" (Fine and Kleinman, 1983: 97), they equate it with social structure, and claim that the approach is suited to dealing with macro-sociological concerns. We should point out that network analysis is somewhat reminiscent of the sociometric technique used by some psychologists and sociologists in the recent past, which yielded "sociograms," or diagrams depicting the preferred or actual associates among members of a group.

Perhaps readers will gain a clearer, more concrete understanding of networks through a summary of Faulkner's (1983) research study. Faulkner interviewed, over an eight-year period, several hundred composers of background music for commercial television and feature films in Hollywood. Because composers work on a free-lance, job-to-job basis, they are continually constrained to curry favor with television producers, movie directors, and other composers (who may recommend them for the better jobs). Those composers who are most successful in securing work on films likely to become "hits" are those able to move from the periphery to the center of a complex social network of these gatekeepers. We observe here, as in so many other occupational careers, the important role of influential "contacts." In this study of an entire industry, music for commercial television and movies, the analysis is unusual in that it combines ethnographic material with quantitative techniques.

In another study of the Hollywood film industry, Faulkner and a co-author (Weiss and Faulkner, 1983), taking network analysis as their point of departure, develop and use an "event analysis" approach. This entails enumerating all relevant activities in an organization, in this case the productivity (i.e., screen credits) of 3800 producers, directors, screenwriters, and cinematographers. As in Faulkner's study of composers, the unequal distribution of credits is accounted for in the following statement:

> A few in the top tiers dominate the business by collaboration with one another, monopolizing credits, and limiting access to work for less experienced freelancers. ...Like most art and craft worlds, the film business is dominated by an elite and manifests severe inequalities in the control over resources, the distribution of rewards, access to continuity in the labor market, and so forth (Weiss and Faulkner, 1983: 120).

It should be noted that this study makes the not uncommon assumption among interactionists (and exponents of other perspectives) that interactions on the micro-structural level cumulate into aggregate regularities. This is not the place to debate this assumption.

A paper mentioned in our discussion of emotion merits attention here as well. Zurcher (1985) adopts a dramaturgical stance in analyzing a war game involving United States military reservists. Viewing the exercise as a "mesostructural phenomenon," connecting the larger military structure with the immediate world of face-to-face interaction among the participants, he reveals both the congruences and the discrepancies between the organizational scripting of emotions and behavior, on the one hand, and the actual "performances" (i.e., the emotions and behavior actually manifested), on the other. These findings are evocative, obviously, of the processual concepts of act-construction, role-making, and negotiation.

Three final summaries remain to be presented, those by Farberman (1975), Couch (1984), and Das (1988), the first of them a major work and all three of them approaching their subject from a *broad, general* interactionist perspective, rather than a specific one. Farberman's (1975) research on the automobile industry illustrates the manner in which large-scale economic organizations set the conditions that constrain the actions of other collectivities within an industry. Denzin's similar study of the liquor industry, it will be recalled, was summarized earlier. Farberman shows us that manufacturers set pricing policies that require new-car dealerships to undertake high-volume and low-profit-per-car sales. These pricing policies, in effect, create a market structure that induces new- and used-car dealers to engage in a number of criminal activities. While this "criminogenic market structure" benefits the manufacturers by increasing their total profits, it has an adverse effect for the dealers, who are under constant pressure to generate capital for fixed-profit new-car inventories. In short, Farberman's investigation clearly demonstrates that many illegal acts in the automobile industry are not simply the products of individuals but, rather, a direct outgrowth of the legally-established structure of the market.

Couch's highly ambitious monograph, *Constructing Civilization* (1984), constitutes another of the relatively few macro-level studies by presentday interactionists. Stressing the important intertwining of temporality (i.e., the sense of time) and sociation (i.e., human relationships), Couch explores the broad processes of trade, cultural diffusion, and especially, the reckoning of time as sources of such systems. Unfortunately, the book has met with a mixed reception among scholars, some of whom question the validity of the archaeological evidence he examines and, hence, of his conclusions. We have, therefore, limited our comments on the book.

We close this survey of recent interactionist work on social structure by showing that the perspective has, in at least one paper, penetrated into the field of management studies. Das (1988) explores the utility of the interactionist theoretical framework for studies of organizational power and authority, particularly, in business organizations. While the paper describes interactionist assumptions and research methods, it fails to suggest any substantive propositions beyond emphasizing the importance of symbols, symbolism, and symbol processing in business firms.

Unresolved or Neglected Issues

By now it should be apparent that the foregoing survey does not definitively confute those detractors who attribute to symbolic interactionism an astructural bias. At a number of points, we have suggested or implied a disinclination on the part of interactionists to deal with macro-level social arrangements. That this disinclination does not derive from an insuperable, inherent flaw in the perspective is shown by the actual studies — albeit relatively few in number — completed at this level, such as the following recent ones: Hall on the American political system (1972), Farberman on the automobile industry (1975), Denzin on the liquor industry (1978), Busch on agricultural research organizations (1982), Faulkner on the world of Hollywood composers of background music (1983), Weiss and Faulkner on technical specialists in the film industry (1983), and Couch on the rise of civilizations (1984). Thus, if interactionism suffers from the astructural bias, the affliction would have to be considered one of degree, rather than kind.

As we examine the various approaches dealt with in our survey, we note that the above-mentioned "affliction" is manifested, to different extents, in each approach. Looking, first, at role theory, we have seen that it tends to confine itself to micro-level researches, with occasional forays into the meso-level. Additionally, we have expressed misgivings about the static character of social structure as conceived by Stryker and other structural role theorists. On the other hand, while indicating a degree of approval of the processual role theory formulated by Turner and others, we must reiterate that it fails to rise above, at best, the mesostructural level.

The negotiated order approach appears to present the most adequate interactionist framework for the over-all analysis of social structure, despite its tendency to focus on the mesostructure. Strauss, his associates, and numerous other contributors to the development and refinement of the theory and methodology of the approach have placed interactionists in their debt. The numerous studies we have cited reflect the dominance of the approach among interactionists. Yet, two features preclude its acceptance by critics as conclusive disproof of the astructural bias charge: (1) its fluid, processual conception of social structure, and (2) the infrequency with which it has been employed to treat macrostructural arrangements.

The miscellaneous approaches reviewed in our section on network analysis and other approaches are difficult to assess. The best-known study summarized in the section, Farberman's macro-level research, does not make use of any of the approaches we have distinguished. As for the remaining works, while some may hold promise as possible multi-level treatments of structure (e.g., Faulkner's provocative book), it is too soon to know whether the promise will be fulfilled. We have, as yet, observed no appreciable impact of these other studies on the interactionist literature.

Summary and Appraisal

We shall conclude this chapter by summarizing the major ideas in our surveys of the interactionist literatures on emotion and on social structure, and by appraising the extent to which these literatures effectively respond to critics. Although the surveys do not claim to be exhaustive, we consider them highly representative and, hence, appropriate bases for summary and evaluation.

With respect to emotion, it has been shown that the early and middle-period cohorts of symbolic interactionists gave a degree of attention to the subject, but usually only secondarily. On the other hand, the outpouring of published works on emotion by current interactionists has made it a primary focus. For example, a number of writings have addressed the nature of emotion, distinguishing between the organicist, or positivist, model (emphasizing the biological component of emotion over the cognitive component) and the interactionist, or social constructionist, model (emphasizing the interplay between the biological and cognitive components). The interactionist predilection for the constructionist view has issued, most notably, in Hochschild's concepts of "feeling rules" and "emotion work," along with a number of researches demonstrating their applicability.

Questioning the utility of the organicist distinction between "coarse" and "subtle" emotions, we have argued for Shott's classification of human feelings into role-taking and other emotions. Her further classification of role-taking emotions into "reflexive" and "empathic" sub-types is of especial value to interactionists who are concerned with types of emotions.

The social sources of emotions have been identified in both the social structure and culture. Thus, Kemper has emphasized the impact of power and status (structural elements) on the affective dimension of behavior, while numerous other researchers have inquired into the impact of cultural norms (specifically, feeling rules). These two different emphases do not, of course, represent antithetical views but, rather, complementary ones.

A number of treatments of the social effects of emotions have disclosed worthwhile knowledge. The role-taking sentiments, both reflexive and empathic, have been described as vital to social control; collective emotional exaltation has been linked with social solidarity; the commoditization of feelings has been seen to lead to alienation; and emotional interaction has supplanted personal qualities as a source of charisma. In short, just as *ideas* have long been held to have consequences, so, too, do we see that emotions have equally important consequences.

As for unresolved or neglected issues in the interactionist corpus of works on emotion, our chief problematic items are the following: the lack of an over-all theoretical framework for the analysis of affective phenomena, the failure to incorporate them into the current overly rational conception of the act, the slighting of human agency in treatments of their social antecedents, and insufficient concern with their social-organizational consequences. These shortcomings, we have previously pointed out, are shared by all competing paradigms and disciplines.

Turning now to our survey of works on social structure, we can make the following points:

1. The early and middle-period interactionists attended to the subject with greater interest than critics have charged, although much of their attention was of a secondary, or indirect, nature.

2. Recent interactionists have produced an abundance of works on the subject. Included in this output have been: both theoretical and empirical studies; inquiries into economic, political and other institutions; investigations of the history, power, conflict, and other dimensions of social organizations; and studies ranging in scope from the micro-level to the macro-level.

3. Among the approaches employed in the recent works surveyed were: structural role theory, processual role theory, negotiated order, network analysis, event analysis, Goffman's dramaturgical approach, and approaches lacking a clearly specified framework.

4. Common to the most widely-used of the approaches listed above (namely, both forms of role theory, as well as negotiated order theory) is a primary, but not exclusive, focus on micro- and meso- structural concerns.

We come now to an appraisal of the efforts of interactionists, particularly in recent years, to deal with the faults most persistently ascribed to their perspective, those that have engaged our attention in this chapter. The appraisal must be a mixed one. On the one hand, it is clear that interactionists have recently developed a set of ideas about human emotion that are at least the equal in vitality of those found in other paradigms and disciplines. On the other hand, interactionist achievements in the sphere of social structural analysis present a less clear picture. From the standpoint of the critics, especially non-interactionist critics, it is doubtful that our review will be deemed a persuasive argument for retracting the charges of an astructural bias. This is so despite the high volume of writings we have surveyed; for interactionist considerations of what are *generally* regarded as structural features, especially macro-structural phenomena, have increased relatively slightly since the first levelling of the charges.

The conventional critique of symbolic interactionism in this connection has revolved around the perspective's processual emphasis. This emphasis, particularly in the Chicago School, has been held to account for its purported difficulties in handling structure. The view of mind, self, and (particularly) society as *processes*, i.e., as individual or collective behavior, is seen by the critics as an impediment to a full-bodied, enthusiastic concern with social structure.[12]

It can be argued, however — as we shall now proceed to argue — that interactionists have, nevertheless, contributed significantly to the understanding of social structure. We begin by invoking a well-worn metaphor: social structure as a freeze-frame picture of social process. In other words, social structure can be viewed as social process in cross-section, frozen in time. By the same token, social process can be viewed as social structure in longitudinal form, over a period of time, or, continuing the metaphor, as a motion picture film. As Glaser and Strauss (1968: 239-242) have indicated, their felicitous terms "structural process" and "structure in process" recognize that social phenomena are not fixed, stable, or static entities; rather, they are dynamic, with a constant potentiality for change. Thus, the fundamental interactionist postulate of process in social life need not be abandoned; for interactionist purposes, structure can fruitfully be conceptualized in processual terms. In proposing this view, we explicitly repudiate a structure-process dualism, whether on ontological or epistemological grounds. We do not consider structure and process different things, but merely different analytical facets of the same thing; nor do we believe sociologists should study either one to the exclusion of the other. Both are equally important to the understanding of social life. Just as human relationships (the conceptual unit of social structure) and human interaction (the conceptual unit of social process) are but two sides of the same coin, so are their respective matrices (social structure and social process) themselves similarly linked. Putting the matter succinctly and in different words: The structural features of society are maintained and changed by the *actions* of people, and are not fixed and autonomous, or self-regulating.

By way of illustration of our general point, let us look briefly at a prototypical macro-level structural phenomenon, relations among social classes. Depiction of such relations from an interactionist standpoint would entail attention to collective definitions and acts both within each class and between classes. How members of each class view themselves in relation to members of the other classes, and how members of the various classes interact both as individuals and as collectivities — these facts would be indispensable to an understanding of class relations.

If the foregoing argument is acceptable, it calls for a reformulation of the entire issue of the astructural bias. That issue should not be stated in terms of whether symbolic interactionism can, or does, deal with social structure. Rather, the issue should be stated as follows: How useful is the interactionist conception of *structure as process*?

NOTES

1. The word "personic" is Coutu's neologism pertaining to meaningful behavior of persons.

2. Scheff (1983), too, has espoused the "coarse-subtle" typology. In view of his above-mentioned ideas on "universal expressive needs," this espousal is quite understandable.

3. We are indebted to Guy E. Swanson's (1985) instructive review of Denzin's sometimes obscure book.

4. Another provocative analysis of specific emotions is to be found in Stanford M. Lyman's *The Seven Deadly Sins: Society and Evil*. Revised and Expanded edition (1989), in which he discusses the traditionally designated vices of unbridled gluttony, greed, vanity, lust, envy, anger, and sloth.

5. Hochschild refers to strong and weak "status shields," the former being exemplified by the fact that high status and authority confer on potential targets of anger a relatively high degree of immunity.

6. A partial exception is an article by Mills and Kleinman (1988). They use data from a variety of sources to develop a four-fold classification of relations between emotions and cognition: Individuals may respond to situations in (1) a reflexive and emotional manner, (2) an unreflexive and emotional way, (3) a reflexive and unemotional way, or (4) neither a reflexive nor an emotional way.

7. The reader should note that the discussion of current interactionist studies is not all-inclusive. Due to limitations of space, we have chosen to present only some works that are representative of the interactionist approach to social structure.

8. For another analysis of Blumer's attention to social structure, see the article by David Maines (1988), who also has examined the concern of symbolic interactionists, in general, with social structure (Maines, 1977).

9. Space limitations do not enable us to list—much less comment on—Blumer's many works on industrial relations; hence, we restrict our commentary to one representative work. In like manner, and for the same reason, we shall comment on only one of his works on race relations.

10. The reader should also consult the following works on labeling: Daniels (1970), Emerson (1969), Hunt (1985), Scott (1965), Stoddart (1982), and Sudnow (1965).

11. Interestingly, one of the few works by an interactionist directly addressing the subject of power, Arnold M. Rose's *The Power Structure* (1967), fails to employ an interactionist analytical scheme. This failure, however, is not surprising to those familiar with his voluminous works, given Rose's eclectic drifting in and out of symbolic interactionism.

12. To recommend, as is done in Chapter 10, that symbolic interactionism deal with social structure by abandoning such "presuppositions" (assumptions) as voluntarism and supplementing such "presuppositions" as interaction represents, in our view, a gratuitous counsel of despair. If such advice were to be followed it would be tantamount to eviscerating the interactionist perspective (at least its Chicago version), transforming it in fundamental ways. This would be comparable to discarding the assumption of class struggle from Marxist sociology, or the assumption of equilibrium from structural-functional theory.

12

SOME RECENT DIRECTIONS IN SYMBOLIC INTERACTIONISM

Gil Richard Musolf

Introduction

This chapter will discuss some of the new directions in symbolic interactionism (SI): postmodernism, the study of emotions, the social reproduction of gender, discourse-analysis, and dramaturgy. An attempt is made to outline the most recent themes of these subsets of SI, rather than to present an exhaustive account of all relevant research. I will conclude with a summary of the directions in which interactionism is heading, according to leading spokespersons.

Postmodernism

A number of recent publications have contributed significantly to illuminating the postmodern project in sociological theory (Alexander, 1991; Antonino, 1991; Baker, 1990; Balsamo, 1989; Brown, 1990; Denzin, 1989a, 1989b, 1990a, 1990b, 1991a, 1991b; Farberman, 1991; Hilbert, 1991; Lemert, 1991; Lynch and Bogen, 1991; Maynard, 1991; Peters, 1990; Plummer, 1990a, 1990b; Richardson, 1991a, 1991b; Richardson and Lockridge, 1991; Schneider, 1991; Seidman, 1991a, 1991b; and Young, 1991;). Clearly, the so-called postmodern leaning is now a major direction, affecting all those working in the field of sociological theory, but especially those engaged in SI. Many are drawing affinities between postmodernism and SI. Some similarities do exist. But the argument presented here is that the differences outweigh the similarities. This critical juncture in interactionism's history calls for a thorough elaboration of postmodern themes and a critique of postmodernism.

Major Themes

Every cultural artifact, practice, routine, and lived experience is now seen as a "text." The concept of text has expanded to include every object of scrutiny that one can critically discuss, that one can deconstruct as a form of communicative action politically constituted. Two themes emerge here that pervade all postmodern projects: everything is text, everything is political. "Every representation is always a representation from some point of view, within some frame of vision" (Brown, 1990: 188); finding *whose* point of view and *whose* frame of reference is a project of deconstruction. Postmodernism is not theory but metatheory; that is, it consists of arguments about the state and hope of theory.

Knowledge is seen as particular rather than general, predictability is absent and chaos ubiquitous, and the ontological instability and variety of the world render scientistic schemes inadequate to capture multifaceted, polyvocal, localized narratives (Young, 1991).

The deconstruction method of postmodernism means *relativizing* all texts, articulating their connections to culture, class, gender, race, ethnicity, patriarchy, ideology, sexual orientation, religion, history, institutions, power, hegemony, linguistic conventions, author and reader. No text is sacred to deconstruction, that is, to being relativized: "scientific texts themselves are seen as rhetorical constructions" (Brown, 1990: 188). In fact, the argument is that science has been privileged, "thereby creating a vast realm of submerged, discredited discourses, knowledges, and communities" (Seidman, 1991b: 187). Postmodernism unmasks "the grand narrative myth of science as a cumulative, empirical enterprise" (Denzin, 1989: 5).

Seidman (1991a: 131–132) argues that the problem of sociological theory (to which postmodernism is a reaction) is its failure to relativize and its presumption to produce a "logic of society," a mirror of the social universe. Seidman also argues (1991b: 183–184) that postmodernism in the United States had is origins in social movements of the 1970s, such as the gay rights movement. Denzin (1990: 145) attributes postmodern theory to the reaction against the conservatism of the 1980s. These movements were reactions of the marginalized, a movement to empower voices in politics and policy that had been silenced. Lemert (1991: 167) locates postmodernism's social origins in the fragmentation of the world:

> since midcentury the world has broken into its political
> and cultural parts. The very idea of the world revolving
> on a true axis has proven finite. The axial principles of
> the twentieth-century world—European culture, Brit-
> ish administration, American capitalism, Soviet poli-
> tics—have come apart as a matter of *fact*, not theory.
> [Consequently, there have emerged] multiple identities
> and local politics.

Antonio (1991: 155) traces postmodernism's intellectual heritage to Nietzsche's perspectivism and his argument that all interpretation masks a will to power.

The postmodern theme is, thus, more than a call for relativization, it is a claim that "concepts, explanations, theories bear the imprint of the particular prejudices and interests of their creators" (Seidman, 1991a: 134). Thus, the social embeddedness of the author renders generalization suspicious. Like Tip O'Neill's phrase that all politics is local, postmodernism argues the same for sociological theory. Doubt is the essential postmodern sensibility (Richardson, 1991: 173). In fact, generalization is a practice of "bad faith, [for] concealed in the will to truth is a will to power, a will to form humanity" (Seidman, 1991a: 135). No discourse is privileged, cynicism reigns. For example, all great modern generalization theorists, Marx, Weber, and Durkheim, are vitiated because they were Eurocentric. But they, the postmodernists charge, were more than bad theorists, they concealed "hegemonic aspirations and national chauvinistic wishes" (Seidman, 1991a: 139). Realism and scientism, two such Eurocentric and power-lusting guises, are subjected to deprecation in order to achieve their derogation.

Language does the concealing. Language was once regarded as unobtrusive, as merely a way of expressing truth (Baker, 1990: 233). But language cannot articulate an objective truth; that is, "language is not merely an apparatus of transmission" (Baker, 1990: 233). Instead, "language is a constitutive force, creating a particular view of reality. This is as true of writing as of speaking, and as true of science as of poetry" (Richardson, 1991: 174). Language is merely the game of scholars. The language of sociological theory has silenced the polyvocal voices, the social narrative, and multiculturalism. This has political consequences: "If the available narrative is limiting, people's lives are limited, textually disenfranchised" (Richardson, 1991b: 37). Listening to previously silenced voices that matter can have positive benefits: "Hearing them helps individuals to replot their lives. New narratives mean new lives. The transformed life, in turn, becomes a part of the cultural heritage affecting future stories, future lives" (Richardson, 1991b: 37).

Language is regarded as so natural that we do not recognize it as socially constituted, a problem of reification. Writing and speaking reality are forms of persuasion (Baker, 1990: 234), and persuasion is achieved through rhetoric. Rhetoric, which was a pejorative in the modernist period, has been elevated to the essence of knowledge construction in the postmodern. Sociological theorists are "experts honing their rhetorical skills [who] can produce some pretty compelling stuff" (Schneider, 1991: 300). What is important is not the truth or rationality of theory but its social or political consequences (Seidman, 1991a: 137).

That a text cannot be extricated from its social context is a major tenet in the sociology of knowledge. The postmodern addition is that no text can be divorced from its author; that is, an argument is made that the author pervades and constructs the text with a moral or political view in mind, shaping as much of reality and policy for others and the world as possible. Theorizing, for example, is indicted for trying to establish textual authority through the guise of having the author disappear from the text; that is, the "analytic voice remains the ordering, authorial one" [whose purpose is] providing the context or 'framework' with which to 'see,'; explain[ing] is to wield power" (Schneider, 1991: 306). As some argue, "Postmodernism says show your process; interrupt your textual staging" (Richardson and Lockridge, 1991: 336).

Certain affinities to the sociology of knowledge appear. But appearances are deceiving. The sociology of knowledge was not in search of truth, of trying to discover whose point of view was correct. But it did not necessarily argue against an objective truth. In fact, the sociology of knowledge argued for recognition of the genetic fallacy, that just because a historically and politically situated author has said something does not vitiate its soundness. The soundness of an argument is independent of the author and can be determined.

The postmodernist argues that no way of knowing, no epistemology, can escape the fact that it is created by a human being through a linguistic convention that has been shaped socially, culturally, historically, and politically just as has its author. All accounts of reality are not just social constructions but political constructions. Attempts to obfuscate this through abstraction, universalization, and generalization have political consequences — a detachment from everyday life leaving "little bearing on major social conflicts and political struggles or on important public debates over current social affairs" (Seidman, 1991a: 133).

The essence of the modernist epistemology was the "disjunctive polarity between truth and its medium of expression" (Baker, 1990: 233). There is no postmodernist epistemology, only "epistemic suspicion" (Seidman, 1991a: 135). Absolute or objective reality is considered nonexistent. What is taken for absolute or objective reality represents the view of power-holders and historically constituted practices. Or, as Denzin (1990: 148) states: "Truth and knowledge are ideological constructions, based on the power formations that exist in any society at any moment in time." There is no scientific method that can present or capture objective reality or truth. Scientific method and all symbols that convey reality do so through conventions embedded in and inextricable from a social, cultural, historical, political relationship among object-person-representations. "Humans *enact* truth not by legislating it scientifically, but by performing it rhetorically" (Brown, 1990: 189); to revise a cliche, truth is in the eye of the beholder. But what is defined as true, that is, the reality that must be obeyed, is in the eye of the beholder with power and persuasion. Richardson (1991: 173) argues that "power positions have been concealed behind notions of general, universal, Archimedean truth."

However, Brown asserts that representation is not necessarily pernicious or conniving, but that it is inherently produced by a process that cannot escape its connection to subjectivity (1990: 189). Since all theory and reason is relative, no theory or method is universal. Postmodernism thus brings a new consciousness to linguistic, or any symbolic, construction. All authors should "maintain and apply the consciousness and the practice of rhetorical awareness" (Brown, 1990: 189). Sociological methodology has been charged as one of the culprits that train students to generalize and thus silence voices: "Most American sociologists are taught that it is best to translate the incalculable richness of being into a highly disciplined linguistic architecture" (Young, 1991: 328). Rather than any disciplined architecture, the call is for narrative and storytelling.

But it is not just the author that produces texts or interpretations. This is one area where postmodernism and SI meet. A major tenet of SI is that the meaning of any object (a text, for example) depends on how the subject responds to it. Meaning does not inhere in the object but is an emergent of interpretation and response. But SI does assume that meanings are intersubjective. Postmodernism embeds the reader of a text in the creative construction of reality and meaning. Readers have as much to do with producing meaning as authors, and since there are innumerable readers, there are countless interpretations of reality. The reader is a situated subject who, through her or his own history of lived experience, engages the text to produce unique and irrefragable meanings. We, as readers, by virtue of our indelible biographies, bring interpretive predispositions or schemata to encode texts we read or witness in any way. We actively shape the text we view and read. Human beings have no epistemologically unobtrusive way to witness or convey reality, a venerable premise traceable to Kant's *Critique of Pure Reason*.

Another theme of postmodernism is that knowing the world, that is knowledge, experience, and understanding, are limited and uncircumscribable. We can grasp only a fraction of lived experience and human knowledge. Reality is a prey not to be captured, only perennially stalked. So far as that goes, it, too, is an old and venerable theme. The postmodern world is too complex, interdependent, changing, and multicultural for any legitimate absolute. Agnosticism, ambivalence, and ambiguity are the current mentality.

Brown, expressing a minority position among postmodernists, argues that just because there are as many interpretations of reality as there are authors and texts does not mean that intersubjectivity is abandoned. Since people share aspects of lived experience—class, gender, race, for example,—intersubjectivity, communication, social order, and a normative order are possible.

But this intersubjectivity is limited to small social worlds. Brown (1990: 192) applies Pierre Bourdieu's concept of the "habitus" to note that a consensual reality provides social utility. A habitus is a framework for viewing reality and guiding behavior shared by a social world. Yet Seidman (1991: 141) claims that even commonalities such as gender do not produce intersubjectivity.

Another theme is that realities of others can be marginalized, excluded, demonized. For example, reflect on Anita Hill's version of reality, how it was marginalized and demonized through a concerted political effort. The Thomas/Hill confrontation was the quintessence of postmodernism writ large. All versions of reality arise from lived experience, represent a point of view, and have proponents and opponents. Our everyday lives and experiences can become a text subjected to as many interpretations as there are those who are affected by them or who witness them or who come across accounts of them.

At the end of the Thomas/Hill confrontation, the postmodern theme prevailed; everyone pontificated on which version of reality was correct, true, and objective. The postmodern theme is that you cannot discern that which is not there, truth. There were as many interpretations—the pastime of the entire nation for over a week—as there were readers of the Hill/Thomas text. Readers of the text shared aspects of their lived experience—sexual harassment or being accused—with the versions of reality presented by participants, witnesses, handlers, and on and on. There is a competition for official reality, but so that social order is achieved, one version of reality dominates, vitiating the robustness and legitimacy of competing discourses (Brown, 1990: 192). For example, a vote on reality, the Senate vote to confirm Thomas, was taken so that social order could continue.

The Hill/Thomas confrontation was also postmodernist in essence because the presentation of reality was totally rhetorical. There was no evidence to uncover. A version of who was telling the truth could only be constructed through persuasion. In fact, there were persuasion teams (the Democratic and Republican senators), persuasion witnesses, and persuasion commentators. No objective reality could be uncovered. The most reiterated phrase was that "only two people know for sure what happened." The media event was entirely a rhetorical strategy, a communicative construction of reality.

Baker is troubled by the nihilism postmodernism may engender. The "permanently imminent self-critique" that postmodernism wages on all texts may leave us enervated for political action. If all theory and truth is relativized, then does scholarship become socially and politically meaningless, is political practice lacking any "secure philosophical grounding," will "doubt incapacitate?" (Baker, 1990:

238–240). Baker's way out of the dilemma is to advocate a self-reflexive politics, that we have a telos and should readily admit to and advocate it. Acknowledging our telos does not vitiate it (Baker, 1990: 239–245). Seidman argues that theorists should be activists, openly encouraging moral debate and moral and social values. Because of an activist sensibility, Richardson (1991: 173–174) argues that "post- modernism appeals to and benefits marginalized people who have been locally and historically denied access to power, or people who can empathize with those so marginalized."

A Postmodern Study

Denzin (1990) employs the postmodern theme that there are as many versions of reality as there are readers, in order to debunk an early work by the founder of ethnomethodology, Harold Garfinkel. This essay is a useful one to explore because it has the benefit of extended criticism.

Denzin provides a reading of how tricky, slippery, and elusive reality, or accounts of it, is, by arguing that Garfinkel and others at UCLA Medical Center were duped by a transsexual named Agnes.

Denzin's purpose is to (1) critique the notion that "the appearance of a thing is the thing," and (2) to deconstruct the presumption that a version of reality, a narrative production, can be divorced from an author (Denzin, 1990: 200). This is the postmodern theme that writer, text, and subject matter are inseparable.

Garfinkel's account of Agnes's lived experience, which she gave to Garfinkel in the course of 35 hours of taped conversation (according to Denzin's account and rereading), is flawed because Garfinkel saw Agnes as she presented herself to be. Denzin makes a more stinging critique, motive imputation, that Garfinkel was willing to do this so that Agnes would be "material for his theory" (Denzin, 1990: 204).

Briefly, Agnes is presented as a woman who wanted to become physiologically female by having her genitalia removed, that is, the penis removed and made into a vagina. Agnes presented herself as a woman who was living undetectedly as a female, a biological victim who had male genitalia but was "completely feminized in her secondary sex characteristics" (Garfinkel, quoted by Denzin, 1990:

203). She persuaded the team of physicians to perform the operation. Five years later these physicians learned "that she had never had a biological defect that had feminized her but that she had been taking estrogens since age 12" (Garfinkel, quoted by Denzin, 1990: 203).

Denzin explains the duping through postmodern themes, that Garfinkel failed to separate himself from the text he was coproducing along with Agnes; he failed to be "rhetorically aware," that is, conscious of his involvement in his interpretation, especially since he was using Agnes as material to prove his theory. Garfinkel's work, Denzin opines, "described Garfinkel's version of Agnes's reality, not her version" (Denzin, 1990: 208). Harold Garfinkel was also rhetorically unaware that he was framing Agnes, Procrustean fashion, within a patriarchal, oedipalized, scientific version, a version taken to be true rather than a relative version of theorizing embedded in a historically situated time-frame, the 1950s.

Harold and Agnes cannot be separated because Agnes also was a conscious agent in her account of reality. She allowed herself to be portrayed in a way that would serve her personal ambitions and the scientific ambitions of the text writers.

Denzin's (1990: 201) project is to persuade us that social science data are a fiction, though not a falsehood. He seeks to debunk the myth that reality is captured in sociological texts (213); while arguing that there are alternative, elusive versions of subjects and reality (214). He presents the essential postmodern theme, the tenuousness of interpretation (214).

Hilbert (1991: 264) castigates Denzin for "false premises and mischaracterizations," contending that "in 20 years he has refused to learn anything" about ethnomethodology or the argument in Garfinkel's study. Hilbert maintains that Garfinkel's study was not to get at the "true" story of Agnes, whatever it may be, but to study Agnes's methods of constructing femininity. Studying peoples' methods—ethnomethods—is the aim of ethnomethodology, which Hilbert argues Denzin fails to notice or understand. Denzin goes on to create a psychoanalytic fabrication that purports to capture the true Agnes. Hilbert argues this is privileging an account that is complete nonsense. Lynch and Bogen (1991) argue that the Denzin piece is not worth reading and that postmodernism needs to be distinguished from absurdities like Denzin's. Maynard (1991) also suggests Denzin misreads Garfinkel. Denzin's response (1991b) is that his main purpose was to present an alternative reading and point out the failure to separate author and text. The article and critiques illustrate a contradiction of postmodernism, for, since no voice is privileged every reading and critique of others' readings becomes entangled in politics and verbiage.

Postmodernism and Interactionism: A Few Similarities

Balsamo (1989: 377) holds that the cultural critique that defines postmodernism has always had a tradition in SI. Also, SI research, through ethnographic studies, has always attempted to give voice to those suppressed and silenced, illuminating the mosaic of American culture (Balsamo, 1989: 377). One theme shared by SI and postmodernism is that there is always an ongoing reification of the socially constructed world. Reification is misreading the social construction of the world—of any text—as though it is natural, unconnected to human subjectivity and intention. It is a misreading that is encouraged by powerholders for obvious reasons: reification has disarming, obfuscatory political consequences. If any social order or text is seen as natural, then the way it is seen can be argued as the way it should be, which eclipses critique and social reconstruction. SI has directed sociologists to the partiality of voices and the gloss of reification, for example, most recently, in questioning "the common-sensical belief in a transcendental 'feminine nature'" (Balsamo: 1989: 373). Classic SI arguments, such as that the self and identity are socially constructed — in fact, that they are "always already" constructed — are shared with postmodernism (Balsamo, 1989: 373).

Farberman (1991: 480) views SI as the "first truly enlightened, post-modern social science." A self-reflexive actor concept and a methodology opposed to the "strait-jacket of a strict, logical, operational positivism" (Randall Collins, quoted in Farberman, 1991: 480) makes SI a "vanguard social science that will lead us into the third millennium" (Farberman, 1991: 481). I would add that SI has always incorporated partiality of perspectives through its argument that behavior is guided by a definition of the situation.

There are methodological similarities. The postmodern artistic/ humanistic approach to knowledge is advocated by Ellis (1991: 44) as a way of understanding emotions. Denzin even states (1990:151– 152) that

> All of [SI's] cardinal tenets (with the exception of one), including respect for the empirical world, fitting theory to that world, entering that world and becoming near to it, listening to the voices that speak, and writing their interpretations, are postmodernist. [The exception]: What puts interactionists outside the postmodern space is the assertion that there is an empirical world *out there* that must be respected.

Though I have argued elsewhere (Musolf, 1992) that Denzin is on the right track in trying to incorporate into interactionism a critical, cultural studies project through giving silenced voices space to speak, and by calling for subversive readings and a political economy of meaning to undermine capitalist patriarchy, I disagree with Denzin's wholehearted embrace of the postmodern project. Especially damaging to Denzin's project of political subversion through cultural critique (see below) is the notion that there can be no truthful representation of the empirical world that is out there. Plummer argues (1990b:156) that any affinity between SI and postmodernism "must be seen as an ambiguous and tenuous one." It is time for SI to dissociate itself from radical postmodernism for the following reasons.

Critique of Postmodern Themes

The postmodern metatheory argument fails in a number of ways. First, the Eurocentric argument. Postmodernists, while correctly condemning Eurocentrism are themselves Eurocentric.

For example, the social development that a Marx or Weber described and toward which, they argued, the world was turning is lambasted by postmodernists. Yet postmodernists project the cultural doom and gloom of Western society "on a global scale [that] are parodies of classical grand narratives" (Antonio, 1991: 156).

Seidman (1991b: 186) is correct in his condemnation that the Enlightenment project "has perpetuated Eurocentric, androcentric values and interests that marginalize and oppress non-Europeans and many women," and that Enlightenment critique has had "flattened concepts of liberation and domination which conceal and obfuscate heterogeneous struggles" (Seidman, 1991b: 187). But, as Farberman (1991: 485) counters, the point is to extend Enlightenment critique, not to abandon it: "the point and purpose of the Enlightenment is the progressive enhancement of everyday life for an ever expanding number of ordinary people on planet Earth." This means speaking truth to power:

> attention should be given to a sustained methodological and theoretical penetration of elite power shields [and] to the situation and circumstances of specific segments of humanity who, from the marginal positions that they occupy, nevertheless, have begun the long march toward emancipation (Farberman, 1991: 484).

But if one's critique is viewed as subjective whining rather than some measure of the true nature of oppression, no one will listen. The struggle is to build a consensus for action around oppression,

> not to turn vices into virtues, by talking approvingly about the segmentation and fragmentation of reality into slivers of insulated, isolated, micro universes, and seeing in them a laudable, multi-centered, freedom. That is not freedom at all, but rather an autonomy based on anonymity and antipathy (Farberman, 1991: 483).

Seidman nearly implies that the Enlightenment is a concern for Eurocentric emancipation and liberation with a malicious unconcern for others' oppression. But the whole progress of Enlightenment politics, however slow, at times retrograde, and still uncompleted, is toward greater inclusion of and emancipation for the remaining nonprivileged, suppressed, and silenced.

The postmodern argument against totalization is also dubious. The notion that presenting a local perspective is less distortive or totalizing ignores the postmodern stricture that an author always orders her or his text: "worldwide, national, regional, and local portrayals are all homogenizing totalizations" (Antonio, 1991: 157).

The privileged storytelling narrative is also open to critique. Antonio notes that the narrative and storytelling mode degenerates into a tower of babel: "A consistent perspectivist method would decompose each [story] into a myriad of inchoate subnarratives" (Antonio, 1991: 157). The extreme relative sensibility (the anything goes, no matter what you say I'm o.k., you're o.k. nonsense) will lead to no wisdom: "Storytelling does not distinguish between myth and reality" (Antonio, 1991: 158). It can offer no referent for judgment, nor does it seek to do so. But that does not enable us to be moral citizens, rather it makes us politically impotent. It disarms critique so that one can offer no praise or condemnation (Antonio, 1991: 158). Thus, the postmodern appeal to bring values back in is a *non sequitur*. Values are a way to both judge and reason with another.

The abandoning of reason is a quagmire. If reason is to be relegated to the dustbin of history, then Antonio (1991: 158) asks why we should bother to give credibility to avowed self-serving polemics. Alexander (1991: 147) critiques the relativist sensibility by arguing that "sociological theory can be a legitimate and socially important enterprise only if it can make a claim to reason." It does this by trying to achieve some generalizibility beyond personal perspective and social group. The denial of any objectivity, and that there is only subjectivity, is a logic of solipsism and political conservatism (Alexander, 1991: 149). It is conservative precisely because the marginalized can make no claim to reason if the postmodern sensibility is accepted.

In an articulate defense of positivism, Peters (1990: 226) argues for disciplined inquiry and the creation of a disciplined self that will help us "suspend passion, interest and prejudice." Such a sensibility — he argues that it is the essence of a positivist social science — will promote civic life, prevent us from overestimating the value of our opinions, and contribute to diversity in beliefs and lifestyles.

Peters repudiates values, passion, and politics in scientific work, thereby endowing the social scientist's work with political virtue, while others void of circumspection promote "dogmatic, fierce, and stiff opinions." Positivism eschews judgment and thereby "passionate intolerance and violence" (Peters, 1990: 228). Certainly such ideals have not been achieved by positivism, but the ideology of an objective social science is a laudable aim and, as Peters contends, one that will be around for some time to come. It also empowers the social scientist, for "objectivity will continue to back up our professional claims to authority when we speak in public" (Peters, 1990: 226). Farberman (1991: 477), also, argues that the trained social scientist should not abandon the authority years of training provide. Discourse needs to promote civility, scientific inquiry, self-discipline, diversity, rationality, and harmony; the postmodern threat, according to Peters (1990), would destroy discourse and its institutional foundations.

The universalism/generalization and anti-relativism charge is tenuous. Seidman (1991: 132) argues that "sociological theory aims to denude itself of its contextual embeddedness." But this is only partially true. Sociology has at least argued for decentering and deconstruction through methods to correct against the gloss of universalization and generalization. Cross-cultural research through our sister discipline of anthropology is most obvious. Relativizing theoretical statements according to class, race, and gender (the big three) is basic sociology, as is relativizing theory through a number of variables: rural-urban, education, age, religion, religiosity, political affiliation, core-periphery or developed-underdeveloped, and on and on. These variables provide (though they are not always utilized) a critical epistemology against any gloss of generalization and universalization. The sociology of knowledge, a basic method of theorizing, has argued for socially contextualizing theory. Think of Gunter Remmling's book in the sociology of knowledge, *Road to Suspicion* (1967). Suspicion yes, total relativization, no. A sociology of knowledge is a critical epistemology to sociological theory. It does not abandon sociological theory, but informs us how to proceed with suspicion, with caution, but to proceed. The sociology of sociology and the sociology of science also have offered these same strictures. Seidman (1991b: 187) argues that "we render science immune from social criticism [and] neglect the social role of science." But that is incorrect. Books such as Roger Krohn's *The Social Shaping of Science* (1971) have pointed out just what Seidman argues has been ignored. Rather than postmodern nihilism and the hope of the demise of sociological theory, theorizing will still be guided by truth-seeking norms, which even though violated, are still worth pursuing (Antonio, 1991: 159).

The postmodern abandoning of objective evaluative criteria, and instead judging theory by its political consequences and its pragmatic ability to shape the material or cultural world, is also flawed. Seidman (1991b: 188) holds that postmodernists

> substitute a pragmatic for a realist strategy. Instead of appealing to reality to judge the truth of my social discourse, I propose that we judge our social stories by their consequences. Does the discourse do what I intended? The advantage of this strategy is that it sets up its own standards of criticism.

The association of relativism with pragmatism has had a long history in sociology. Werner Stark, writing in *The Sociology of Knowledge* in 1960, trounced such simplistic notions.

> Such relativism is a natural and necessary concomitant of pragmatism. If different societies exhibit or represent different systems of action and interaction, and if the truth is whatever happens to fit in with these individual systems, then every society must in strict logic possess a materially different concept of the truth (Stark, 1960: 335).

As Stark opines, reason and truth-seeking may not always lead to wisdom or accuracy. Our errors often humble us, but on the other hand:

> Assuredly they will lead us farther than pure pragmatism ever can, for the latter would incarcerate us in the tiny territory delimited by human practices and purposes, the petty princedom of utility. Humble no doubt we should be; but there is no point in being humbler than we need. Little as we are, we are large enough to conceive of verities finer than those that underlie our successful manipulation of the material world (Stark, 1960: 342).

As a sociology of knowledge theorist, rather than a postmodernist, I would agree that Karl Mannheim's conception of relationism, which is explained by Stark, is the appropriate way to present theory that guards against the gloss of universalism and generalization:

> By the concept of relationism he means that if we formulate a truth, we should not do so in abstract and absolute terms, but must always include in the formula the concrete conditions to which it is related, i.e., under which it really holds good. For instance; we would not say "x is true," but "x is true, provided there are a, b, c"; not: "all men want to maximize their money incomes," but "all men want to maximize their money incomes if they live in a society which has private property as its fundamental institution and is rational, competitive . . ." (Stark, 1960: 338).

And, of course, glosses such as "all" and "men" should be replaced by other qualifiers. We should speak and write more probabilistically; that is the theoretical sensibility of SI. Qualifying is what good sociology does. It does not conceive of things in such absolutist terms as postmodernists charge. Indeed, sociology, more so than any other discipline, except for anthropology, has argued for a relational sensibility without devolving into the void of relativity.

Postmodernism, presenting itself as the ultimate in critique, ironically, abandons critique. Embracing all subjectivity as equally legitimated voices with a story to tell, abandons critique in favor of "reductionist pragmatism" (Alexander, 1991: 150). If any particularistic interest is legitimate, then this can easily engender "misunderstanding, prejudice, and anticivil conflict" (Alexander, 1991: 150). The claim that one can advocate morality particularistically is untenable since "moral arguments themselves involve abstract, universal issues" (Alexander, 1991: 150). For example, Richardson's hope that narrative should benefit and appeal to marginalized people is dashed since their appeals will, to the postmodernist, be just another assertive subjectivity that has no epistemological privilege. Marginalized positions will be deprecated as merely relative subjectivity masking their will to power rather than representing the truth of the oppressed, such as would a more traditional Marxist approach. Richardson (1991a: 176–177) even rejects the postmodern wish to be a moral advocate as suspicious, another "undisclosed lust after power" and argues that sociologists "do not command special moral/political/intellectual privileges".

Richardson, however, reflecting the postmodern sensibility of ambivalence, is herself aware of this quandary. She has correctly pointed out how postmodernists themselves have silenced feminism: "The egregious subsuming of feminism under deconstructionism is neither intellectually accurate nor politically benign" (Richardson, 1991b: 32). She further recognizes the problem by noting that giving voice to the previously silenced is not enough, that relativization can reduce profound, emancipating critique, such as hers in particular and feminism in general, to the status of nagging.

> As the speechless are given voice and the power to name and be named through feminist practice, the postmodernist theorist would disempower them by erasing their names, deconstructing their stories, and undermining their grounds for authority. Forging a writing-union between feminism and postmodernism is, thus, a seriously difficult task (Richardson, 1991b: 36).

A difficult task indeed! How this perspicacious scholar will incorporate enfranchising silenced voices (with authority to speak truth to power) while arguing that everything is relative and staged, is a dilemma. On the one hand is the Scylla of generalization, which silences, on the other is the Charybdis of relativization, which delegitimizes the voice of the oppressed. Will postmodernism honor the voice of the oppressed only to make her a Cassandra? Richardson is abundantly percipient to navigate these straits in future theoretical work.

Antonio (1991: 159) points out that abandoning reason or reasonableness, or some form of privilege, is a political and personal danger since it makes us vulnerable to hucksterism and can increase social divisions. The postmodern notion of critique is an "aromatic brew of anti-intellectualism" and is dangerous because it naively assumes that a multiplicity of equally legitimated/privileged voices can achieve social reconstruction, a belief that polyvocalism alone "is an act of elite bashing that will oust a patriarchal establishment of white, male, heterosexuals which will result in democratic redress" (Farberman, 1991: 477). All oppressed, all suppressed and silenced voices, must be allowed to speak. But that does not mean one eclipses critique as compensation for oppression. Consensus building and united action are necessary. The call should be: oppressed of the world, unite!

Summary

Postmodernism is avowedly critical, political, reflexive; it advocates that theory be a moral and political practice, to bring values back in; and, that truth and validity are rhetorical constructions by authors and readers embedded in a historically situated social surround (Brown, 1990: 194). It passionately calls for the end to patriarchal, elitist, and Eurocentric views of the world. For that it should be applauded. But critique should not abandon the notion of community and communication. Postmodernism does not share SI's attempt at intersubjectivity through the significant symbol, role-taking, sympathetic introspection, the generalized other, empathy, social worlds, primary groups, subcultures, meaning, social act, joint action, and the social self. Postmodernism advocates polyvocalism, a notion that since our social origins and lived experiences are unique, we interpret everything differently and share no common ground. As Plummer (1990a:138) noted: "relativity becomes nihilism . . . ambiguity becomes absurdity . . . I and Me are decentered to nonexistence, and flux [becomes] mere chaos." Postmodernism does not present any coherent or consistent frame of reference. Yes, life is indeterminate and probabilistic, but not anarchic or deranged. Selves and interaction are social, which presupposes shared meaning and interpretation. Postmodernists have ignored the fundamental nature of interaction, selves, and social life. It is basically a free-for-all, king-of-the-hill notion of analysis. Those with the best rhetoric persuade their way to the top, regardless of a coherence or a correspondence with the truth. And since those in power possess the means of persuasion, postmodernism condemns the oppressed, who can no longer speak truth to power. Postmodernism is a fad, and while certain interactionists seem committed to such a stance, others appear to have jumped on the bandwagon just as they did with semiotics.

Structuring Emotions and Reproducing Gender

Emotions

The SI position on emotions, plus recent research from within that general framework, is briefly sketched here. Although the sociology of emotions is a new focus area, especially within SI, Meltzer and Herman point out in this volume that Mead, James, Dewey, Cooley, and Blumer devoted attention to the subject. The sociology of emotions has been divided into two branches: those whose framework is organistic and those whose perspective is constructionist (Adler, Adler, and Fontana, 1987). The constructionist view, how "physiological processes are molded, structured, and given meaning," is the focus of the following review (Adler, Adler, and Fontana, 1987: 225).

Rosenberg (1990) has outlined an SI perspective on emotions. His work can serve to supplement the overview provided by Meltzer and Herman in this volume. The following paragraphs are a summary of his schema.

Rosenberg's argument is that the foundation of emotions is physiological, but that through human reflexivity we attribute meaning to organismic processes to define, control, and manipulate our emotions. Reflexivity—the actor defining, interpreting physiological arousal—constitutes the nature of an emotion. Emotions are socially constructed through interaction between an actor and her or his social habitat. One's interpretation is affected by previous and ongoing socialization. Reflexivity affects any state of arousal subject to interpretation in three fundamental and transforming ways: emotional identification, emotional display, and emotional experiences.

Physiological arousal does not constitute an emotion; arousal must be defined, interpreted, and given meaning. An emotion is the result of the interplay between arousal and cognitive interpretation. Emotional identification is problematic because arousal is often ambiguous: "Different emotions may have similar manifestations"

(1990: 5). For example, fear and joy may be the same physiologically. At times we have mixed emotions simultaneously: e.g., fear and excitement. It is only through understanding our situation and experience reflexively that we can define our emotions as mixed. There may be no differentiating physiological marker between fear and excitement. Another problem in emotional identification is that we define feeling idiosyncratically: "Internal experiences are unique and incommunicable" (1990: 5). There may be no word, or we may not know the word, for what we are feeling. We are uncertain of our feelings.

The social environment can also affect our cognitive interpretation of any arousal state. People, through causal assumptions acquired during socialization, define arousal states. We know that during certain situations the arousal that we notice should be normatively defined. Cultural expectations contribute to the defining process by providing socialized actors an "emotional logic." Certain events— e.g., funerals, celebrations—demand certain emotions. Failing to make this culturally induced logical connection between arousal and interpretation is dangerous deviance: "Society takes this emotional logic very seriously. Failure to adhere to it constitutes one of the defining features of mental disorder" (1990: 6).

Rosenberg also believes that emotions are causes of behavior. One may attribute falling asleep to boredom, or cheering at a football game to excitement. One observes one's behavior, the circumstances under which it occurred, and then attributes an emotion as the cause.

Referent others are also used to infer the nature of our arousal. We conform to a "social consensus," i.e., we tend to interpret our initial arousal according to how others are defining their emotional experience. States of arousal are emotionally defined so that they correspond to a "cultural scenario." Love may be one's emotional identification for feelings and physiological processes experienced around a potential partner and that match cultural criteria. The point is that the interpreting process is affected by socialization and cultural scripts. There is an element of social constraint in the interpreting process.

Rosenberg argues that emotions have "action implications," we should act in accordance with the emotion we are experiencing. But, insightfully, he (1990: 7) points out "because of these action implications people may be motivated to avoid emotional interpretations that have threatening consequences." Because human beings interpret arousal states, they may misinterpret. For example, when working at a counseling agency white males have told me about receiving unemployment compensation with no intention of working while, almost in the same breath, they condemn minorities as lazy, for not working when they can. Here is a textbook case of someone experiencing an arousal state (perhaps guilt) but interpreting it as anger at others. One could say one is projecting anger at oneself onto others.If I feel guilty about not working, then I must actively seek work. However, if I can define my arousal as anger at others, then I can avoid seeking work and feel superior to others. The SI position on emotions thus makes a contribution to the mental health field through illustrating people's capacity for self-delusion.

Rosenberg (1990: 7) contends that motivational influences cause misinterpretation: "In view of the importance of emotions in the lives of human beings, it is not surprising that motivational factors should play a role in their identification." Emotions are what we define (or misdefine) our arousal states to be.

Emotional display is quite different from emotional identification. It involves agency in both the exhibition and concealment of emotions. Rosenberg (1990: 8) locates emotional display "squarely in the realm of dramaturgy or impression management". It is producing "intended effects" on others so that they interpret the situation in accordance with how one is emotionally staging the scene.

People engage in emotional display for a variety of purposes. One is to convince others that one is a moral actor, so, for example, one may display grief over someone's death when one is really quite happy. To violate normative expectations would be deviance and would prompt negative sanctions. According to Hochschild, whose work on emotions is summarized in the chapter by Meltzer and Herman, there are "feeling rules," a phrase now part of the sociological lexicon. We are "emotional actors." Emotional display or concealment through such tools as verbal devices, facial expressions, and the use of physical objects helps us to manipulate situations and others' impressions in order to achieve desired ends.

Emotional display has costs: suspicion and doubt. These pervade human relationships and make us cynical. SI shares the postmodern theme here. But I would add a positive note to Rosenberg's malaise.

Awareness of the pervasiveness of emotional display can arm us against the hucksterism so prevalent in our society. Televangelism is just one area where people's inability to attend to the speciousness of emotional display has cost billions.

Emotional experience is not so easy for the individual to affect and can be outside one's control. We can display emotions, convey the proper expression to others to support social situations and social roles, but can we directly manipulate emotional experience, how we actually feel? Rosenberg (1990: 10) contends "that people unable to exercise direct control over their emotional experiences adopt the strategy of attempting to control the *causes* of these experiences."

A mental cause is central to the notion that "how we think affects how we feel," the major insight of the cognitive theory of depression. If we want to control our emotions, then we attempt to control our thoughts. Thus, as active agents we can indirectly alter, or attempt to alter, emotional experience. We can also do this through "selective exposure," by avoiding that which depresses and seeking that which brings joy. Rosenberg can be faulted for contending that this process is not "difficult." One cannot have selective exposure or easily think positive thoughts if one has lost a child, a farm, a job, etc.

Another way to alter emotional experience is through the body. We can exercise, drink alcohol, and take drugs—all producing physiological arousal—to try to bring about the desired experience. We can do this because the body—to the self-reflexive actor—is an object of manipulation. The self-reflexive human being actively defines and produces emotional identification, emotional display, and emotional experience.

The most significant collection in the new sociology of emotions is David D. Franks and E. Doyle McCarthy's edited volume *The Sociology of Emotions: Original Essays and Research Papers* (1989). The following offers a review of how these sociologists are drawing links between emotions and the social and cultural context of late capitalist western society. I shall begin by outlining those of their theoretical insights consistent with SI and then make brief comments on the research papers.

McCarthy argues that a sociology of emotions can be built out of traditional social psychology and the sociology of knowledge: "Each views mental structures as manifestations of particular cultural and social developments; each conceives social factors as intrinsic to mentality" (1989: 51). The logical place to start for McCarthy is to expand upon the work of G.H. Mead.

Emotions are social emergents that develop in social relations. The fact that emotions are socially embedded in group processes explains their commonality (we all share in group processes) and their differences (we all belong to different groups and social worlds). Emotions are situationally constituted and thus vary according to the diversity of situations a class, race, gender, society, and culture encounter. Emotions are thus not biological, personal, or universal in mode of expression. Emotions are a product of socialization and social interaction, and thus McCarthy's argument (1989: 68) correctly notes that Cooley's position "of unsocialized feelings is theoretically indefensible."

As Franks and McCarthy (1989: xix) caution, there may be universal emotions, such as anger, "but this in no way undermines the argument that emotions are cultural and historical ways of experiencing and acting capable of considerable variation in both what is felt and in the meaning of what is felt."

Gordon (1989:115) agrees with McCarthy's view and goes on to note that interpretation of emotions is also socially embedded, "Sociology's most significant insight into emotions may be that individuals interpret emotional experience within socially constructed frameworks of meaning." Gordon (1989:115) argues that there exists an "emotional culture" through which people "communicate, perpetuate, and develop their knowledge about and attitudes toward emotions." In our emotional culture, actors define the meaning of an emotion by attributing it to either an institutional or impulsive orientation.

An institutional meaning of an emotion centers on control over feeling and expression, conforming to norms, values, and collective standards. An impulsive meaning of an emotion centers on spontaneity, lack of inhibition, and abandon. Our society has both institutional norms and impulsive ones. We should express emotion according to certain institutional standards, say, at a funeral. But an individualistic culture cultivates impulsive expressions as a way of self-discovery. However, even impulsive emotion is not divorced from social embeddedness: "From a sociological standpoint, impulse is not antithetical to self-control: standards and techniques for being impulsive are socially learned and negotiated" (Gordon, 1989: 128).

Gordon (1989: 132) concludes that the social construction of emotions cannot be conceived of as a personal process; it is guided by norms, vocabulary, beliefs, and our entire emotional culture. This emotional culture guides our emotional expressions whether we define and give meaning to our emotions through an institutional or an impulsive orientation. Again, here we notice SI's sensibility to interpret human behavior dialectically, emerging as a process between constraint and agency.

Hochschild, whose early work on emotions is detailed in this volume, explains that "different cultural prisms for men and women" can affect the way a couple interprets gratitude. This can affect their relationship, for "crucial to a healthy economy of gratitude is a common interpretation of reality, such that what feels like a gift to one, feels like a gift to the other" (1989: 96). But couples, because of gender differences, interpret reality differently.

Hochschild focuses on how changes in the economy, where women have taken 80% of the new jobs since 1980, have not produced the corresponding cultural shift to accommodate women's lives at home. She employs William Ogburn's concept that there is a "cultural lag" in sanctioning, supporting, and encouraging men to work at home. This gender "culture lag" is in behavior and attitudes, for when it comes to housework and childrearing, men still believe they are "women's work" and do not participate in the social reproduction of the household.

Hochschild dichotomizes gender culture into a traditional view and an egalitarian one. Where men and women fall in their attachment to one of these views will shape the way they define gratitude for certain social acts. Their views will also shape the quality of their relationship, how they feel about the spouse: warm and grateful, or cold and resentful.

In a traditional family, if a man helps out at home this may be viewed as a gift by the husband and received as one by the wife. If the wife works outside the home this may be intended as a gift by the wife and felt as one by the husband. A family such as this, interpreting reality the same way, can have a rich economy of gratitude.

In an egalitarian family, traditional gift giving over providing income or social reproduction of the household is changed. Men do not view their wives working as a gift but as a social expectation. Women do not view their husbands doing housework or childrearing as a gift since they are expected to share in the social reproduction of the household as well as the financial maintenance of it. If both interpret reality this way and both correspond with the appropriate behavior, i.e., sharing financial responsibility and social reproduction, this too may bring about a happy household. Gifts that are given over and above expectations will engender gratitude.

Problems arise when couples misperceive and misreceive gifts due to their attachment to different gender cultures. The problem is that men are, by and large, attached to traditional gender culture resulting in spousal exploitation; for example, women who work full-time still do 80% of the housework and childrearing. Men's acceptance of women working, the new economy, has not generated a new culture, men doing housework; consequently, a cultural lag prevails in taking responsibility for social reproduction of the household:

> The most common form of "misgiving" occurs when the man offers a traditional gift—hard work at the office—but the woman wants to receive a "modern" gift—sharing child-rearing and housework. Similarly, the woman offers a "modern" gift—more money, while the man hopes for a traditional gift—like home cooking. As external conditions create a "gender gap" in the economy of gratitude, they disrupt the ordinary ways in which a man and woman express love (Hochschild, 1989: 102).

Obviously, because our economy necessitates a dual-income to stay financially afloat, women will be giving modern gifts, but men (who adhere to traditional gender culture) will not be reciprocating. The unrequited condition will only cause bitterness and resentment and deteriorate the marriage. Men will not feel gratitude for their wives working to the extent that they will share in the social reproduction of the household. Women will feel no gratitude for an occasional "helping out" approach. A different interpretation of reality will lead to an impoverished economy of gratitude.

As Hochschild notes, women are adapting to their changing environment, the economy, but men are not adapting to their changing environment, women. The tenacity of traditional culture impedes men's progress, for work has always had high value but housework has never been esteemed; therefore, "these changes are likely to feel to women like moving "up" and to men like moving "down" (Hochschild, 1989: 109).

Hochschild has shown how cultural variation produces the emotion of gratitude. What one defines as a gift, and what a gift means, that is, how one responds to it, depends on how it is interpreted through the constraint of a gender culture and the social context of a changed economy.

Clark (1989) used a multiplicity of research techniques to study sympathy. She found sympathy an emergent of social interaction and that sympathy rules vary by subculture

A way of feeling is socially embedded in and representative of an age, which is analogous to classifying an age according to a *Weltanschauung* or what Edwin G. Boring referred to as a *Zeitgeist*. Clanton (1989: 179) thus suggests that "patterns of emotional experience change in response to changes in society and culture." He uses this tenet of the sociology of emotions to explore the way jealousy is conceptualized and experienced in two different time frames.

In the first time-frame, 1945–1965, jealousy is conceptualized as proof of love, natural, and good for marriage. In the second time-frame, 1970–1980, jealousy is conceptualized as unnatural, a product of learning which should be unlearned, and bad for marriage. Jealousy becomes a human defect, a product of low self-esteem.

Clanton traces the social roots of this change in mentality to changes in love relationships. He argues that in the 1950s and early 1960s, the emphasis was on "relationship commitment or togetherness." In the 1970s the emphasis was on "personal freedom" in marriage and relationships. The goal of personal freedom is seen as "part of a larger trend in favor of more freedom, more experimentation, and a more positive view of pleasure" (Clanton, 1989: 187). He views the social roots of this conceptual change in jealousy as part of the counter-culture and youth-culture that was burgeoning in the 1970s. Again, the argument of the sociology of emotions is to conceptualize emotions as embedded in history and culture.

Weigert and Franks (1989) attribute the emotion of ambivalence to the ongoing change, incompleteness, competing ideologies, multiple interpretive frameworks, and complexity of contemporary society. Our culture promotes ambivalence through contradictory values and symbolic forms expressed in a mainstream and counterculture. Social organizations engender ambivalence through their adherence to universalistic norms and their practice of informally operating on particularistic ones. The contemporary family breeds ambivalence since members find it hard to reconcile personal and group goals. An individualistic culture supports personal achievement, and yet it also socializes us to be committed to our families. There are interactional ambivalences, for example, when we question if we are acting toward another on the basis of sex or love. Gender culture produces ambivalence in females: should they work, should they rear children, or should they try to do both? Contradictory messages are given to women currently socialized in the United States.

Weigert and Franks characterize ambivalence as the modern temper, an existential condition.[2] There is no authority to legitimize absolutes, a postmodern theme that echoes back to Nietzsche. Since we are responsible for the world and our actions, since there are no more supernatural guidebooks that can provide succor for our existential loneliness and isolation, this leaves us with uncertainty, angst, and ambivalence as to what is believable, what is the good society, and what is the good life. Now that we know we are the authors of our world, that knowledge costs us certainty and security: "The post-modern context generates intense ambivalence as a paradoxical concomitant of the human control over, and responsibility for, nature, society, and self" (Weigert and Franks, 1989: 220).

Swanson (1989) maintains that what is of value to us is embedded in our culture. Virtues and emotions, such as honesty, courage, gratitude, temperance, humility, meekness, justice, repentance, kindness, forgiveness, faith, hope, and love, are socially constituted. The self emerges through social interaction, through role-taking with various significant others and the generalized other. When we role-take, we not only internalize a cognitive perspective on the world (a way to think) but we internalize an affective framework as well (a way to feel). Culture socializes us to ways of thinking and ways of feeling, which, of course, will vary by subculture and other traditional variables.

Franks (1989: 154) outlines "how human interpretation of affective behaviors reflects and maintains power structures and stratification systems." In this structural analysis, Franks points out the way asymmetrical resources in relationships, such as power and status, influence battered wives to define the situation as their own fault. Victims, the powerless in general, are more accurate at role-taking. In this process, the powerless often adopt the standpoint of the other. This is especially the case in close personal relationships. In the case of battered women, this leads to self-accusation rather than attributing the cause to where it surely belongs, to a violent and inexcusable display of emotion.

The sociology of emotions is growing, which is leading to new methods of inquiry. Ellis (1991a, 1991b) has argued that an untapped way sociologists can study how people define emotions is through introspection. She advocates (1991b: 125) that SI and the new sociology of emotions need to focus on "studying emotions emotionally, examining our own emotions, and concentrating on introspective narratives of lived experience." "Introspection as a social process" she argues, "is active thinking about one's thoughts and feelings" (1991b: 128). A sociological introspection can also reveal the cultural influence on the interpretive process. Ellis uses introspection to study her own and others' emotions, noting how norms and situations require emotional display, how emotions can be mixed, contradictory, and redefined. She also illustrates, through self-reports and the reports of others, how emotions are controlled and managed, and the strategies for doing emotion work.

Ellis (1991b: 139) argues that: "Advancing the case for an emotional sociology does not mean arguing against empiricism or rigor." She is following a venerable history in SI methodology, arguing that one can incorporate scientific and humanistic methods to explore subjectivity.

Summarizing, we notice that SI is focusing on the dialectic between cultural constraint and human agency, that emotional frameworks are internalized just as are cognitive frameworks, and that, therefore, emotions have social and cultural roots that vary historically. One can define an epoch by a characteristic or representative emotion, such as ambivalence, or notice the effect a changing social context has on the repute of an emotion such as jealousy.

The Social Reproduction of Gender

The social reproduction of gender has occupied the research projects of many interactionists, but this is a development of very recent origin and one shared by other theoretical orientations. Historically, gender has not been a topic of much interest to interactionists. They previously directed about as much attention to it as they did to social class—which is to say next to nothing. Furthermore, while minorities have been studied by interactionists, minority women typically have not.[3]

The work reviewed here demonstrates that SI can make significant contributions to illustrating the effect that organization, structure, culture, gender, and power have on interaction and the reproduction and reification of gender stereotypes and oppression.[4]

Padavic (1991) reports participant observation research that demonstrates how gender is reconstituted in daily interaction within a hostile social context, the all-male, blue-collar work world. Gender is a process of negotiation, but interactants do not negotiate from equal positions; that is, men have more resources than women on the basis of historical and institutionalized positions of privilege. Work cultures that affirm masculinity provide another social constraint impeding women's integration into nontraditional jobs (1991: 280). The symbolic production of masculinity and reified notions of what constitutes femininity are tenaciously guarded by men, since they both provide the only self-esteem enhancing, psychic rewards men receive from jobs that produce alienation. Men's belief that they are masculine doing masculine work that only "real men" can do—a self-defining though self-deluding label of superiority—allows them to define a situation of oppression (their job) as one of privilege.

Padavic's research was conducted at a coal power plant. At the plant, male-bonding and masculinity production are accomplished through rituals of buying food and denigrating women through jokes, put-downs, and humiliating portrayals of nude women. Padavic chronicles the torments that men put women through when she (Padavic) enters a previously all-male preserve, the blue-collar social world: teasing, pushing, being tossed back and forth in the air among workers, threats of bodily harm, and paternalism.

This treatment to assert dominance produced self-fulfilling notions of femininity. Padavic, to disprove stereotypes, acted in a way that created safety hazards, but more significant, the harassment created doubts in her mind as to whether she could perform the job. Through this treatment "gender ideology" and stereotypical gender behavior are recreated. Traditional femininity was reconstituted in Padavic by men because they, as a group, were in a position of power to do so. When another female arrived who was physically and behaviorally opposite the feminine stereotype, she posed an immediate threat to masculinity. Since she did not affirm their notions of femininity, she was ignored, never helped, and despised.

Other SI scholars working in this tradition[5] are Richardson (1986, 1988), who has researched the way a patriarchal society reproduces gender inequality even in extramarital affairs; Martin (1978), who has shown that in pursuing a job as a policeperson women are relegated to a subordinate status and excluded from the mentoring process; Hammond (1980), who demonstrated that women medical students endure an unrelieved status degradation ceremony; West (1984), who revealed that even a pinnacle status, such as physician, is no counter to the master status of gender, for women physicians are easily interrupted by their patients as opposed to men; and Wolf (1986), who theorized how a culture of inferiority is internalized by women (and minorities and the poor) through the everyday process of role-taking from a sexist, racist, and classist generalized other. Women, having internalized the cultural myth of inferiority, socially reproduce gender ideology through false-conscious attitudes and behavior.

Mary Glenn Wiley (1991), working within Stryker's structural SI and self-identity perspective, has researched gender differences in levels of stress. The self is made up of hierarchical identities; that is, some identities are more important to us than others. Those that are most important to us have salience and engender our commitment. We act in ways to confirm our identity. Two of the major identities in our society are work and family. Affecting these identities is the master status of gender. A gender culture socializes men and women to define work and family in different ways so that the meaning, obligations, and rewards of work and family are gendered, that is, still today, both through attitudes and behavior, men are committed primarily to work and women to family. But many women are committed to work and family and thus have two identities and two commitments. Wiley (1991: 497) points out that an identity perspective identities two major sources of stress: "conflict between behaviors that confirm different identities of similar salience, and inadequate performance of behaviors that confirm highly salient identities."

Today, men and women work. However, because of a gendered culture that does not support equality in the sharing of housework and childrearing, there is a gendered commitment to work and family with consequences for differential stress. For men there is not as much conflict between family and work identities. Men do not come anywhere near equally participating in housework and childrearing; "Work is allowed to infringe on men's family time and responsibilities" (Wiley, 1991: 499). However, "A woman's family identity is predominant and her work identity is not allowed to interfere" (1991: 499). Men have primarily one identity, work, and a strong commitment to it, with a helping-out mentality at home. Many women today have two salient identities and commitments, work and family. They work at work and then go home and work at family. Women perform two jobs exposing them to greater stress. Because their commitments are stretched, their role performance suffers in both job and family, causing additional stress. Naturally, then, women who "choose" to work suffer greater stress due to a double burden and to the fact that almost total responsibility for family impairs work and family performance, adding additional stress and lowered self-esteem. Women's careers suffer and inequality in the home is reproduced.

Discourse/Conversation-Analysis

The goal of this section is to familiarize the reader with discourse-analysis and its relationship to SI.

Boden (1990) presents a thorough account of the relationship between discourse or conversation-analysis and SI, which, she claims, are "complementary frameworks." I agree, and the methods of discourse-analysis will be fruitful for interactionists to pursue. She notes, however, that the driving force of discourse-analysis has been ethnomethodology. Its intellectual origins are also due to the pioneering work of Harvey Sacks, Emanuel Schegloff, and Gail Jefferson. Both Sacks and Schegloff were students of Erving Goffman.

Talk, which Boden defines as "language-in-action", is the data to be explored. Language is the epitome of the significant and shared symbol. Interactionists looking for a method that is more quantitative than participant observation may find discourse-analysis fertile, since it is "highly empirical, grounded firmly in a form of data that can be repeatedly analyzed" (Boden, 1990: 247). Conversation-analysis is primarily micro-research, employing audio or video recordings of natural, that is, unstaged, ordinary social occasions. Any obtrusive research, such as interviews or experiments is avoided. As Adler, Adler, and Fontana have commented (1989: 226), the focus is on "the production of natural language in situ." Diversity of conversation is as vast as the social settings studied. Talk is viewed as "the very heart of social interaction." The postmodern theme is also here, since one aspect of discourse-analysis is "letting subjects tell their own narratives" (Boden, 1990: 257). The sociological goal of discourse-analysis is to "uncover the formal properties of inter-action, and, in that sense, the project is 'highly Simmelian'" (Boden, 1990: 248).

Boden (1990: 250) shows that conversation is ordered and ordering, and that turns in conversation shape the conversation. The argument that conversation orders interaction echoes a fundamental SI tenet: "social order and social structure are not external to action but rather produced *in and through the local structures of interaction*" (Boden, 1990: 250).

Turn-taking in conversation is the major way that interaction is structured, a "central social act." Turn-taking itself is structured through turn allocation and turn transfer. Conversation, then, has a structure that operates as social constraint:

> The organizational features of conversation are treated as structures in their own right and are taken to oper-ate—like other social structural factors—independently of specific actors, psychological dispositions, or at-tributes of particular individuals (Boden, 1990: 250–251).

Talk is the quintessence of what Blumer referred to as joint action, "the orientation of one actor to another" (Boden, 1990: 253). In talking, people possess power. For example, turns structure the sequence of interaction, and power can be built up out of turn-taking dynamics. One of the ways conversation-analysis is making a connection to macrostructure and the study of power is researching language interaction in institutional settings (Adler, Adler, and Fontana, 1989: 227).

For example, Molotch and Boden (1985: 273) show how politicians staging an investigation into malfeasance "invoke routine conversational procedures to accomplish power." In analyzing the Watergate Hearings, the authors ingeniously portray how Senators establish power over witnesses. Authority to regulate the question and answer format derives from status, that is,

> the organization of talk is tied to social structure generally—to the political, economic and historic forces of which talk is inevitably a part. [Thus] purposive control over the very grounds of verbal interchange, conversational procedures become mechanisms for reifying certain versions of reality at the expense of others, and thus become a tool of domination (Molotch and Boden, 1985: 273).

What the research reveals is that Senators, and by implication all those who can determine the format and rules of conversation, maintain dominance in interaction and reproduce structures of domination:

> The capacity to deprive another of the grounds of talk is founded in a social location that lies outside that particular talk and is reflexively reproduced through it. Conversations *contain* these power relations in that individuals begin with different capacities to manipulate the tacit procedures and architecture of talk (Molotch and Boden, 1985: 285).

Those who own the means of communication and the means to regulate conversation possess the means to construct reality.

The fact that others can structure conversation does not necessarily mean that such constraint has negative outcomes. Garcia's (1991) research on the conversation of meditations induces her to conclude that an interactional organization constrains the type of argument allowed in mediated disputes so that they can be resolved. Resolution usually occurs because "mediation provides an interactional structure that minimizes disputing" (1991: 819). The success of mediation derives from how turn-taking is formally structured.

Turn-taking and "arguing techniques," which are explicitly prescribed and proscribed in mediation, contrast with the informal and unbridled nature of interaction in everyday disputes: "Research on arguing in ordinary conversation in informal settings shows that it involves adjacent, directly addressed exchanges of oppositional turns" (1991: 819). Garcia (1991: 820) identifies arguing techniques in ordinary disputes: "repetition of the previous speaker's utterance, escalation of volume, acceleration, and denying or negating the previous speaker's utterance". This type of open-ended conversation promotes the continuation of disputing and actually foments the exacerbation of hostility. Accusations do not elicit agreement, since this would be an admission of guilt; rather, denials and counter-accusations proliferate (1991: 821). Disputes are maintained and escalated, that is, "[o]nce an argument has begun, its structure contains the seeds of its continuance" (1991: 821).

Mediation provides the interactional organization that structures turn-taking so that resolution of conflict is possible. The mediator controls who is speaking, when one can speak, what one can speak about, and to whom one speaks (which is to the mediator). Other interactional aspects, such as a delay between accusation and denial while the mediator mulls over the charge and then queries the other party, counseling by the mediator that the purpose is to come to agreement, the downgrading of accusations by participants when a third-part is present, and not mentioning the putative reprehensible party, and the like, also promote the structure of agreement. This normative structure changes the nature of accusations and denials, especially since they are addressed to the mediator. Discussion with a mediator through his/her queries structures the deescalation of accusations and denials, and thus institutionalizes a structure for agreement.

Thus, the way we talk to one another is a new area of research ripe for interactionists.[6]

Dramaturgy

Chapter 5 provides a brief overview of the dramaturgical genre. Here, I will simply outline some recent arguments about where dramaturgy should find new data, as well as some recent appraisals of Erving Goffman's work.

Lyman (1990) feels that dramaturgy has been limited in its scope of analysis and that a "drama in the routine" focus is needed. Sociologists should pay attention to habits, those everyday events which are unremarkable, autonomous, regular, though reoccurring. These routines, or habits, are the glue of social interaction and social order. By studying the interruption and invasion of habits and routines, sociologists acquire insights into deviance and social change. What is at first deviance can be the harbinger of social change and eventual institutionalization of new habits and routines. Drama is in everyday life, and as everyday routines are transformed there occurs the transformation of society.

Phil Manning (1991: 72) believes that sociological theory can be viewed as analysis through metaphor, that "metaphor is not so much a word or a sentence as a *conceptual system or model*." As every sociologist is aware, theater is the metaphor through which Goffman wrote sociological theory. Or is it? Manning presents a rereading of Goffman challenging the taken-for-granted assumption that Goffman persisted in the dramaturgical analysis of social life.

He contends that Goffman found the dramaturgical metaphor inefficacious between the first and second publications of *The Presentation of Self in Everyday Life*, 1956, 1959. According to Manning (1991: 76–77), by the time of the second edition, Goffman had dropped the "two selves thesis" (Manning's phrase) of a self that is a performer and a cynical manipulator. The 1959 version downplays earlier cynicism and advances the multiple selves thesis. Manning (1991: 78) holds that the first edition pursued the metaphor "optimistically," while the second edition, recognizing the inadequacy of the metaphor, viewed the metaphor "pessimistically." By the time of *Frame Analysis* (1974), a dramaturgical metaphor is no longer an adequate one to describe the world, for, Goffman recognized that all the world is not a stage (Manning, 1991: 81). The metaphor also did not differentiate between performer and character.

Manning believes that Goffman's project shifted to explicating the rules of everyday interaction, how rules were constraints, resources, and guides to behavior. Goffman's explicit concern was with how people follow and manipulate rules. Rules became Goffman's metaphor in his attempt to formalize everyday behavior. However, according to Manning, Goffman was dubious of how successful any formalization project could be.

Cahill (1992), in an evaluation of Goffman, points out that Goffman explored social life through both dramaturgy and ritual. Interaction was similar to a "religious ceremony *filled with ritual observances*" (1992: 186). Cahill (1992: 186), however, does not notice any incongruity between the two types and argues that "these two characteristics of social interaction—drama and ritual—are complementary." Because of Goffman's untimely death, how he would have made compatible his metaphors (theater and rules) for describing everyday behavior, and the possibility of using both frameworks in formalizing social life, were left unresolved.

For those wishing to explore many of the classical statements in dramaturgical analysis (for example, writings by Goffman, Foote, Burke, Stone, Messinger, R. Turner, E. Becker, Scott and Lyman, and P. Berger) as well as some new explorations, Dennis Brissett and Charles Edgley's second edition of *Life as Theater: A Dramaturgical Source Book* (1990), is recommended. Though the editors review the theoretical foundations and critiques of dramaturgy, the book does not address the many ways postmodernism has affected sociological theory, including dramaturgical analysis.

The back cover promises that the articles "reflect the latest thinking and work being done within this point of view." Excluding the introduction, all of the twenty-six articles have been previously published. Of those twenty-six, one is from the 1920s, one is from the 1940s, two are from the 1950s, five are from the 1960s, seven are from the 1970s, and ten are from the 1980s. Of the ten from the 1980s, only three date from 1985; the rest are earlier. Either the blurb is misleading, or else such a scarcity of contemporary publications from a 1990 edited work augurs ill for the dramaturgical perspective. Since I want to limit my analysis to recent work, I shall comment solely on the three works originally published in 1985.

Pin and Turndorf describe how we stage-manage dramaturgical performances of our ideal selves at social gatherings. Their article continues the landmark work of Goffman in *Behavior in Public Places* (1963). They depict many insightful observations concerning how people strive to portray ideal selves, a risky adventure since presentation pitfalls are frequent.

Kolb uses Goffman's concepts of props, front stage and back region, dramatic realization, and what actors "give" and what they "give off" to demonstrate how mediators manage the impression of rapport, intimacy, and legitimacy in order to persuade their clients to accept proposals and settlements. Though these articles are the "latest thinking and work," they continue to mine a mother lode discovered by Goffman.

Welsh likewise employs Goffman's concepts to portray how, through impression management, political power is transformed into authority. He (1990: 400) develops a "critical dramaturgy" by contending that the capitalist state, through dramaturgical means, "constitutes a mystification of the character of American political life in that the objective outcomes of the state's presentation of self as a system permitting democratic participation is not matched by its performance." Characterizing the state as a performer, Welch has forged a slightly[7] new direction for dramaturgy, employing the perspective to achieve a more comprehensive political sociology.

According to Welsh (1990: 400), the state serves the "interests of privileged social categories" but presents itself as existing "for the benefit of the totality of society." "Dramaturgy is particularly useful" to the manipulators of statecraft, for through it they achieve the "mystification of political life" (Welsh, 1990: 400). Welsh (1990: 400–408) asserts that the "political consciousness" of American citizens is manipulated by dramaturgical techniques in such areas as (1) elections, whereby we merely have "the prerogative of choosing a master;" (2) issues, whereby "political definitions of reality are elaborated in the name of the people by those at the apex of the pyramidal power structure;" (3) political debate, whereby "debates give off expressions of negativity, opposition and choice, but actually function to mystify the one-dimensional character of the political system;" (4) policy failures, whereby we attribute blame to the "personal qualities of the public officials involved [rather than to] system failures;" (5) the crisis of bureaucracy versus democracy, whereby "the state con[s] the populace into believing it is attempting to resolve the crisis in favor of accountability;" and (6) patriotism, whereby "the legitimacy of a crisis-ridden state can be renewed by military adventures." Welch thus expands the applicability of dramaturgical concepts, which had been primarily utilized to depict the presentation of self, to entities such as the state.

Mangham and Overington (1987) also extend the dramaturgical perspective by applying it to organizations. Organizations perform, and the dramaturgical model is one way to interpret their performance. The authors claim "that there is originality in our work," and its purpose is "to stimulate critical extension and application of our conceptual model [dramaturgy] among social scientists" (Mangham and Overington, 1987: 2). But the book is primarily about social interaction among senior managers within corporations. Here again, the authors "claim this book to be a first, contemporary attempt to use the theatrical model as a general conceptual resource for understanding social interaction in organizations" (4). While it might be true that this is the first *exclusively dramaturgical* portrait of organizations and interaction within them, utilizing SI concepts to analyze interaction within organizations dates from at least 1963 with the publication of A. Strauss and others' classic essay (it gave birth to the negotiated order perspective) "The Hospital and its Negotiated Order." Two other sociologists that come to mind here are Donald Roy (whose work dates from the 1950s) and Herbert Blumer.

Much of the book, though informative for newcomers, sums up concepts and themes familiar to those conversant with this perspective. Chapters review traditional dramaturgical notions, such as reality is interpreted through metaphors, that the theater offers a particularly rich metaphorical wardrobe for conceptualizing social life, and that everyday interaction can be portrayed dramaturgically. I shall limit my comments to what the authors claim is original in their work, an analysis of the social interaction of senior managers within a corporate organization.

Mangham and Overington summarize participant observation research obtained while employed as consultants to organizations. They argue that senior managers who surround board tables debating corporate policy and direction are performers and that their presentations are elaborately staged. Policy is vigorously debated as each manager proffers his/her plan on new corporate directions. The performances are a mixture of bravado and bravura. The uncertainties of the market, the economy, and product or service acceptance makes each manager's bid for the helm a precarious ploy. The manager in charge of corporate direction can substantially advance or shatter her/his career. The board meeting agenda resembles a plot with the denouement uncertain. Different division heads—personnel, finance, sales, and legal—audition for the lead, or present themselves as the protagonist, the one to be listened to, the one to gain the applause of the Chief Executive Officer, CEO.

When senior managers make their "power play," the authors conceptualize it as a frame that can easily deteriorate. The division heads represent characters, and like actors, they must not appear to be playing the part:

> Should anyone present signal that he is not invested in the part that he is proffering then, again, the appearance will be shattered. In such circumstances, as in theatre, others present are made aware of the actor *as such*, the person behind the role; the appearance of Joe, or whatever, *as* planner, personnel manager or whatever fails to be an imposing one and we glimpse the actor behind the part (Mangham and Overington, 1987: 102).

Such a poor performance can have career-devastating consequences. Senior managers, through their performances, are creating reality, they are staging a definition of the situation and want the CEO to role-take from their perspective. In the corporate world, playing the lead is paramount, the actual direction of the corporation, secondary. Those who have the lead often enough become corporate celebrities, are in line for a vice presidency, and are sure to be nominated for that ultimate corporate Oscar, the next CEO.

One might have the impression that corporate managers are dower, austere people, pouring over corporate statistics and market research, rationally calculating corporate policy. However, these authors "maintain that a great deal of interaction which occurs in organizations is expressive, constituting objectification of feelings rather than anything else" (1987: 107). The corporate board meeting is a ritual which "has been elaborated over a long time; all concerned are thoroughly versed in the combats they enact" (1987: 107).

Sometimes the CEO may reject the plans of all department heads, giving no applause for any of their performances. Mangham and Overington (1987: 109) note that at this point, the players switch from performance to rehearsal, "they construct and interpret a revised situational script". The CEO, as producer and director, lets each division head rewrite the script and offer an improvisation. Careers are on the line. Again, this is not a rational, dispassionate discussion of the facts. The important outcome, the only outcome from the players' definition, is to be cast in the leading role. The CEO's decision confers "power and status and the ruling—whatever it is, even if it were to be that of a Solomon—would be the occasion for emotion" (1987: 114). One's performance is gauged to achieve individual advancement and the loss of a lead is a time of personal sadness rather than relief that the corporation has a new direction. Every board meeting is a chance to curry favor, advance one's career; the corporate interest, though presented as one's ostensible concern, is merely the obligatory script in a masquerade.

The authors continue their analysis by noting that social interaction in organizations has staging, settings, costumes, properties, and cues: "The setting, the built environment, be that a room or an entire building, provides us with a clue as to the behavior appropriate to it. Experience and cultural expectation has taught us to expect little grey men in little grey offices dispensing little grey platitudes" (1987: 121). The board meeting is a built environment. Though participants encircle a table, the CEO is in the limelight, antagonists competing for power and status face each other, and lesser lights play bit parts in the gloomy regions opposite the CEO.

The many-storied corporation has secretaries and clerks on the bottom floors, middle management on the middle floors, and top management on the top floors. The more power and status one has the more likely one is to have an office with space and privacy. Physical setting is organized to shape behavior, particularly, "to reduce the ambiguity of social position and power by making distinctions between social actors" (1987: 124). The authors paint an elaborate, in-depth portrait of the landscape of organizations, and thus, how organizations perform. But much of this material on the built environment is not really new to sociologists.

For a book that blends dramaturgy and postmodernism, T.R. Young's *The Drama of Social Life* (1990) is worth exploring. His purpose is "to carry the postmodern critique into the realm of dramaturgy" (1990: 9). Young amplifies the critical dramaturgy project envisioned by Welsh. In fact, one of the chapters is coauthored by Welsh, and Young acknowledges that Welsh has shaped his "thinking on critical dimensions in dramaturgical analysis for the past seven years" (1990: ix). Young claims that his "essays explore and include new topics salient to a critically transformed dramaturgical analysis that have been excluded hitherto" (1990: 13). Such a claim to originality is dubious. Yet these essays do attempt to go beyond what Young refers to as the sociology of fraud. He does not blame Goffman for this; rather, the reprehensible are those who have exploited his insights to manipulate and aggrandize. A more modest claim of originality is Young's exploration of the emancipatory uses of dramaturgy. Since much of Young's book revolves around postmodern issues, which have been reviewed, and the critical dramaturgy project, also reviewed, I shall limit my comments to Young's application of a postmodern dramaturgy to emancipatory issues.

Young (1990: 273–274) suggests that one must subject theater to three tests to determine its emancipatory caliber: the content must offer a more equitable vision of life, the medium must present "new ways to use color, line, form, texture, materials," and the mode of production of an artistic event must not put the artist above others who help produce it. He posits that dramaturgy should focus on presenting life as it could and should be, guided by emancipatory values: "community, democratic self-management, social justice, and the integrity of the natural and human environment" (1990: 275). Like motherhood, we are all for it! However, Young has abandoned a concern for dramaturgy, or the theater, as a metaphor to portray everyday life. Rather, he is proffering some prescription for radical theater. His goals are laudable: "Radical theatre must show how an oppressed population might get from one set of relationships to another" (1990: 227). Young's essay is not on how a dramaturgical analysis of social life can bring about emancipatory change, as one might infer from a putative sociological work on dramaturgy, but on the potential of theater to serve as the catalyst for social revolution.

The contention that revolution will come from those who attend radical theater, or that radical theater can socially transform the world, is naive, and contravenes much of what Young has argued in earlier chapters. Such an analysis opens up a can of worms: who is the revolutionary class? Is the working class going to start attending the theater? The theater is a far too limited medium to attract the mass following necessary for social revolution. Young's appeal is to radical chic and the literati who would like to see more productions on alienation and exploitation (so would I), rather than to those in the arena of social policy who need to formulate concrete proposals to alter the maldistributions in our society.

If Young is thinking of more popular media, his argument is still quixotic. It has been argued that the media manufacture a passive consciousness that allows the power elite to rule by consent. This is the traditional definition of hegemony. But the media are not going to present radical television, which would only fall on deaf ears. The media are powerful corporations, so formats or messages that might remanufacture consciousness along radical lines would be eschewed. There are too many important aspects that Young fails to address, or to use the postmodernist jargon, the "presence of absence" is visible.

Focusing on new avenues of research, such as the board meetings of senior corporate executives, dramaturgy offers insight into the drama of everyday life. There is promise in the critical dramaturgy project as it can expose the way the media, politicians, and the state stage events. Critical dramaturgy can also unmask the powerful influence the media have as agents of socialization, creating forms of consciousness and media selves.

Semiotics and SI

Semiotics, the science of signs, has increasingly garnered the attention of interactionists since the 1980s. Semiotics has its intellectual origins in the work of the Swiss linguist, Ferdinand de Saussure. Since the term and what it stands for may be confusing to students, I shall present a cursory review of semiotics. To do so, I shall draw from interactionist writings on semiotics, especially from Peter Manning's 1987 book, *Semiotics and Fieldwork*.

A sign is comprised of the signifier and the signified. In language, the signifier refers to the word spoken and the signified to the concept, which may be abstract or concrete, real or imaginary. Signs are crucial to interactionists because language, the most elaborate sign system ever devised, is fundamental to interactionists' understanding of human behavior. Understanding language as signs, that is, something that arbitrarily represents something else, helps us to understand humans' symbolic interaction. Those sharing a common culture share the meaning of signs, that is, those signs mean the same thing to a wide variety, or cross-section, of the population. Signs become conventional; it seems natural that green means go and red means stop. But a sign does not necessarily indicate that meaning is shared. Also, the sign does not entail interaction. The significant symbol is the term for shared meaning in interaction. People's behavior and gestures are symbolic and conventional also: the "hello," the "thank you," and the handshake.

Interactionists argue that the way humans respond to objects determines their meaning. By knowing what things mean to individuals we come to understand why they behave toward them (respond) as they do. Simply said, understanding the meaning people attach to their world is a way of understanding their behavior: "Language symbols do not merely stand for something else—they also indicate the significance of things for human behavior, and they organize behavior toward the thing symbolized" (Lindesmith, Strauss, and Denzin, 1988: 54).

Understanding signs helps us to understand both social order (people responding to signs in the same way, such as a traffic light that flashes green for go and red for stop) and social conflict (people responding to signs in diametrically opposed ways, such as is the case in the definition of "life" and "privacy" in the abortion controversy).

Language allows us to perceive the world that is out there. We are signifying, typifying creatures, organizing our environment in a way that makes sense to us. We signify and typify through the concepts and categories of language. Concepts and categories organize the vast array of the empirical world that bombards our senses so that we can select out those objects relevant to our plans of action. Through concepts we can adapt and make adjustive responses, that is, employ reflective thought in responding to a mutable environment. Language and signs are human constructions, or social inventions, just as are concepts and categories, through which we construct and interpret reality. Our behavior is based on our interpretations or definitions of the situation utilizing the concepts and categories of language (Lindesmith, Strauss, and Denzin, 1988: 55).Most of the time nothing out of the ordinary happens. But sometimes our concepts and categories of interpretation lead us humorously astray, since we do not have any direct knowledge of objects or things-in-themselves but only things-as-they-appear. Through concepts and categories we can misinterpret and misdefine situations, or others' gestures and behavior, a frequent human malady.

Since signs, significant symbols, and language in general are such a vital aspect of understanding human behavior, and since symbolic interaction is the study of people interacting in a social context who are self-indicating and making adjustive responses to the symbolic behavior of others, do semiotics and symbolic interactionism complement each other?

In 1986, the journal *Symbolic Interaction* published a debate on the plausibility of integrating semiotics and SI. MacCannel (1986: 161), while not calling for an integration, does advance the notion that there can be a *"partnership, rapprochement, alignment, and linkage"* between the two perspectives. He wants interactionists to be "semiotically aware", and I think that they are. Harman (1986: 148), however, believes that MacCannel "overrates the usefulness of semiotics for sociological analysis, and downgrades the interpretive side of symbolic interactionism." Harman (1986: 150) agrees that "symbolic interactionism and semiotics are similar in that they entail the study of representation." But there are differences that should not be glossed; mainly, "symbolic interactionism has moved in the direction of the study of the construction and negotiation of social reality through 'significant symbols,' while semiotics has tended to focus on the unidirectional spread of the image from source to reader" (Harman, 1986: 151). Harmon's critique clarifies that the significant symbol for SI entails so much more than does the sign as used by semioticians. The significant symbol centers on shared meanings in interaction, both of which can be ignored by those studying signs. Semiotics, for example, can, and has, included the study of art, photographs, movies, and literature, etc. These studies may help us understand human behavior. However, SI is concerned with human beings engaging in symbolic interaction within a social context. Past SI strongholds, such as the study of socialization and role-taking, appear to be absent from semiotics. Even Manning (1987: 26) points out that semiotics does not

> seek to describe the motives of individual actors who animate social life, nor indeed has it any concern for individuals, their morals, attitudes, values, or behaviors except as they are symbolized within a system of signs.

Thus, I would agree with Harman that interactionists should be circumspect about jumping on the semiotic bandwagon. However, two leading interactionists, Norman Denzin and Peter Manning, both have used semiotics to broaden their sociological studies.

Norman Denzin's third edition of *The Research Act* (1989), has a chapter titled "Film, Photography, and Sociology." Denzin (1989: 210) celebrates the beginning of "visual sociology," a focus on "photography, audio-visual recordings, documentary films, and Hollywood-made movies." He notes that sociologists have long used film to study human behavior, such as Birdwhistle's studies of kinesics, and that in 1982 the journal *Video Sociology Quarterly* was founded.

Denzin argues that we interact with film, that watching a movie is an emotional experience, and that films are cultural productions that help to reproduce institutional arrangements. Films—and our role-taking from the perspective of the director—contribute to the social construction of reality.

The film is replete with signs, which Denzin argues are not necessarily shared: "No visual text evokes the same meanings for all viewers. In the process of interacting with the text, viewers develop readings and interpretations that are uniquely their own" (1989: 229). The signs in a film always tell two stories, one literal, one inferred. One must go beyond a realist interpretation and offer a subversive one, that is, how any text "is always filtered through preconceptions and biases" (1989: 230). These preconceptions and biases help reproduce the social structure of domination, that is, "the gender, race, ethnic, and class relationships in society" (1989: 223). Films are full of signs that help reproduce things-as-they-are and make things-as-they-are seem natural, the problem of reification. Or, from the perspective of Ronald Barthes, "those signs that are hyperelevated into matters of trust, and shared reality that approaches the unquestioned, are myths" (in Manning, 1987: 27).

Denzin has used semiotics to broaden SI to include a political economy of meaning, to show through subversive readings that a film, or any text, can reproduce ideology and myth—which may be very oppressive—so that life as portrayed in the movies appears natural, normal, as the reality we all (stereotypically) know.

Manning's aim is to blend the insights of fieldwork (a methodological tradition of Chicago School SI, though, also, associated with British social anthropology) and semiotics. Fieldwork, as Manning (1987: 9–20) states, centers on gathering empirical data through association with, and even living among, those studied. Semiotics tries to

> derive explanation of cases from general rules or principles and to discern and make obvious the underlying pattern, model, or order that obtains among various forms of communication such as music, art, literature, and formal scientific languages (1987: 9).

These two perspectives appear to come from opposite ends of academic discourse; yet, Manning contends (1987: 10) that "all such opposites are false and misleading. They contain truth that can arise from exploring an apparent paradox." Semiotics is nomothetic while fieldwork is ideographic, that is, the former favors law-like theory, the latter, well-crafted description. Though, as Manning (1987: 16) reminds us, "the potential for generalized explanation within the Chicago style of fieldwork is considerable." Human Ecology and the Concentric Zone perspectives are two prominent examples.

Manning thus combines fieldwork and semiotics to study the police, which work I shall briefly review. Manning has concerned himself with how messages are defined in police departments in the United States and Britain. His research delineates how organizational structure, codes, and technology all affect the interpretation of an incoming message.

The organizational structure has an ideology that converts incoming calls into communications relevant for police. Any call for help to a police station goes through several levels of conversion where the meaning of the call is transformed: "Through this work of encoding, formatting, interpreting, and placing in context, police processing converts or transforms calls into jobs and produces a layering of meanings that moves a long way from the social world of the person who makes the original call" (Manning, 1987: 54–55).

There are various ways the police can interpret a call and this has consequences for how the police respond. Certain calls are coded in a certain way. Certain signs in the call, or the way the call comes to the attention of a police officer, influence how that police officer will respond:

> These are learned ways of connecting expression and content, and grouping various signs so composed into meaningful action-units. It is a kind of mental sorting and classification that one does everyday, but it is crucial to understand it in this organization, because it is the basis on which the police are mobilized and take action (Manning, 1987: 59).

For example, one of the most important signs to decode is if the call can be interpreted as a crime or noncrime call. A crime call is one that is sought after by police officers. Police officers will thus assess the call, listen for the telltale signs that this is one where action will happen. In fact, officers may drop what they are doing or encroach upon others' turf just to pursue a call that has the sign of "something heavy going down:"

> This connotative meaning adds a potential for competition with other officers, stealing and "jumping" calls (taking a call directed to another unit and trying to be the first on the scene to make the arrest, apprehend the suspect, and so on), and lying (Manning, 1987: 64).

Thus officers have to assess the subtext of what is being said. Interpreting or decoding texts and subtexts is something we all do. A text can be viewed "as a set of interlocking signs understood by the application of several codes" (Manning, 1987; 39–40). Texts communicate meaning, and they do so denotatively and connotatively. Texts and words have more than one meaning, but to know the meanings we have to know the codes. For example, it is common knowledge that political rhetoric produces text as code, commonly referred to as "buzz words." It is so unsubtle that any rube can apply the proper code to deconstruct the text. In this political season we have to interpret political phrases both denotatively and connotatively. What does "diversity"connote if it is a Democrat talking about employment policy, what does "protecting everyone's civil rights" connote if it is a Republican talking about the same thing?

Semiotics may help SI by broadening its scope of analysis, but there is a real danger of becoming literary critics with a social bent, rather than using the basic concepts of SI to understand human behavior.

The Future

In the last twelve years, beginning with Maines (1981), interactionists have been speculating on the future of interactionism. Responding to Nicholas Mullins's premature postmortem on SI, Maines argued, instead, that a rich diversity was underway, that SI was developing affinities with other interpretive theories, such as critical theory, phenomenological sociology, labeling theory, sociolinguistics, attribution theory, the negotiated order, historical analysis, and strategic interaction. He discussed the move to an emphasis on social organization and was right on target. It is here that SI has continued to make strong corrections to an earlier astructural bias. Maines also accurately predicted the coming methodological diversity in SI, as well as the decline of the "Twenty Statements Test" as a much favored device. Many of the current trends, such as discourse-analysis, were suggested by Maines's (1981: 477) argument that an ever-stronger focus would be on sociolinguistics, "the most fundamental area of substantive continuity in the perspective insofar as it links the early interactionists' views on communication and society with contemporary research and scholarly inquiry."

Stryker (1987) sees a vitalization in SI already taking place. After a decline in the 1960s and 1970s, the 1980s vitalization is based on SI's influence on a variety of theoretical and empirical works of non-SI researchers, such as Anthony Giddens and Randall Collins, European action theorists, and psychological social psychologists. Stryker also sees new theoretical developments within SI, such as William Corsaro's work on childhood socialization, David Snow's work on social movements, Clark McPhail's work on collective behavior, C. Norman Alexander's situated identity theory, David Heise's affect control theory, Anselm Strauss's negotiation perspective, Stryker's structural SI and self-identity theory, and the perspectives of role theory and expectation states theory. Methodological diversity is also contributing to the vitalization.

Adler, Adler, and Fontana (1987) argue that everyday life sociology, of which SI is a subset, has been highly critical of macrosociology. The critique is based on macrosociology's determinism, its subject/object dualism, and its failure to both incorporate the concept of the self-reflexive actor and to view social structure as a dependent variable emerging out of social interaction. They predict that three avenues of research will define everyday sociology in the future: existential sociology, the sociology of the emotions, and conversation-analysis. They accurately predict the rise of the latter two, but existential sociology does not appear as popular as it was only a few years ago.

One insight Adler, Adler, and Fontana (1987: 228) have into the workings of the discipline of sociology is the increasing use of everyday sociology by macro theorists. This use centers on bringing agency back into sociological analysis. The notion that individuals are creative agents in shaping structure, social worlds, and context, even though they are "always already" constrained by them, now seems to be accepted by selected mainstream macrosociologists. It is in these "micro-macro syntheses that many of the most far-reaching theoretical advances of everyday life can be found" (Adler, Adler, and Fontana, 1987: 229). Recent events in Eastern Europe and the Soviet Union are bound to heighten interest in interactionism's variety of everyday sociology with its theory of agency.

Potentially, the most fruitful micro-macro synthesis on the horizon is cultural studies, just now becoming known to a wider SI audience. A number of interactionists have been mining cultural studies for a more critical SI (Denzin, 1989b, 1990b, 1991b; McCall and Becker, 1990; and Cagle, 1989). As Denzin (1990b: 146–147) puts it: "Cultural studies directs itself to the problem of how the history that human beings make and live spontaneously is determined by structures of meaning that they have not chosen for themselves."

Cultural Studies refers both to the British School of Cultural Studies (BSCS) and to the American Cultural Studies project, reflected in the work of James Carey. BSCS scholarship has been under the direction of Stuart Hall at the Birmingham Centre of Contemporary Cultural Studies.

The BSCS shares some similarities with SI (Musolf, 1992). The most notable is a redirection of scholarship to include concepts of human agency. Also, BSCS needed a methodology to reflect this concern and was influenced by the Chicago School ethnography of Howard Becker and Erving Goffman (Cagle, 1989). BSCS and SI share the theme of the social construction of meaning. SI has not, however, been as explicitly political as BSCS.[8]

One recent SI study that shows how selves are a product of structures of meaning that they have not chosen, is John P. Hewitt's *Dilemmas of the American Self* (1989). The self can be viewed as a dialectical product influenced by both a contradictory culture that advocates, let us say, leading a life that has to be socially worthwhile but also materially rewarding and, on the other hand, the agency of the self as it resolves these dilemmas. The self is a unique product as human agency and cultural constraint interact to shape the human being, each generation of selves having to resolve new dilemmas.

Plummer (1991) has been one of the latest to gaze into the crystal ball. He predicts that contributions will continue to come from interactionist research standbys such as deviance and medical sociology.

Plummer's (1991: xi–xvii) gaze reveals seven themes that he feels will dominate interactionism as it moves into the next century. The first is a greater emphasis on macrointeractionism, represented in its most ambitious form in Carl Couch's *Constructing Civilizations*. The second is innovative methodologies, such as the study of language through metonymy, synecdoche, and irony, that are being experimented with by Peter Manning and Joseph Gusfield. Third is a move toward a more systematic interactionism, reflected in the research guides of Barney Glaser and Anselm Strauss, *The Discovery of Grounded Theory*, and John Lofland's, *Analyzing Social Settings*. Fourth is a connection to semiotics. Fifth is the increasing importance of a theory of emotion. Sixth is the increasing politicization of interactionism. The seventh is that interactionism is becoming so diverse that one must speak of "interactionist sociologies", abandoning the classic Chicago and Iowa Schools distinction. However, I would argue that the distinction is still useful, for many recent developments can be subsumed under the typology. Virtually all of the new developments are compatible with the Chicago School tradition. The antipositivist, postmodern theme that many interactionists are taking up is sure to work a hardship on the Iowa School, as was predicted by Maines.

Zurcher (1989) opines that there is a creative renewal in SI by pointing to the diversity of papers presented at the 1987 Stone Symposium. Unfortunately, Zurcher never spells out where SI is going. However, Joel Best's imaginative constructionist approach to social problems is taking SI in a promising direction.

Denzin (1989: 6) feels that interactionists "must abandon the modernist project that has organized the SI project since 1937." Second, he argues that any interactionist project (though he would argue any theoretical project) that "aims for a science of the social as a totality must be abandoned" (Denzin, 1989: 6). Thus, Denzin believes interactionism is too conservative, which can be corrected by absorbing postmodern sensibilities. Given the profusion of articles published in SI journals and elsewhere on postmodernism, Denzin's gaze appears accurate.

An opposite prediction (and one I believe inaccurate) is prophesied by Saxton (1989), who holds that SI is in danger of disappearing. He cites declining numbers of undergraduate and graduate students interested in SI, eroding SI faculty, and loss of SI training programs, to suggest that there is a "greying of SI." He cites the need for establishing national programs. His postmortem is wrongheaded, I believe. Currently, the newest program that I know of is at the University of South Florida, where they are establishing an Institute for Interpretive Human Studies.

Conclusion

Where SI is headed, is, of course, ultimately unknowable, since, as the grammarian Harry Shaw has argued, the "foreseeable future" is a trite oxymoron. Significant research will continue in emotions, discourse-analysis, social organization, cultural studies, and the social reproduction of gender. The alliance between postmodernism and SI, most notable in the work of Norman Denzin, is yet too recently formed to tell how long it will last or how fruitful it will be. I have argued that that direction has pitfalls. I think the best and most promising work in SI is research into what I have called "the social reproduction of gender." Such scholars as Judith M. Hammond, Arlie Russell Hochschild, Susan E. Martin, Irene Padavic, Laurel Richardson, Candace West, Mary Glenn Wiley, and Charlotte Wolf are articulating the impact that structure, organization, culture, gender, and power have on everyday interaction, and they are contributing substantially to reducing further SI's alleged astructural bias. Dierdre Boden's work in discourse-analysis is also contributing to illuminating the impact of power on everyday life. The future of dramaturgy appears questionable. What can be argued, as does Joel Charon (1992: 225) in an assessment of the field, is that "increasingly sociologists are using symbolic interactionism in their analysis of socialization, culture, society, and social structure." As this book makes clear, there are still substantial criticisms that can be levied against SI, but interactionists are responding to their critics. There is an affinity between leading practitioners and leading critics of SI. That relationship has been productive, propelling a self-renewing SI to its current position as the leading perspective for interpreting everyday life.

NOTES

1. I would like to thank Bernard N. Meltzer and Larry T. Reynolds (colleagues, friends, and mentors) for comments on an earlier version of this chapter. All errors, of course, remain with the author.

2. For a thorough study of mixed emotions from an SI perspective, see: Andrew J. Weigert, *Mixed Emotions: Certain Steps toward Understanding Ambivalence*, Albany: State University of New York Press, 1991. See also *Emotions and Violence*, Thomas Scheff and Suzanne Retainger. New York: Lexington Books, 1991.

3. For a notable exception to this see Norma Williams, *The Mexican American Family*, Dix Hills: General Hall, 1990.

4. For an overview of the relationship between women and the interactionist tradition see Mary Jo Deegan and Michael Hill, *Women and Symbolic Interaction*, New York: Unwin Hyman, 1989.

5. For an in-depth review of Richardson, Martin, Hammond, West, and Wolf see Gil Richard Musolf, "Structure, Institutions, Power, and Ideology," *Sociological Quarterly* 33 (1992).

6. For a recent study see R.S. Perinbanayagan's *Discursive Acts*, cited in the references. Also, see, Deirdre Boden and Don H. Zimmerman's *Talk and Social Structure*, Berkeley: University of California Press, 1991.

7. I use the word "slightly" because SI has been used by interactionists in the field of political sociology since at least 1969. See Richard S. Brooks "The Self and Political Role: A Symbolic Interactionist Approach to Political Ideology." *Sociological Quarterly* 10 (Winter 1969) 22–31. Also, Peter Hall's work has contributed to the field of political sociology.

8. For a fuller discussion of the BSCS and its relationship to SI see Gil Richard Musolf, "Structure, Institutions, Power, and Ideology," *Sociological Quarterly* 33 (1992); Stuart Hall, "Cultural Studies and the Centre: Some problematics and problems," Pp. 15–47 in *Culture, Media, Language*, edited by Stuart Hall et al. London: Hutchinson 1980; Carey Nelson and Lawrence Grossberg, *Marxism and the Interpretation of Culture*, Urbana: University of Illinois Press 1988; Norman K. Denzin, "Empiricist Cultural Studies in America: A Deconstructive Reading," *Current Perspectives in Social Theory,* 1991, 11:17–39; and Norman K. Denzin, *Symbolic Interactionism and Cultural Studies: The Politics of Interpretation,* Oxford: Blackwell, 1992.

REFERENCES

Adler, Patricia A., Peter Adler, and Andrea Fontana
    1987   "Everyday Life Sociology." Pp. 217–236 in W.R. Scott and J.S. Short
            (Eds.), *Annual Review of Sociology*. Palo Alto: Annual Reviews, Inc.
Albas, Cheryl, and Daniel Albas
    1988   "Emotion Work and Emotion Rules: The Case of Exams." *Qualitative*
            Sociology 11: 259–274.
Alexander, Jeffrey C.
    1988   "The 'Individualist Dilemma' in Phenomenology and Interactionism."
            Pp.222–256 in Jeffrey Alexander (Ed.) *Action and Its Environments:*
            Toward A New Synthesis. New York: Columbia University Press.
    1991   "Sociological Theory and the Claim to Reason: Why the End is Not in
            Sight." *Sociological Theory* 9:147–153.
Alexander, Jeffrey C., et al.
    1987   *The Micro– Macro Link*. Berkeley: University of California Press.
Altheide, David
    1988   "Mediating Cutbacks in Human Services: A Case Study in the Nego-
            tiated Order." *Sociological Quarterly* 29: 339–355.
Antonio, Robert J.
    1991   "Postmodern Storytelling Versus Pragmatic Truth-Seeking: The Dis-
            cursive Bases of Social Theory." *Sociological Theory* 9: 154–163.
Averill, James R.
    1989   *Anger and Aggression: An Essay on Emotion*. New York: Springer
            Verlag.
Bacharach, Samuel B. and Edward J. Lawler
    1981   *Bargaining: Power, Tactics, and Outcomes*. San Francisco: Jossey-Bass.
Baker, Scott
    1990   "Reflection, Doubt, and the Place of Rhetoric in Postmodern Social
            Theory." *Sociological Theory* 8: 232–245.
Baldwin, James Mark
    1895   *Mental Development in The Child and The Race*. New York: Macmillan.
Baldwin, John D.
    1985   "Social Behaviorism on Emotions: Mead and Modern Behaviorism
            Compared." *Symbolic Interaction* 8: 263–289.
    1986   *George Herbert Mead: A Unifying Theory for Sociology*. Newberry Park:
            Sage Publications.
Balsamo, Anne
    1989   "Imagining Cyborgs: Postmodernism and Symbolic Interactionism."
            Symbolic Interaction 10: 369–379.

Bartelt, Pearl W., Mark Hutter and David W. Bartelt
    1986   "Politics and Politesse: Gender, Deference and Formal Etiquette." *Studies in Symbolic Interaction* 7: 199–228.

Becker, Howard S.
    1960   "Notes on the Concept of Commitment." *American Journal of Sociology* 66 (July): 32–40.

Becker, Howard S.
    1963   *Outsiders.* New York: Free Press.
    1982   *Art Worlds.* Berkeley: University of California Press.
    1986   *Doing Things Together: Selected Papers.* Evanston: Northwestern University Press.

Block, Fred
    1973   "Alternative Sociological Perspectives: Implications for Applied Sociology." *Catalyst* 7: 29–41.

Blumer, Herbert
    1936   "Social Attitudes and Nonsymbolic Interaction "*Journal of Educational Sociology* 9: 515–523.
    1939   "Collective Behavior." Pp. 219–280 in Robert E. Park (Ed.), *An Outline of the Principles of Sociology.* New York: Barnes and Noble.
    1948a   "Sociological Theory in Industrial Relations." *American Sociological Review* 13: 271–278.
    1948b   "Public Opinion and Public Opinion Polling." *American Sociological Review* 13: 542–554.
    1949   "Group Tension and Interest Organization." Pp. 1–5 in *Proceedings of the Second Annual Meetings* Industrial Relations Research Association
    1953   "Psychological Import of The Human Group." Pp. 185–202 in Muzfer Sherif and M. D. Wilson (Eds.), *Group Relations at the Crossroads.* New York: Harper and Row.
    1954a   "Social Structure and Power Conflict." Pp. 232–239 in Robert Dubin and Arnold Rose (Eds.), *Industrial Conflict.* New York: McGraw-Hill.
    1954b   "What is Wrong with Social Theory?" *American Sociological Review* 19: 3–10.
    1956   "Social Science and the Desegregation Process." *Annals of the American Academy of Political and Social Science* 304: 137–143.
    1958   "Race Prejudice as a Sense of Group Position." *Pacific Sociological Review* 1: 3–7.
    1959   "Suggestions for the Study of Mass-Media Effects." Pp. 197–208 in Eugene Burdick and A.J. Brodbeck (Eds.), *American Voting Behavior.* Glencoe, IL: The Free Press.
    1960   "Early Industrialization and the Laboring Class." *The Sociological Quarterly* 1: 5–14.
    1962   "Society as Symbolic Interaction" Pp. 179–192 in Arnold Rose (Ed.), *Human Behavior and Social Process.* Boston: Houghton Mifflin.
    1966a   "Sociological Implications of the Thought of G. H. Mead." *American Journal of Sociology* 71: 535–544.
    1966b   "The Idea of Social Development." *Studies in Comparative International Development* 2: 3–11.

1969a   "Fashion: From Class Differentiation to Collective Selection." *Sociological Quarterly* 10: 275–291.

1969b   *Symbolic Interaction.* Englewood Cliffs, NJ: Prentice Hall.

Boden, Deirdre

1990.   "People are Talking: Conversation Analysis and Symbolic Interaction." Pp. 244–274 in Howard S. Becker and Michal M. McCall (Eds.) *Symbolic Interaction and Cultural Studies*, Chicago: University of Chicago Press.

Bodenhafer, W. B.

1920–1921 "The Comparative Role of the Group Concept in Ward's *Dynamic Sociology* and Contemporary American Sociology." *American Journal of Sociology* 26: 425–474.

Braroe, N.W.

1975   *Indian and White: Self-image and Interaction in a Canadian Plains Community.* Stanford: Stanford University Press.

Brissett, Dennis and Charles Edgley (Eds.)

1990   *Life as Theater: A Dramaturgical Source Book.* 2nd edition. New York: Aldine de Gruyter.

Brittan, Arthur

1973   *Meanings and Situations.* London: Routledge and Kegan Paul.

Brooks, Richard S.

1969   "The Self and Political Role: A Symbolic Interationist Approach to Political Ideology." *Sociological Quarterly* 10: 22–31.

Brown, Richard Harvey

1990.   "Rhetoric, Textuality, and the Postmodern Turn in Sociological Theory." *Sociological Theory* 8:188–197.

Bucher, Rue

1970   "Social Process and Power in a Medical School." Pp. 3–45 in Mayer Zald (Ed). *Power and Organizations.* Nashville, Tennessee: Vanderbilt University Press.

Bucher, Rue, and Joan Stelling

1969   "Characteristics of Professional Organizations." *Journal of Health and Social Behavior* 10: 3–15.

Burke, Peter

1977   "The Self: Measurement Requirements from an Interactionist Perspective." Unpublished version of a paper presented to the section on Social Psychology, American Sociological Association, Chicago, September 5.

Busch, Lawrence

1980   "Structure and Negotiation in the Agricultural Sciences." *Rural Sociology* 45: 26–48.

1982   "History, Negotiation, and Structure in Agricultural Sciences." *Urban Life* 11: 368–384.

Busch, Lawrence and William B. Lacy

1983   *Science, Agriculture, and the Politics of Research.* Boulder, CO: Westview Press.

1984   *Food Security in the United States.* Boulder, CO: Westview Press.

Busch, Lawrence, William B. Lacy, Jeffrey Burkhardt, and Laura R. Lacy
1991 *Plants, Power, and Profit: Social, Economic, and Ethical Consequences of the New Biotechnologies.* Oxford: Basil Blackwell.

Busch, Lawrence and Carolyn Sachs
1981 "The Agricultural Sciences and the Modern World System." Pp.131–56 in Lawrence Busch (Ed), *Science and Agricultural Development.* Totawa, NJ: Allanheld, Osmun.

Cagle, Van M.
1989 "The Language of Cultural Studies: An Analysis of British Subculture Theory." Pp. 301–313 in Norman K. Denzin (Ed.), *Studies in Symbolic Interaction Volume 10,* Greenwich, CT: JAI Press.

Cahill, Spencer
1992. "Erving Goffman." Pp. 185–200 in Joel Charon, *Symbolic Interactionism,* Englewood Cliffs, NJ: Prentice-Hall.

Cavan, Sherri
1966 *Liquor License: An Ethnography of Bar Behavior.* Chicago: Aldine.

Charon, Joel
1992 *Symbolic Interactionism: An Introduction, An Interpretation, An Integration.* Fourth edition. Englewood Cliffs, NJ: Prentice Hall.

Cicourel, Aaron
1968 *The Social Organization of Juvenile Justice.* New York: Wiley.
1974a *Cognitive Sociology.* New York: Free Press.
1974b *Theory and Method in a Study of Argentine Fertility.* New York: Wiley.

Clanton, Gordon
1989 "Jealousy in American Culture, 1945–1985: Reflections from Popular Literature." Pp. 179–193 in David D. Franks and E. Doyle McCarthy (Eds.) *The Sociology of Emotions: Original Essays and Research Papers,* Greenwich, CT: JAI Press.

Clark, Candace
1989 "Studying Sympathy: Methodological Confessions." Pp. 137–151 in David D.Franks and E. Doyle McCarthy (Eds.) *The Sociology of Emotions: Original Essays and Research Papers,* Greenwich, CT: JAI Press.

Clarke, Adele E.
1987 "Research Materials and Reproductive Science in the United States, 1910–1940." Pp.323–350 in Gerald L. Geison (Ed), *Physiology in the American Context, 1850–1940.* Bethesda, MD: American Physiological Society.
1990a "Controversy and the Development of Reproductive Sciences." *Social Problems* 37(1): 18–37.
1990b "A Social Worlds Research Adventure: The Case of Reproductive Science." Pp.23–50 in Susan E. Cozzens and Thomas F. Gieryn (Eds), *Theories of Science in Society.* Bloomington, IN: Indiana University Press.
1991a "Embryology and the Rise of American Reproductive Sciences, circa 1910–1940." Pp.107–32 in Keith R. Benson, Jane Maienschein, and Ronald Rainger (Eds), *The Expansion of American Biology.* New Brunswick, NJ: Rutgers University Press.

1991b   "Social Worlds/Arenas Theory as Organizational Theory." Pp.119–57
         in David R. Maines (Ed), *Social Organization and Social Process:
         Essays in Honor of Anselm Strauss*. New York: Aldine De Gruyter.

Clarke, Adele E. and Elihu M. Gerson
1990   "Symbolic Interactionism in Social Studies of Science." Pp.179–214 in
         Howard S. Becker and Michal M. McCall (Eds), *Symbolic Interaction
         and Cultural Studies*. Chicago: University of Chicago Press.

Clough, Patricia T.
1986   "The Failures of Women's Consciousness: A Brief History of a Woman's
         Group." *Studies in Symbolic Interaction 7:* 291–304.

Coleman, James C.
1987   "Microfoundations and Macrosocial Behavior." Pp. 153–173 in Jeffrey
         C. Alexander et al, (Eds.) *The Micro-Macro Link*. Berkeley: University
         of California.

Collins, Randall
1975   *Conflict Sociology*. New York: Academic Press.
1981   "On the Micro-Foundations of Macro-Sociology." *American Journal
         of Sociology* 86: 984–1014.
1985   *Three Sociological Traditions*. New York: Wiley.

Collins, Randall, and Michael Makowsky
1972   *The Discovery of Society*. New York: Random House.

Cooley, Charles H.
1902   *Human Nature and Social Order.New* York: Scribner's.
1909   *Social Organization*. New York: Scribner's.
1918   *Social Process*. New York: Scribner's.

Coser, Lewis
1976   "Sociological Theory from the Chicago Dominance to 1965 " *Annual
         Review of Sociology* 2: 145–160.

Couch, Carl
1984a   *Constructing Civilizations*. Greenwich, CT: JAI Press.
1984b   "Symbolic Interaction and Generic Sociological Principles." *Symbolic
         Interaction 7:* 1–14.

Couch, Carl J. and Robert A. Hintz (Eds.)
1975   *Constructing Social Life: Readings in Behavioral Sociology from the
         Iowa School*. Champaign, IL: Stipes.

Couch, Carl, Stanley L. Saxon, and Michael A. Katovich
1986   *Studies in Symbolic Interaction: The Iowa School*. Greenwich, CT: JAI
         Press.

Coutu, Walter
1949   *Emergent Human Nature*. New York: Alfred A. Knopf.

Cuzzort R. P.
1969   *Humanity and Modern Sociological Thought*. New York: Holt, Rinehart,
         and Winston.

Daniels, Arlene K.
1970   "The Philosophy of Combat Psychiatry." *American Behavioral Scien-
         tist* 14: 169–178.

Das, Hari
  1988   "The Relevance of a Symbolic Interactionist Approach in Understanding Power: A Preliminary Analysis." *Journal of Management Studies* 25: 257–267.
Day, Robert and JoAnne V. Day
  1977   "A Review of the Current State of Negotiated Order Theory: An Appreciation and Critique." *Sociological Quarterly* 18: 126–142.
Denzin, Norman K.
  1969   "Symbolic Intractionism and Ethnomethodology: A Proposed Synthesis." *American Sociological Review* 34: 922–934.
  1974   "The Methodological Implication of Symbolic Interactionism for the Study of Deviance." *British Journal of Sociology* 25: 269–282.
  1978   "Crime and the American Liquor Industry." *Studies in Symbolic Interaction* 1: 887–918.
  1984   *On Understanding Emotion.* San Francisco: Jossey-Bass.
  1985   "Emotion as Lived Experience." *Symbolic Interaction* 8: 223–240.
  1989a   "Thoughts on "Critique and Renewal in Symbolic Interactionism." Pp. 3–8 in Norman Denzin (Ed.) *Studies in Symbolic Interaction,* Volume 10, Greenwich, CT: JAI Press.
  1989b   "Reading/Writing Culture:" Interpreting the Postmodern Project." *Cultural Dynamics* 2: 9–27.
  1989c   *The Research Act: A theoretical Introduction to Sociological Methods.* Englewood Cliffs, NJ: Prentice Hall.
  1990a   "Harold and Agnes: A Feminist Narrative Undoing." *Sociological Theory* 8:198–216.
  1990b   "The Spaces of Postmodernism: Reading Plummer on Blumer." *Symbolic Interaction* 13: 145–154.
  1990c   "Presidential Address: *The Sociological Imagination* Revisited." *Sociological Quarterly* 31(1): 1–22.
  1991a. "Back to Harold and Agnes." *Sociological Theory* 9:280–285
  1991b   "Empiricist Cultural Studies in America: A Deconstructive Reading." *Current Perspectives in Social Theory* 11:17–39.
  1992   Norman K. Denzin, *Symbolic Interactionism and Cultural Studies: The Politics of Interpretation,* Oxford: Blackwell..
Deutscher, Irwin
  1973   *What We Say, What We Do.* Glenview, IL: Scott, Foresman.
Dewey, John
  1896   "The Reflex Arc Concept in Psychology." *Psychological Review* 3: 357–370.
  1917   "The Need for Social Psychology." *Psychological Reivew* 24: 266–277.
  1922   *Human Nature and Conduct.* New York: Holt.
  1925   *Experience and Nature.* New York: W.W. Norton.
  1931   "George Herbert Mead." *Journal of Philosophy* 28: 309–314.
Dreitzel, Hans P.
  1970   *Recent Sociology* No. 2. London: Macmillan.

Durkheim, Emile
  1964   *The Division of Labor in Society.* New York: Free Press.
Eames, S. Morris
  1973   "Mead and the Pragmatic Conception of Truth." Pp. 135–152 in Walter R. Corti (Ed.), *The Philosophy of George Herbert Mead.* Winterhur, Switzerland: Amrisuiler Burcherei.
Emerson, Robert M.
  1969   *Judging Delinquents: Context and Process in Juvenile Court.* Chicago: Aldine.
Ellis, Carolyn
  1991a   "Sociological Introspection and Emotional Experience." *Symbolic Interaction* 14:23–50
  1991b   "Emotional Sociology." Pp. 123–145 in Norman K. Denzin (Ed.) *Studies in Symbolic Interaction* Volume 12, Greenwich, CT: JAI Press.
Ezorsky, Gertrude
  1967   "Pragmatic Theory of Truth." Pp. 427–429 in Paul Edwards (Ed.), *The Encyclopedia of Philosophy* Vol. 5. New York: Macmillan.
Farberman, Harvey
  1975a   "Symposium on Symbolic Interaction: An Introduction." *Sociological Quarterly* 16: 435–437.
  1975b   "A Criminogenic Market Structure: The Automobile Industry." *Sociological Quarterly* 16: 438–457.
Farberman, Harvey A.
  1991   "Symbolic Interaction and Post-modernism: Close Encounter of a Dubious Kind." *Symbolic Interaction* 14:471–488.
Faulkner, Robert R.
  1983   *Music on Demand: Composers and Careers in the Hollywood Film Industry.* New Brunswick: Transaction.
Filmer, Paul, et al.
  1972   *New Directions in Sociological Theory.* London: Collier, Macmillan.
Fine, Gary Alan
  1983   "Symbolic Interaction and Social Organization: Introduction to the Special Feature" *Symbolic Interaction* 6: 69–70.
  1990   "Symbolic Interactionism in the Post-Blumerian Age." Pp.117–57 in George Ritzer (Ed), *Frontiers of Social Theory: The New Synthesis.* New York: Columbia University Press.
Fine, Gary Alan and Sherryl Kleinman
  1983   "Network and Meaning: An Interactionist Approach to Structure." *Symbolic Interation* 6: 97–110.
Fletcher, C. Richard, et al.
  1974   "The Labelling Theory of Mental Illness." Pp. 43–62 in Paul Roman and Harrison Trice (Eds.), *Explorations in Psychiatric Sociology.* Philadelphia: F.A. Davis.
Frank, Arthur W.
  1979   "Reality Construction in Interaction." *Annual Review of Sociology* 5: 167–191.
Franks, David D.

1985 "Introduction to the Special Issue on the Sociology of Emotions." *Symbolic Interaction* 8: 161–170.

1987 "Notes on the Bodily Aspect of Emotions: A Controversial Issue in Symbolic Interaction." *Studies in Symbolic Interaction* 8: 219–233.

1989 "Power and Role-Taking: A Social Behaviorist's Synthesis of Kemper's Power and Status Model." Pp. 153–177 in David D. Franks and E. Doyle McCarthy (Eds.) *The Sociology of Emotions: Original Essays and Research Papers*, Greenwich, CT: JAI Press.

Franks, David D. and E. Doyle McCarthy

1989 "Introduction." Pp. xi–xx in David D. Franks and E. Doyle McCarthy (Eds.) *The Sociology of Emotions: Original Essays and Research Papers*, Greenwich, CT: JAI Press.

Fujimura, Joan H.

1987 "Constructing Doable Problems in Cancer Research: Articulating Alignment." *Social Studies of Science* 17: 257–93.

Gallmeir, Charles P.

1987 "Putting on the Game Face: The staging of Emotions in Professional Hockey." *Sociology of Sport Journal* 4: 347–362.

Garcia, Angela.

1991 "Dispute Resolution Without Disputing: How the Interactional Organization of Mediation Hearings Minimizes Argument." *American Sociological Review* 56: 818–835.

Garfinkel, Harold

1952 "Perception of the Other." Unpublished Ph.D. dissertation, Harvard University.

1967 *Studies in Ethnomethodology.* Englewood Cliffs, NJ: Prentice-Hall

1968 "The Origins of the Term Ethnomethodology." Pp. 5–11 in Richard J. Hill and Kathleen S. Crittenden (Eds.), *Proceedings of the Purdue University Institute for the Study of Social Change.*

Gerson, Elihu M.

1983 "Scientific Work and Social Worlds." *Knowledge* 4: 357–377.

Gerth, Hans and C. Wright Mills

1954 *Character and Social Structure.* London: Routledge and Kegan Paul.

Giddens, Anthony

1984 *The Constitution of Society.* Berkeley: University of California Press.

Glaser, Barney G. and Anselm L. Strauss

1968 *Time for Dying.* Chicago: Aldine Publishing Company.

Goffman, Erving

1956 "Embarrassment and Social Organization." *American Journal of Sociology* 62: 264–271.

1959 *The Presentation of Self in Everyday Life.* Garden City, NY: Doubleday.

1961a *Asylums: Essays on the Social Situation of Mental Patients and Other Inmates.* Garden City, NY: Doubleday.

1961b *Encounters.* Indianapolis: Bobbs-Merrill.

1963a *Behavior in Public Places.* New York: Free Press.

1963b *Stigma: Notes on the Management of Spoiled Identity.* Englewood Cliffs, NJ: Prentice-Hall.

1967   *Interaction Ritual: Essays in Face-to-Face Behavior.* Garden City, NY: Doubleday.

1969   *Strategic Interaction.* New York: Ballantine.

1974   *Frame Analysis: An Essay on the Organization of Experience.* Cambridge: Harvard University Press.

Gonos, George

1977   "Situation Versus Frame: The Interactionist and Structuralist Analyses of Everyday Life." *American Sociological Review* 42: 854–867.

Goodwin, Charles

1979   "The Interactive Construction of a Sentence in Natural Conversation." Pp. 97–122 in George Psathas (Ed.), *Everyday Language: Studies in Ethnomethodology.* New York: Irvington.

Gordon, Steven L.

1989   "Institutional and Impulsive Orientations   in Selectively Appropriating Emotions to Self." Pp. 115–135 in David D. Franks and E. Doyle McCarthy (Eds.) *The Sociology of Emotions: Original Essays and Research Papers*, Greenwich, CT: JAI Press.

Gouldner, Alvin W.

1961   "Metaphysical Pathos and the Theory of Bureaucracy." Pp. 71–81 in Amitai Etzioni (Ed.), *Complex Organizations.* New York: Holt, Rinehart and Winston.

1970a   *The Coming Crisis of Western Sociology.* New York: Basic Books.

1970b   "Review of N. J. Smelser and J.A. Davis' *Sociology.*"*American Sociological Reivew 35:* 332–334.

Gross, Edward, and Gregory P. Stone

1964   "Embarrassment and the Analysis of Role Requirements." *American Journal of Sociology* 70: 1–15.

Habermas, Jurgen

1970   *Toward a Rational Society.* Boston: Beacon Press.

Hadwiger, Don F.

1982   The Politics of Agricultural Research. Lincoln: University of Nebraska Press.

Hall, Peter M.

1972   "A Symbolic Interactionist Analysis of Politics." *Sociological Inquiry* 42: 35–75.

1985   "Asymmetric Relationships and Processes of Power." *Studies in Symbolic Interaction, Supplement 1:* 309–344.

1987   "Interactionism and the Study of Social Organization." *Sociological Quarterly* 28: 1–22.

Hall, Peter M. and Dee Ann Spencer Hall

1982   "The Social Conditions of Negotiated Order." *Urban Life* 11: 328–349.

Hammond, Judith M.

1980   "Biography Building to Insure the Future: Women's Negotiation of Gender Relevancy in Medical School." *Symbolic Interaction* 3:35–49.

Harman, Lesley D.

1986   "Sign, Symbol, and Metalanguage: Against the Integration of Semiotics and Symbolic Interaction." *Symbolic Interaction* 9 (147–160)

Hazen, Haim

1986 "Body Image and Temporality among the Aged: A Case Study of an Ambivalent Symbol." *Studies in Symbolic Inferaction* 7: 305–329.

Heritage, J. C., and D.R. Watson
1979 "Formulations as Conservational Objects." Pp. 123–162 in George Psathas (Ed.), *Everyday Language: Studies in Ethnomethodology.* New York: Irvington.

Hewitt, John P.
1989 *Dilemmas of the American Self.* Philadelphia: Temple University Press.

Hilbert, Richard A.
1991 "Norman and Sigmund: Comment on Denzin's "Harold and Agnes."' *Sociological Theory* 9: 264–268.

Hirschman, Albert
1970 *Exit, Voice and Loyalty.* Cambridge: Harvard University Press.

Hochschild, Arlie R.
1975 "Sociology of Feeling and Emotion: Selected Possibilities." Pp. 280–307 in Marsha Millmen and Rosabeth M. Kanter (Eds.) *Another Voice: Feminist Perspectives on Social Life and Social Science.* Garden City: Anchor Press/Doubleday.
1979 "Emotion Work, Feeling Rules, and Social Structure." *American Journal of Sociology* 85: 551–575.
1983 *The Managed Heart: Commercialization of Human Feeling.* Berkeley: University of California Press.
1989 "The Economy of Gratitude." Pp. 95–113 in David D. Franks and E. Doyle McCarthy (Eds.) *The Sociology of Emotions: Original Essays and Research Papers*, Greenwich, CT: JAI Press.

Horowitz, Irving
1971 "Review of Howard S. Becker's *Sociological Work: Method and Substance.*" *American Sociological Review* 38: 278–284.

Hosticka, Carl J.
1979 "We Don't Care About What Happened, We Only Care About What Is Going To Happen: Lawyer-Client Negotiations of Reality." *Social Problems.* 26: 599–610.

Huber, Joan
1973 "Symbolic Interaction as a Pragmatic Perspective: The Bias of Emergent Theory." *American Sociological Review* 38: 278–284.

Hunt, Jennifer
1985 "Police Accounts of Normal Force." *Urban Life* 13: 315–341.

James, William
1890 *Principles of Psychology.* New York: Holt.

Jefferson, Gail
1979 "A Technique for Inviting Laughter and Its Subsequent Acceptence Declination." Pp. 79–96 in George Psathas (Ed.), *Everyday Language: Studies in Ethnomethodolgy.* New York: Irvington.

Kanter, Rosabeth M.
1972 "Symbolic Interactionism and Politics in Systematic Perspective." *Sociological Inquiry* 42: 77–92.

Karp, David A., and William C. Yoels
1979 *Symbols, Selves and Society.* New York: J. P. Lipincott Company.

Kemper, Theodore D.

1 978a   *A Social Interactional Theory of Emotions.* New York: John Wiley and Sons.

1978b   "Toward a Sociology of Emotions: Some Problems and Some Solutions." *The American Sociologist* 13: 30–41.

1981   "Social Constructionist and Positivist Approaches to the Sociology of Emotions." *American Journal of Sociology* 87: 336–362.

1987   "How Many Emotions Are There? Wedding the Social and the Automatic Components." *American Journal of Sociology* 93, 263–289.

Killian, Lewis M.

1968   *The Impossible Revolution?* New York: Random House, Inc.

1970   "Herbert Blumer's Contributions to Race Relations." Pp. 179–190 in Tamotsu Shibutani (ed.), *Human Nature and Collective Behavior.* Englewood Cliffs, N.J. Prentice Hall.

Kolb, Deborah M.

1990   "To Be A Mediator: Expressive Tactics in Mediation." Pp. 317–332 in Dennis Brissett and Charles Edgley (Eds.) *Life as Theater: A Dramaturgical Source Book,* New York: Aldine de Gruyter.

Kolb, William

1944   "A Critical Evaluation of Mead's I' and Me' Concepts." *Social Forces* 22: 291–296.

Krueger, E. T., and Walter C. Reckless

1934   *Social Psychology.* New York: Longmans, Green and Company.

Kuhn, Manford H.

n.d.   "Lectures on the Self." Mimeographed. Iowa City, IA.

1954   "Factors in Personality: Socio-cultural Determinants as Seen Through the Amish." Pp. 43–60 in Francis L.K. Hsu (Ed.), *Aspects of Culture and Personality.* New York: Abelard-Schuman.

1960   "Self-Attitudes by Age, Sex, and Professional Training." *Sociological Quarterly 1:* 38–55.

1964   "Major Trends in Symbolic Interaction Theory in the Past Twentyfive Years." *Sociological Quarterly* 5: 61–84.

Kuhn, Manford, and Thomas S. McPartland

1954   "An Empirical Investigation of Self-Attitudes. *American Sociological Review 19:* 68–72.

Lacy, William B. and Lawrence Busch (eds)

1988   *Biotechnology and Agricultural Cooperatives: Opportunities and Challenges.* Lexington: Kentucky Agricultural Experiment Station.

Latour, Bruno

1986   *The Pasteurisation of French Society.* Alan Sheridan (Tr.) Cambridge: Harvard University Press.

Lauer, Robert, and Warren Handel

1977   *Social Psychology: The Theory and Application of Symbolic Interacionism.* Boston: Houghton Mifflin.

Law, John

1984   "How much of Society Can the Sociologist Digest at one Sitting?: The Macro' and the Micro' Revisited for the Case of Fast Food." *Studies in Symbolic Interaction* 5: 171–196.

Lee, Grace Chin

1945   *George Herbert Mead: Philosopher of the Social Individual.* New York: King's Crown Press.

Lemert, Charles
    1991   "The End of Ideology, Really." *Sociological Theory* 9: 164–172.

Lemert, Edwin
    1974   "Beyond Mead: The Societal Reaction to Deviance." *Social Problems* 21: 457–468.

Leonard, William N., and Marvin G. Weber
    1970   "Automakers and Dealers: A Study of Criminogenic Market Forces." *Law and Society* 4: 407–424.

Lichtman, Richard T.
    1970   "Symbolic Interactionism and Social Reality: Some Marxist Queries." *Berkeley Journal of Sociology* 15: 75–94.

Lindesmith, Alfred R., Anselm L. Strauss, and Norman K. Denzin.
    1988   *Social Psychology.* Englewood Cliffs, NJ: Prentice Hall.

Lofland, John
    1970   "Interactionist Imagery and Analytic Interruptus." Pp. 35-45 in Tamotsu Shibutani (Ed.), *Human Nature and Collective Behavior.* Englewood Cliffs, NJ: Prentice-Hall.

Lofland, Lyn H.
    1985   "The Social Shaping of Emotion: The Case of Grief." *Symbolic Interaction* 8: 171–190.

Luckenbill, David F.
    1979   "Power: A Conceptual Framework." *Symbolic Interaction* 2: 97–114.

Lyman, Stanford
    1989   *The Seven Deadly Sins: Society and Evil. Revised and Expanded Edition.* Dix Hills, NY: General Hall.

Lyman, Stanford M.
    1990   "The Drama in the Routine: A Prolegomenon to a Praxiological Sociology." *Sociological Theory* 8:217–223.

Lynch, Michael, and David Bogen
    1991   "In Defense of Dada-Driven Analysis." *Sociological Theory* 9: 269–276.

McCall, George, and J.S. Simmons
    1978   *Identities and Interaction.* New York: Free Press.

McCall, M. and Howard S. Becker
    1990   "Introduction." Pp. 1–15 in Howard S. Becker and Michal M. McCall (Eds.) *Symbolic Interaction and Cultural Studies*, Chicago: University of Chicago Press.

McCarthy, E. Doyle.
    1989   "Emotions are Social Things: An Essay in the Sociology of Emotions." Pp. 51–72 in David D. Franks and E. Doyle McCarthy (Eds.) *The Sociology of Emotions: Original Essays and Research Papers*, Greenwich, CT: JAI Press.

McHugh, Peter
    1968   *Defining the Situation.* New York: Bobbs-Merrill.

McNall, Scott, and James Johnson
    1975   "The New Conservatives." *Insurgent Sociologist* 5: 49–65.
MacCannell, Dean
    1986   "Keeping Symbolic Interaction Safe from Semiotics: A Response to Harman." *Symbolic Interaction* 9 161–168.
Maines, David
    1977   "Social Organization and Social Structure in Syrnbolic Interactionist Thought." Pp. 235–259 in A*nnual Review of Sociology*. Palo Alto, CA: Annual Reivews.
    1979   "Mesostructure and Social Progress." *Contemporary Sociology* 8: 524–527.
    1981   "Recent Developments in Symbolic Interaction." Pp. 461–486 in Gregory P. Stone and Harvey A. Farberman (Eds.) *Social Psychology Through Symbolic Interaction*, 2nd. ed. New York: John Wiley.
    1982   "In Search of Mesostructure: Studies in the Negotiated Order." *Urban Life* 11: 267–279.
    1988   "Myth, Text and Interactionist Complicity in the Neglect of Blumer's Macrosociology." *Symbolic Interaction* 11: 43–57.
Maines, David R., and Joy C. Charlton
    1985   "The Negotiated Order Approach to the Analysis of Social Organization." *Studies in Symbolic Interaction, Supplement 1:* 271–308.
Malinowski, Bronislaw
    1944   A *Scientific Theory of Culture*. Chapel Hill: North Carolina University Press.
Manis, Jerome
    1972   "Common Sense and Analytic Sociology." *Sociological Focus* 5: 1–15.
    1984   *Serious Social Problems*. Boston: Allyn and Bacon.
Manis, Jerome and Bernard N. Mettzer
    1967   *Symbolic Interaction: A Reader in Social Psychology*. Boston: Allyn & Bacon.
    1972   *Symbolic Interaction: A Reader in Social Psychology*. Second edition. Boston: Allyn & Bacon.
    1978   *Symbolic Interaction: A Reader in Social Psychology*. Third edition. Boston: Allyn & Bacon.
Mangham, Iain, and Michael A. Overington
    1982   "Performance and Rehearsal: Social Order and Organizational Life." *Symbolic Interaction* 5: 205–222.
Mangham, Iain L. and Michael A. Overington
    1987   *Organizations As Theatre: A Social Psychology of Dramatic Appearances*.New York: John Wiley and Sons.
Manning, Peter K.
    1977   "Rules in Organizational Context: Narcotics Law Enforcement in Two Settings." *The Sociological Quarterly* 18: 44–61.
Manning, Peter
    1987   *Semiotics and Fieldwork*. Beverly Hills,CA: Sage.
Manning, Phil.

1991   "Drama as Life: The Significance of Goffman's Changing Use of the Theatrical Metaphor." *Sociological Theory* 9:70–86.

Martin, Susan E.
1978   "Sexual Politics in the Workplace: The Interactional World of Police-women." *Symbolic Interaction* 1:44–60.

Martindale, Don
1960   *The Nature and Types of Sociological Theory.* Boston: Houghton Mifflin.
1981   *The Nature and Types of Sociological Theory.* Second Edition. Boston: Houghton Mifflin.

Maryl, William W.
1973   "Ethnomethodology: Sociology Without Society." *Catalyst* 7:15–28.

Mast, Sharon
1983   "Working for Television: The Social Organization of TV Drama." *Symbolic Interaction* 6: 71–83.

Maynard, Douglas W.
1991   "Goffman, Garfinkel, and Games." Sociological Theory 9: 277–279.

Mead, George Herbert
n.d.   "The Principal Features of the Social Psychology of George Herbert Mead." Mimeographed. No Author.
1900   "Suggestions Toward a Theory of Philosophical Disiplines." *Philosophical Review 9:* 1–17.
1912   "The Mechanism of Social Consciousness." *Journal of Philosophy* 9:401–406.
1927   "The Objective Reality of Perspectives." Pp. 75–85 in E.S. Brightman (Ed.), *Proceedings of the International Congress of Philosophy.* New York: Longmans, Green.
1932   *The Philosophy of the Present.* La Salle: Open Court. Edited by Arthur Murphy.
1934   *Mind, Self and Society: From the Standpoint of a Social Behaviorist.* Chicago: University of Chicago Press. Edited by Charles W.   Morris.
1936   *Movements of Thought in the Nineteenth Century.* Chicago: University of Chicago Press. Edited by Charles W. Morris.

Mehan, Hugh, and Huston Wood
1975   *The Reality of Ethnomethodology.* New York: Wiley.

Meltzer, Bernard N.
1957 &
1964   *The Social Psychology of George Herbert Mead.* Kalamazoo: Center for Sociological Research, Western Michigan University.
1978   "The Social Psychology of George Herbert Mead." Pp. 15–27 in Jerome G. Manis and Bernard N. Meltzer (Eds.), *Symbolic Interaction: A Reader in Social Psychology.* Third Edition. Boston: Allyn & Bacon.

Meltzer, Bernard N., and John W. Petras
1970   "The Chicago and Iowa Schools of Symbolic Interactionism." Pp. 3–17 in Tomatsu Shibutani (Ed.), *Human Nature and Collective Behavior.* Englewood Cliffs, NJ: Prentice-Hall.

Meltzer, Bernard N., John W. Petras, and Larry T. Reynolds

1975   *Symbolic Interactionism: Genesis, Varieties and Criticism.* London: Routledge & Kegan Paul.

Mesler, Mark
1989   "Negotiated Order and the Clinical Pharmacist: The Ongoing Process of Structure." *Symbolic Interaction* 12: 139–157.

Miller, David L.
1973   *George Herbert Mead: Self, Language and the World.* Austin: University of Texas Press.

Mills, C. Wright
1966   *Sociology and Pragmatism.* New York: Oxford University Press.

Mills, Trudy, and Sherryl Kleinman
1988   "Emotions, Reflexivity, and Action: An Interactionist Analysis." *Social Forces* 66: 1009–1027.

Mitchell, Jack
1978   *Social Exchange, Dramaturgy and Ethnomethodology.* New York: Elsevier.

Molotch, Harvey L. and Deirdre Boden
1985   "Talking Social Structure: Discourse, Domination and the Watergate Hearings." *American Sociological Review* 50: 273–288.

Mullins, Nicolaus
1973   *Theories and Theory Groups in Contemporary American Sociology.* New York: Harper & Row.

Musolf, Gil Richard.
1992.   "Structure, Institutions, Power, and Ideology: New Directions Within Symbolic Interactionism." *Sociological Quarterly* 33 Number 2.

Nicolas, Martin
1970   "Text of a Speech Delivered at the A.S.A. Convention." Pp. 274–278 in Larry Reynolds and Janice Reynolds (Eds.), *The Sociology of Sociology.* New York: McKay.

Novak, George
1975   *Pragmatism Versus Marxism: An Appraisal of John Dewey's Philosophy.* New York: Pathfinder Press.

O'Toole, Richard and Anita O'Toole
1981   "Negotiating Interorganization Orders." *Sociological Quarterly* 22: 29–41.

Padavic, Irene
1991   "The Re-Creation of Gender in a Male Workplace." *Symbolic Interaction* 14:279–294.

Parsons, Talcott
1964   "Recent Trends in Structural-Functional Theory." Pp. 145–158 in E.W. Count and G. T. Bowles (Eds.) *Fact and Theory in Social Science.* Syracuse: Syracuse University Press.

Perinbanayagan, Robert S.
1982   *The Karmic Theater: Self, Society and Astrology in Jaffna.* Amherst: University of Massachusetts Press.
1992.   *Discursive Acts.* Greenwich CT: JAI Press.

Peters, John Durham

1990 "Rhetoric's Revival, Positivism's Persistence: Social Science, Clear Communication, and the Public." *Sociological Theory* 8:224–231.

Peterson, Trudy H.
1980 Farmers, Bureaucrats, and M*iddlemen: Historical Perspectives on American Agriculture.* Washington, D.C.: Howard University Press.

Petras, John W.
1966 "The Genesis and Development of Symbolic Interactionism in American Sociology." Unpublished Ph.D. Dissertation. University of Connecticut.

Petras, John W., and Bernard N. Meltzer
1973 "Theoretical and the Ideological Variations in Contemporary Interactionism." *Catalyst* 7: 1–8.

Pin, Emile J. and Jamie Turndorf
1990 "Staging One's Ideal Self." Pp. 163–181 in Dennis Brissett and Charles Edgley (Eds.) *Life as Theater: A Dramaturgical Source Book*, New York: Aldine de Gruyter.

Plummer, Ken
1990a "Herbert Blumer And The Life History Tradition." *Symbolic Interaction* 13:125–144.
1990b "Staying In The Empirical World: Symbolic Interactionism and Postmodernism: A Response to Denzin." *Symbolic Interaction* 13:155–160.
1991 "Introduction: The Future of Interactionist Sociologies." Pp. ix–xix in Ken Plummer (Ed.) *Symbolic Interactionism: Volume I: Foundations and History*, Hants, England: Edward Elgar Publishing.

Polner, Melvin
1979 "Explicative Transactions: Making and Managing Meaning in a Traffic Court." Pp. 227–255 in George Psathas (Ed.), *Everyday Language: Studies in Ethnomethodology.* New York: Irvington.

Psathas, George
1979 *Everyday Language: Studies in Ethnomethodology.* New York: Irvington.

Regan, Thomas G.
1980 "Negotiating Community Mental Health: A Review and Analysis of the Experiences of the Fundy Mental Health Center" Presented at Annual Meetings of the Canadian Sociology and Anthropology Association, Montreal, Quebec.
1985 "Bargaining in Regard to a Governmental Directive: The Question of Limits to Negotiated Orders." Paper presented at Qualitative Research Conference, University of Waterloo, Waterloo, Ontario.

Reynolds, Janice M., and Larry T. Reynolds
1973 "Interactionism, Complicity, and The Astructural Bias." *Catalyst* 7:76–85.

Reynolds, Larry T.
1969 "The Sociology of Symbolic Interactionism." Unpublished Ph.D. dissertation, Ohio State University.

Reynolds, Larry T., et al.

1970   "The Self in Symbolic Interaction Theory." Pp. 422–438 in Larry T. Reynolds and Janice M. Reynolds (Eds.), *The Sociology of Sociology.* New York: McKay.

Reynolds, Larry T., and Carol L. McCart
1972   "The Institutional Basis of Theoretical Diversity." *Sociological Focus* 5: 16–39

Reynolds, Larry T., and Bernard N. Meltzer
1973   "The Origins of Divergent Methodological Stances in Symbolic Interactionism." *Sociological Quarterly* 14: 189–199.

Reynolds, Larry T., and Janice M. Reynolds
1979   "The Nature of Social Control." *Western Sociological Review:* 159–171.

Reynolds, Larry T., Janice M. Reynolds, and Charles Bowden
1979   "Varieties of Theoretical Expression and Informal Patterns of Interaction. Pp. 21–38 in Norman K. Denzin (Ed.), *Studies in Symbolic Interaction.* Greenwich, Ct: JAI Press.

Richardson, Laurel.
1986   "Another World." *Psychology Today* Feb.:22–27.
1988   "Secrecy and Status: The Social Construction of Forbidden Relationships." *American Sociological Review* 53:209–219.
1991a.   "Postmodern Social Theory:Representational Practices." *Sociological Theory* 9:173–179.
1991b   "Speakers Whose Voices Matter:Toward A Feminist Postmodernist Sociological Prax." Pp. 29–38 in Norman K. Denzin (Ed.) *Studies in Symbolic Interaction,* Volume 12, Greenwich, CT: JAI Press.

Richardson, Laurel and Ernest Lockridge
1991   "The Sea Monster: An Ethnographic Drama." *Symbolic Interaction* 14:335–340.

Riesman, David, Reul Denney, and Nathan Glaser
1950   *The Lonely Crowd.* New Haven, CT: Yale University Press.

Roebuck, Julian
1986   "Sociability in a Black Outdoor Drinking Place." *Studies in Symbolic Interaction* 7: 161–197.

Ropers, Richard
1973   "Mead, Marx, and Social Psychology." *Catalyst* 7: 42–61.

Rose, Arnold M.
1962   *Human Behavior and Social Processes.* Boston: Houghton Mifflin.
1967   *The Power Structure.* New York: Oxford University Press.

Rosenberg, Morris
1990   "Reflexivity and Emotions." *Social Psychology Quarterly* 53:3–12.

Ryave, A. Lincoln, and James N. Schenkin
1974   "Notes on the Art of Walking." Pp. 264–275 in Roy Turner (Ed.), *Ethnomethodology: Selected Readings.* Harmondsworth, Middlesex, England: Penguin.

Sachs, Harvey

1972 "On the Analyzability of Stories by Children." Pp. 329–345 in John J. Gumperz and Dell Hymes (Eds.), *Directions in Sociolinguistics: The Ethnography of Communication.* NewYork: Holt, Rinehart & Winston.

Saxton, Stanley L.
1989 "Knowledge and Power: Reading the Symbolic Interaction Journal Texts." Pp. 9–24 in Norman Denzin (Ed.) *Studies in Symbolic Interaction,* Volume 10, Greenwich, CT: JAI Press.

Scheff, Thomas J.
1983 "Toward Integration in the Social Psychology of Emotions." *Annual Review of Sociology 9:* 333–354.
1985 "Universal Expressive Needs: A Critique and a Theory." *Symbolic Interaction 8:* 241–262.
1988 "Shame and Conformity: The Deference-Emotion System." *American Sociological Review 53:* 395–406.

Schegloff, Emanuel, A.
1979 "Identification and Recognition in Telephone Conversation Openings" Pp. 23–78 in George Psathas (Ed.), *Everyday Language: Studies in Ethnomethodology.* New York: Irvington.

Schellenberg, James A.
1978 *Masters of Social Psychology.* New York: Oxford University Press.

Schmitt, Raymond L.
1986 "Embodied Identities: Breasts as Emotional Reminders." Pp. 229–289 in Norman K. Denzin (Ed.) *Studies in Symbolic Interaction.* Greenwich, Ct: JAI Press.

Schneider, Joseph W.
1991 "Troubles with Textual Authority in Sociology." *Symbolic Interaction* 14:295–319.

Scott, Robert
1969 *The Making of Blind Men: A Study of Adult Socialization.* Russell Sage Foundation.

Seidman, Steven.
1991a "The End of Sociological Theory: The Postmodern Hope." *Sociological Theory* 9:131–146.
1991b "Postmodern Anxiety: The Politics of Epistemology." *Sociological Theory* 9:180–190.

Shaskolsky, Leon
1970 "The Development of Sociological Theory: A Sociology of Knowledge Interpretation." Pp. 6–30 in Larry T. Reynolds and Janice M. Reynolds (Eds.), *The Sociology of Sociology.* New York: McKay.

Shibutani, Tamotsu
1955 "Reference Groups as Perspectives." *American Journal of Sociology* 60: 562–569.
1961 *Society and Personality.* Englewood Cliffs: Prentice Hall.

Shibutani, Tamotsu, and K.W. Kwan

1965 *Ethnic Stratification: A Comparative Approach.* New York: Macmillan.

Shott, Susan

1979a "Emotion and Social Life: A Symbolic Interactionist Analysis." *American Journal of Sociology* 84: 1317–1334.

1979b "The Sociology of Emotion: Some Starting Points." Pp. 450–462 in Scott G. McNall (Ed.) *Theoretical Perspectives in Sociology.* New York: St. Martin's Press.

Sjoberg, Gideon, and Roger Nett

1968 *A Methodology for Social Research.* New York: Harper & Row.

Skidmore, William

1975 *Theoretical Thinking in Sociology.* Cambridge, England: Cambridge University Press.

Smelser, Neil J.

1988 "Social Structure." Pp. 103–129 in Neil J. Smelser (Ed.), *Handbook of Sociology.* Beverley Hills: Sage.

Smith, Dusky Lee

1973 "Symbolic Interactionism: Definitions of the Situation from H. Becker and J. Lofland." *Catalyst* 7:62–75.

Spreitzer, Elmer E., and Larry T. Reynolds

1973 "Patterning in Citations: An Analysis of References to George Herbert Mead." *Sociological Focus* :71–82.

Stark, Werner

1960 The Sociology of Knowledge. London: Routledge and Kegan Paul.

Stevens, Edward

1967 "Sociality and Act in George Herbert Mead." *Social Research* 34: 613–631

Stoddart, Kenneth

1982 "Narcotics Enforcement in a Canadian City: Heroin Users' Perspectives on the Production of Official Statistics." *Canadian Journal of Criminaology* 23: 425–438.

Stone, Gregory P., and Harvey A. Farberman

1970 *Social Psychology Through Symbolic Interacfion.* Waltham, MA: Ginn-Blaisdell.

Stover, Stewart S.

1977 "Convergences between Symbolic Interactionism and Systems Theory." *Symbolic Interaction* 1: 89–103.

Strauss, Anselm

1959 *Mirrors and Masks.* New York: Free Press.

1964 *George Herbert Mead on Social Psychology.* Chicago: Phoenix.

1978a *Negotiations: Varieties, Contexts, Processes, and Social Order.* San Francisco: Jossey-Bass.

1978b "A Social World Perspective." *Studies in Symbolic Interaction 1:* I 19–128.

1982 "Interorganization Negotiations." *Urban Life* 11: 350–367.

1984 "Social Worlds and Their Segmentation Processes." *Studies in Symbolic Interaction* 5: 123–139.

Strauss, Anselm, et al.

1963   "The Hospital and Its Negotiated Order." Pp. 147–169 in Elliott Freidson (Ed.), *The Hospital in Modern Society*. New York: Free Press.

Stryker, Sheldon

1980   *Symbolic Interationism*. Menlo Park, CA: Benjamin Cummings.

1981   "Symbolic Interactionism: Themes and Variations." Pp. 3–29 in Morris Rosenberg and Ralph H. Turner (Eds.), *Social Psychology Perspectives*. New York: Basic Books.

1987   "The Vitalization of Symbolic Interactionism." *Social Psychology Quarterly* 50:83–94.

Stryker, Sheldon, and Richard T. Serpe

1982   "Commitment, Identity, Salience and Role Behavior." Pp. 199–218 in William Ickes and Eric Knowles (Eds.) *Personality, Roles and Social Behavior*. New York: Springer-Verlag.

Sudnow, David

1965   "Normal Crimes: Sociological Features of the Penal Code in a Public Defender Office." *Social Problems* 12: 255–264.

1967   *Passing On: The Social Organization of Dying*. Englewood Cliffs, NJ: Prentice-Hall.

Swanson, Guy E.

1985   "Review of N.K. Denzin's *On Understanding Emotion.*" *Symbolic Interaction* 8: 311–314.

1989   "On the Motives and Motivations of Selves." Pp. 3–32 in David D. Franks and E. Doyle McCarthy (Eds.) *The Sociology of Emotions: Original Essays and Research Papers*, Greenwich, CT: JAI Press.

Thayer, H. S.

1967   "Pragmatism." Pp.430–435 in Paul Edwards (Ed.), *The Encyclopedia of Philosophy Vol. 5*. New York: Macmillan.

Thoits, Peggy A.

1985   "Self-Labeling Processes in Mental Illness: The Role of Emotional Deviance." *American Journal of Sociology 91:* 221–249.

Thomas, D.L., D.D. Franks, and J.M. Calonico

1972   "Role-Taking and Power in Social Psychology." *American Sociological Review,* 37: 605–614.

Thomas, Jim

1984   "Some Aspects of Negotiated Order, Loose Coupling and Mesostructure in Maximum Security Prisons" *Symbolic Interaction* 7: 213–231

Thomas, W. I.

1937   *Primitive Behavior*. New York: McGraw-Hill.

Thomas, W. I., and Dorothy S. Thomas

1928   *The Child in America*. New York: Knopf.

Tucker, Charles

1966   "Some Methodological Problems of Kuhn's Self Theory." *Sociological Quarterly* 7: 345–358.

Turner, Jonathan

1974   *The Structure of Sociological Theory*. Homewood, IL: Dorsey Press.

1978   *The Structure of Sociological Theory.* Second edition. Homewood, IL: Dorsey.

1982   *The Structure of Sociological Theory.* Third edition. Homewood, IL: Dorsey.

1986   *The Structure of Sociological Theory.* Fourth edition. Belmont, CA: Wadsworth Publishing Company.

Turner, Ralph H.

1962   "Role-Taking: Process Versus Conformity." Pp. 20–40 in Arnold M. Rose (Ed.). *Human Behavior and Social Process.* Boston: Houghton Mifflin.

1978   "The Role and the Person." *American Journal of Sociology* 84: 1–23.

Turner, Roy

1974   *Ethnomethodology.* Harmondsworth, Middlesex, England: Penguin.

Vaughan, Ted R. and Larry T. Reynolds

1968   "The Sociology of Symbolic Interationism." *American Sociologist* 3: 208–214.

Volkart, Edmund H.

1951   *Social Behavior and Personality.* New York: Social Science Research Council.

Wagner, Helmut R.

1964   "Displacement of Scope: A Problem of Relation between Small-Scale and Large-Scale Sociological Theories. " *American Journal of Sociology* 69: 571–584.

Wallace, Jennifer J.

1988   "Who's in Charge?: Factors Affecting the Negotiation of the Role of Manager in Organizations." Paper Presented at Interactionist Research Conference, Windsor, Ontario Canada.

Wallace, Walter

1969   *Sociological Theory.* Chicago: Aldine.

Warshay, Leon H.

1971   "The Current State of Sociological Theory: Diversity, Polarity, and Small Theories." *Sociological Quarterly* 12: 23–45.

1975   *The Current State of Sociological Theory.* New York: McKay.

1982   "A Tough-Minded Interactionism: Structuralism and Theoretical Breadth; Deductivism, Fictionalism, and Methodological Narrowness." *Symbolic Interaction* 5: 141–147.

Wasielewski, Patricia L.

1985   "The Emotional Basis of Charisma." *Symbolic Interaction* 8: 207–222.

Weigert, Andrew and David D. Franks

1989   "Ambivalence: A Touchstone of the Modern Temper." Pp. 205–227 in David D. Franks and E. Doyle McCarthy (Eds.) *The Sociology of the Emotions: Original Essays and Research Papers*, Greenwich CT: JAI Press.

Weinberg, S. Kirson

1962   "Social Action Systems and Social Problems." Pp. 401-442 in Arnold M. Rose (Ed.), *Human Behavior and Social Processes.* Boston: Houghton Mifflin.

Weiss, Paul R., and Robert R. Faulkner
  1983   "Credits and Craft Production: Freelance Social Organization in the
          Hollywood Film Industry, 1964–1978." *Symbolic Interaction* 6: 111–
          123.
Welsh, John F.
  1990   "Dramaturgy and Political Mystification: Political Life in the United
          States." Pp. 399–410 in Dennis Brissett and Charles Edgley (Eds.) *Life
          as Theater: A Dramaturgical Source Book*, New York: Aldine de Gruyter.
West, Candace
  1984   "When the Doctor is a 'Lady': Power, Status and Gender in Physician-
          Patient Encounters." *Symbolic Interaction* 7:87–106.
Whyte, William H., Jr.
  1956   *The Organization Man.* New York: Simon & Schuster.
Wiley, Mary Glenn
  1991   "Gender, Work, and Stress: The Potential Impact of Role-Identity
          Salience and Commitment." *Sociological Quarterly* 32:495–510.
Willhelm, Sidney M.
  1983   *Black in a White America.* Cambridge, MA: Schenkman.
Wolf, Charlotte
  1986   "Legitimation and Oppression: Response and Reflexivity." *Symbolic
          Interaction* 9:217–234.
Wood, Michael, and Mark L. Wardell
  1983   "G.H. Mead's Social Behaviorism Vs. the Astructural Bias of Symbolic
          Interactionism." *Symbolic Interaction* 6: 85–96.
Wrong, Dennis
  1961   "The Oversocialized Conception of Man in Modern Sociology."
          American Sociological Review 26: 183–193.
Young, T.R.
  1990   *The Drama of Social Life: Essays in Post-modern Social Psychology.*
          New Brunswick, NJ: Transaction Publishers.
  1991   "Chaos Theory and Symbolic Interaction Theory: Poetics for the
          Postmodern Sociologist." *Symbolic Interaction* 14: 321–334.
Zardrozny, John T.
  1959   *Dictionary of Social Science.* Washington, DC: Public Affairs Press.
Zeitlin, Irving
  1973   *Rethinking Sociology: A Critique of Contemporary Sociology.*
          Englewood Cliffs, NJ: Prentice-Hall.
Zurcher, Louis A.
  1985   "The War Game: Organizational Scripting and the Expression of
          Emotion." *Symbolic Interaction* 8: 191–206.
  1989   "Critique and Renewal in Symbolic Interactionism: Reflections on the
          1987 Symposium." Pp. 491–499 in Norman Denzin (Ed.) *Studies in
          Symbolic Interaction,* Volume 10, Greenwich, CT: JAI Press.

SUBJECT INDEX

Act
  philosophy of, 46–48
  social, 46–47
Activity, imaginative, 55
Ahistorical, noninstitutional
      interactionism, 135
Analytic interruptus, 133–134
Apolitical interactionism, 134

Bias, astructural, 154–185, 204–225

Codeterminism, 7
Common sense and interactionism,
      147
Constructed action, 69–70
Contemporary interactionism,
      73–117
  Chicago school, 76–83
  dramaturgical genre, 95–102
  ethnomethodology, 103–117
  Iowa school, 84–94
Conventional interactionism, 73
Criticisms of interactionism,
      128–185
Cultural, temporal limitations,
      135–136

Darwinism, social, 6
Definition of the situation, 40–42
Discourse analysis, 261–264
Dramaturgy, 95–102, 264–272

Early interactionism, 32–70
  summary characteristics, 70–72
Emergence, 8
Emergent theory, bias of, 142–145
Emotions, 182–199, 220–221, 248–258
Emotions slighted, 129

Ethnomethodology, basic concepts
      of, 110
Evolutionism, 6–9
Existential interactionism, 3

Field theory interactionism, 3
Functional psychology, 25–31
  basic assumptions, 25–26
  criterion for truth, 26

Gender 258–261
Gestures, 12, 44, 54–55

Habit, 30–31

Idealism, German, 10–13
Idealist bias, 137–142
Impression management, 96–97,
      99–101
Impulse, 30–31
Indeterminate situation, 23
Interactionism. see Ahistorical,
      Noninstitutional interactionism,
      Apolitical interactionism;
      Common sense and
      interactionism; Contemporary
      interactionism; Conventional
      interactionism; Criticisms of
      interactionism; Early
      interactionism; Existential
      interactionism; Field theory
      interactionism; Interactionism's
        indispensable concepts;
      Phenomenological interactionism;
  Role theory interactionism;
      Unconventional interactionism
Interactionism's indispensable
        concepts, 156–157
Instinct, 27–28, 39

Labeling theory, 3, 101
Life policies, 41
Looking–glass self, 32, 37–38

Metaphysic of meaning, 130–131
Mind, 63–67

Objective psychology, 5
Operationalism, 19, 85
Oral tradition, evils of, 131–132

Participant observation, 83
Personal documents, 42
Phenomenological interactionism, 3
Philosophical anthropology, 3
Plans of action, 24, 50–51, 68
Postmodernism 231–248
Power ignored, 136
Pragmatism, American, 13–25
    characteristics, 16
    definition of, 13–14
Present, philosophy of, 46
Primary group, 32, 35–37

Quaintness and interactionism,
    141–142

Reality construction, 3
Role, 52, 72, 88–90,157
Role taking, 9, 50–51, 60, 67

Role–theory variant of
    interactionism, 3

Science and idealism, 16
Self
    elements of, 60–62
    multiple conception, 28–29
    primary group, 35–37
    self–indication, 58, 66–68
    stages of development, 59–60
    unitary conception, 29
Semiotics 272–277
Sign, 54
Sins of omission, 129–130
Situation of doubt, 23
Social organization, 154–155,
    158–185, 204–224
Society
    self in, 58–59
    society's mental nature, 33–35
    symbols and role taking, 49–56
Sociology
    of the absurd, 3
    without society, 144–145
Stimulus response view criticized, 31
Sympathetic introspection, 35, 79

Unconscious ignored, 129
Unconventional interactionism, 73

Warranted assertion, 23

NAME INDEX

Adler, Patricia, 202, 249, 262, 279
Adler, Peter, 202, 249, 262, 279
Albas, Cheryl, 199
Albas, Daniel, 199
Alexander, Jeffery C., 158, 184, 231, 243, 246
Altheide, David, 215
Ames, Edward S., 17, 45
Angell, James R., 17, 25–26
Antonio, Robert, 231, 239–243
Asch, Solomon, 201
Averill, James, 193

Bacharach, Samuel, 177
Baker, Scott, 231–234, 237–239
Baldwin, James M., 5, 32, 37, 45
Baldwin, John D., 187, 205–206
Balsamo, Anne, 231, 239–240
Bartelt, David W., 161
Bartelt, Pearl W., 161
Becker, Howard S., 142, 148, 151–152, 184, 209, 279–280
Bergson, Henri, 7–8, 45, 56
Best, Joel, 281
Block, Fred, 135
Blumer, Herbert, 74, 76–88, 95, 102, 120–125, 131, 186, 188–189, 202, 206–208, 213, 230, 268
Boden, Deirdre, 261–263, 282
Bodenhafer, W.B., 33
Bogen, David, 231, 239
Braroe, N.W., 209
Brooks, Richard S., 134, 283
Brissett, Dennis, 266
Brown, R.H., 231, 235–237, 248
Bowden, Charles, 154
Burke, Kenneth, 95–96, 266
Burke, Peter, 210

Burkhardt, Jeffery, 179
Busch, Lawerence, 176–180, 183, 185, 220–221, 224

Cagle, Van, 279–280
Cahill, Spencer, 266
Calonico, James, 214
Cavan, Sherri, 167
Charlton, Joy C., 159, 167
Charon, Joel, 282
Cicourel, Aaron V., 111, 115, 117
Clanton, Gordon, 256
Clark, Candace, 256
Clarke, Adele, 171–176, 183
Clough, Patricia, 161
Coleman, James, 170
Collins, Randall, 104–105, 109, 138, 145–148, 167, 278
Cooley, Charles H., 5–6, 9–10, 3–39, 43, 45, 48, 188, 205
Coser, Lewis, 184
Couch, Carl J., 128, 159, 164, 211, 223–224, 280
Coutu, Walter, 189, 229
Cuzzort, Raymond P. 97–98

Daniels, Arlene, 230
Darwin, Charles, 6, 56, 97–98, 190–191
Das, Hari, 223–224
Day, JoAnne V., 158, 162
Day, Robert, 158, 162
Deegan, Mary Jo, 282
Denny, Reul, 99
Denzin, Norman K., 102, 120–125, 131–132, 159, 167, 183–185, 195, 219–221, 224, 231–232, 234, 238–241, 273, 275, 279, 281, 283

308

Deutsher, Irwin, 105
Dewey, John, 7, 10–11, 15–32, 43–45,
    57, 78, 187–190
Dreitzel, Hans P., 106, 108
Duncan, Hugh, D., 95
Durkheim, Emile, 95, 107, 200, 234

Eames, S. Morris, 19
Edgley, Charles, 266
Ellis, Carolyn, 241, 258
Emerson, Robert, 230
Ezorsky, Gertrude, 18, 23–24

Faberman, Harvey, 6, 8, 22, 159, 170–
    171, 184–185, 220–224, 231,
    240, 244
Faris, Ellsworth, 76
Faulkner, Robert R., 180–183, 221–
    225
Ferguson, Adam, 9, 32
Fichte, Johann, 10–11, 44
Filmer, Peter, 105
Fine, Gary Alan, 159, 163, 184, 210,
    221
Fletcher, C. Richard, 150
Fontana, Andrea, 202, 249, 262, 279
Frank, Arthur, 175
Franks, David D., 187, 193–194, 203,
    214, 252, 256–257
Freud, Sigmund, 47, 190
Fujimura, Joan, 174

Gallmeir, Charles P., 199
Garcia, Angela, 263–264
Garfinkel, Harold, 103–115, 238–240
Gerson, Elihu, 172, 176
Gerth, Hans, 189–190
Giddings, Franklin, 45
Giddens, Anthony, 162, 164, 167, 171,
    278
Glaser, Barney, 228, 280
Glazer, Nathan, 99
Goffman, Erving, 88, 95–102, 111,
    133, 148–151, 189–190, 226–
    227, 265–267, 280
Gonos, George, 101
Goodwin, Charles, 111

Gordon, Steven, 253
Gouldner, Alvin W., 138, 148–152
Gross, Edward, 189
Gurwitsch, Aron, 103
Gusfield, Joseph, 280

Habermas, Jurgen, 18, 180
Hadwiger, Don, 179
Hall, Dee Ann Spencer, 159, 217–218
Hall, Peter V., 128, 131, 134, 159–160,
    164, 167–168, 176, 180, 183,
    217–221, 224
Hall, Stuart, 279, 283
Hammond, Judith, 260, 281
Handel, Warren, 16
Harman, Lesley, 274–275
Hazen, Haim, 161
Hegel, G.W.F., 11, 44
Heise, David, 278
Heritage, J.C., 111
Herman, Nancy J., 186–230
Hewitt, John, 280
Hickman, C. Addison, 84, 87–88,
    91–92, 208
Hilbert, Richard, 231, 239
Hill, Michael, 282
Hintz, Robert A., 211
Hirschman, Albert, 170
Hochschild, Arlie R., 190–193, 195,
    197–200, 203, 226, 229, 254–
    256, 281
Homes, Henry, 9
Horowitz, Irving L., 135, 142
Hosticka, Carl J. 215
Huber, Joan, 135–136, 138, 142–145
Hughes, Everett, 95
Hume, David, 9, 32
Hunt, Jennifer, 230
Husserl, Edmund, 103
Hutcheson, Francis, 9
Hutter, Mark, 161

Ichheiser, Gustave, 95

James, William, 12, 15–17, 20–29,
    32, 43–44, 57, 95, 187, 190

Jefferson, Gail, 111, 261
Johnson, James, 135
Judd, Charles H., 25

Kanter, Rosabeth M., 135, 140, 158
Karp, David, 213–214
Kemper, Theodore D., 191, 194–197,
      203, 226
Killian, Lewis, 207, 209
King, Martin L., 201
Kleinman, Sherryl, 159, 163, 221, 229
Knottnerus, John David, 158–185
Kolb, Deborah, 226
Kolb, William, 131
Krohn, Roger, 244
Krueger, E.T., 189
Kuhn, Manford H., 19, 74, 78, 84–94,
      131–132, 186, 208, 211
Kwan, K.W., 209

Lacy, Laura, 179
Lacy, William, 178–179
Lamarck, Jean B., 45, 56
Lauer, Robert, 16
Law, John, 163–164, 167
Lawler, Edward, 177
Lee, Grace C., 43, 45–47, 64
Lemert, Charles, 231
Lemert, Edwin, 131
Leonard, William N., 185
Levi–Strauss, Claude, 46
Lichtman, Richard T., 138, 141–142
Lindesmith, Alfred, 273
Lockridge, Ernest, 231
Lofland, John, 131, 133,–134, 147,
      280
Lofland, Lyn H., 135, 193, 198
Lovejoy, A.O., 15
Luckenbill, David F., 159
Lyman, Stanford, 229, 265
Lynch, Michael, 231, 239

McCall, George, 210
McCall, M., 279
McCart, Carol L., 73, 154
McCarthy, E. Doyle, 252–253
McDougall, William, 191

McHugh, Peter, 111
McNall, Scott, 135
McPhail, Clark, 184, 278
MacCannell, Dean, 274
Maines, David R., 128, 159, 163, 167,
      176–177, 180, 184, 219, 230,
      278
Makowski, Michael, 104–105
Malinowski, Bronislaw, 139
Mangham, Ian, 267–270
Manis, Jerome G., 3, 5–11, 16, 81,
      86, 91, 125–126, 135, 139, 145,
      147, 158
Mannheim, Karl, 245
Manning, Peter K., 217, 272–277, 280
Manning, Phil, 265
Martindale, Don, 10, 12–15, 20, 40,
      43, 47, 57, 76–79
Martin, Susan, 260, 281
Marx, Karl, 25, 232
Maryl, William W., 138, 145–146
Mast, Sharon, 168–169, 183, 185, 218
Maynard, Douglas, 231, 240
Mead, George H., 4–12, 14, 17–19,
      23, 25, 42–54, 56–69, 74, 95,
      129, 186–187, 200, 202, 205–
      206, 213
Mehan, Hugh, 115–117
Meltzer, Bernard, N., 2–3, 5, 7–11,
      16, 22, 24, 27, 30, 32–33, 35–40,
      45–46, 48, 50–51, 54, 56–64,
      66–67, 69, 72–73, 75–76, 79–83,
      85–90, 94, 97–98, 105, 107, 111,
      125–126, 128–130, 154, 158,
      186–230, 282
Merleau–Ponty, Maurice, 103
Mesler, Mark, 215–216
Millar, John, 9
Miller, David L., 5, 7–8, 10, 12, 45
Mills, C. Wright, 6–7, 30, 189–190
Mills, Trudy, 229
Molotch, Harvey, 263
Moore, Addison, W. 17, 45
Morris, Charles, 8, 23
Mullins, Nicolaus, 106, 138, 186, 278
Musolf, Gil, 231–285

Nett, Roger, 80
Nicolaus, Martin, 153
Nimkoff, Meyer, 118
Novak, George, 13–15, 24

O'Toole, Anita W., 218
O'Toole, Richard, 218
Overington, Michael, 267–270

Padavic, Irene, 259, 281
Park, Robert E., 76
Parsons, Talcott, 153
Perinbanayagan, Robert S., 128, 282
Peters, John, 231, 243–245
Peterson, Trudy, 179
Petras, John W. 3, 5, 12, 22, 25, 27, 30,
    32–33, 36–40, 48, 56–57, 66,
    70–73, 75–76, 79–83, 85–90, 94,
    97–98, 105, 107, 128, 137, 158
Piaget, Jean, 74
Pierce, Charles S., 15–21, 23
Pin, Emile, 266
Plummer, Ken, 231, 242, 280
Pollner, Melvin, 111
Prendergast, Christopher, 158–185
Psathas, George 111

Reckless, Walter C., 189
Regan, Thomas G., 218
Reynolds, Janice M., 136–137, 153–
    154, 158
Reynolds, Larry T., 3, 12, 22, 24, 27,
    29–30, 32–33, 36–40, 48, 56–57,
    66, 70–76, 79–83, 85–88, 90, 94,
    97–98, 105, 107, 128, 136–138,
    153–154, 158, 282
Reid, Thomas, 9
Reisman, David, 99, 135
Remmling, Gunter, 244
Richardson, Laurel, 231–236, 246–
    248, 260, 281
Roebuck, Julian, 161
Rogers, Carl, 74
Ropers, Richard, 135
Rose, Arnold, 118–119, 122–125, 134,
    158, 230
Rosenberg, Morris, 249–252

Royce, Josiah, 11, 16, 44
Ruggiero, Guido de, 13
Ryave, A. Lincoln, 111

Sachs, Harvey, 111, 261
Sacks, Carolyn, 180
Saxton, Stanley, 281
Scheff, Thomas, 191, 201–203, 229,
    282
Schegloff, Emanuel A., 111
Schellenberg, James A., 22
Schelling, Friedrick Von, 10–11, 44
Schenkin, James N., 111, 261
Schmitt, Raymond L, 161
Schneider, Joseph, 231
Schutz, Alfred, 95, 103
Scott, Robert, 230
Seidman, Steven, 231, 233–238, 242,
    244–248
Shaskolsky, Leon, 6, 135, 138–140,
    142
Shibutani, Tamotsu, 163, 184, 209
Shott, Susan, 191, 194–195, 199–
    200, 203, 226
Simmel, Georg, 95, 207
Simmons, J.S., 210
Sjoberg, Gideon, 80
Skidmore, William 14–15, 106
Small, Albion, 17
Smelser, Neil, 184
Smith, Adam, 9, 32
Smith, Dusky, 135
Snow, David, 278
Spence, Kenneth, 85
Spencer, Herbert, 6
Spreitzer, Elmer, E., 45, 48
Stark, Werner, 245–246
Stevens, Edward, 131
Stoddart, Kenneth, 230
Stone, Gregory, 6, 8, 22, 189, 266
Stover, Stewart S., 159
Strauss, Anselm, 48, 159, 163, 176–
    177, 184, 208–209, 215, 228,
    273, 280
Stryker, Sheldon, 32, 39, 41–42,
    90, 92–93, 128, 157, 159, 175–
    176, 184, 210–213, 225, 278

Sudnow, David, 111, 230
Sullivan, Harry S., 74
Sumner, William, 6
Swanson, Guy E., 229, 257

Tarde, Gabriel, 45
Thayer, H.S., 13, 15–17, 19, 21, 23
Thoits, Peggy A., 201
Thomas, D.L., 214
Thomas, Dorothy S., 41
Thomas, Jim, 168, 216–217
Thomas, William 1., 5–6, 17, 39–43,
      45, 95, 102
Tucker, Charles, 93, 131
Tufts, J.H., 17, 45
Turndorf, Jamie, 266
Turner, Jonathan H., 135, 153, 158,
      211–212
Turner, Ralph, 210, 212–213, 225
Turner, Roy, 110

Vaughan, Ted R., 3, 158
Veblen, Thorstein, 17
Volkhart, Edmund, 41

Wagner, Helmut R., 158, 162
Wallace, Jennifer J., 218
Wallace, Walter, 103
Wardell, Mark L., 206
Warshay, Leon H., 3, 74, 111
Wasielewski, Patricia L., 201

Watson, D.R., 111
Watson, John B., 57
Weber, Marvin G., 185
Weber, Max, 104, 234
Weigert, Andrew, 256–258, 282
Weinberg, S. Kirson, 16
Weiss, Paul R., 222, 224
Welsh, John, 267, 270
West, Candace, 260, 281
Whitehead, Alfred N., 45
Whyte, William H., Jr., 99
Wiley, Mary Glenn, 260–262, 281
Willhelm, Sidney M., 140
Williams, Norma, 282
Wolf, Charlotte, 260, 281
Wood, Huston, 115–117
Wood, Michael, 206
Wrong, Dennis, 21, 61
Wundt, Wilhelm, 5, 11–13, 19, 44, 57

X, Malcolm, 201

Yoels, William C., 213–214
Young, Kimball, 85
Young, T.R., 231, 235, 270–272

Zadrozny, John T., 122
Zeitlin, Irving, 52, 61, 111, 114, 158,
      166
Znaniecki, Florian, 40
Zurcher, Louis A., 198, 222–223, 281